How

A Ne

Empowering Everyone to be a Problem Solver

Autoliv Received 63 Ideas per Employee
Gulfstream Received 33 Ideas per Employee

Bunji Tozawa
Norman Bodek

Before Kaizen **After Kaizen**

Edited by Kevin Tame, David Hubbard and Steven Hatch

Copyright © 2009 by Norman Bodek
All rights reserved. No part of this book may be reproduced or transmitted in any form by any means, electronic or mechanical, including photocopying, recording, or by any information storage and retrieval system without permission in writing from the Publisher.

PCS Inc.
PCS Press
809 S.E. 73rd Avenue
Vancouver, WA 98664

bodek@pcspress.com
http://www.pcspress.com

Printed in the United States of America

Printing number
1 2 3 4 5 6 7 8 9 10

The cover is a stereogram designed by Gene Levine

Library of Congress Cataloging-in-publication Data

Bodek, Norman.
How to do Kaizen: A new path to innovation
Empowering everyone to be a problem solver

    p. cm.
    Includes index.

ISBN 978-0-9712436-7-5
1. Production management.   2. Industrial Management.
3. Organizational change.   4. Organizational behavior
5. Human relations.

Published with ENNA:

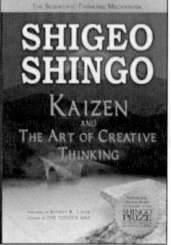

"In this book we learn how Dr. Shingo thinks about problems. You will not be overwhelmed by flowery prose and deep theoretical discussions in a Shingo book; what you will get is a straightforward methodology and examples to illustrate each concept."
Jeffrey Liker, Ph.D., Industrial and Operations Engineering
The University of Michigan and author of *The Toyota Way, Toyota Culture* and *Toyota Talent.*

The greatest value of this book is an opportunity to learn how a master sensei thinks about operations improvement. We see how Dr. Shingo thought both about macro-improvement of value streams and micro-process improvement.
Jeffrey Liker
New York Times best-selling author, The Toyota Way

If you need help in implementing Kaizen contact me at bodek@pcspress.com

Books Previously Published 383

JIT truly is flow—and flow is best medicine in a disruptive ultra-competitive world. This book covers all the bases in telling how. And don't miss the insightful 24-page interview at the end. I think the trailing interview with Erik Hager is great." **Richard J. Schonberger**, author or *Japanese Manufacturing Techniques: Nine Hidden Lessons in Simplicity, The World Class Manufacturing: The Lessons of Simplicity Applied and World Class Manufacturing: The Next Decade*

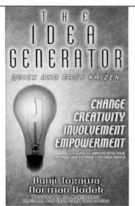

"*The Idea Generator* brings continuous improvement down to Earth--and raises up to the heavens the importance of everybody documenting every implemented idea, however small. It's a message too few understand." - **Richard J. Schonberger, Author or World Class Manufacturing: The Next Decade**

"Lean systems will degrade without ongoing improvement from every employee through a myriad of simple, quick changes. What brings lean structures to life is people—people engaged in continuous improvement. Tozawa and Bodek provide deep insights into this fundamental ingredient of high performance companies." - **Prof. Jeffrey K. Liker, University of Michigan and author of The Toyota Way**

In down times, having an idea program will make the difference. It creates a competitive advantage. - **Gary Corrigan, VP Corporate Communications, Dana Corporation**

In *Rebirth of American Industry*, William Waddell and Norman Bodek call American management onto the carpet. By showing how modern financial accounting (derived from practices from 8 decades past) drives American companies to non-lean measures. Mr. Waddell and Mr. Bodek have clearly demonstrated why American manufacturers continue to come up short when compared to their lean competitors. If unheeded, it could be the epitaph of a once-great manufacturing powerhouse. - **Bill Kluck, President, The Northwest Lean Networks**

Books Previously Published

"Norman Bodek played the key role in the spread of lean techniques around the world. In this wonderful book, he tells how it all happened. Along the way, he weaves in lessons derived from his interaction with the original developers of lean production ideas. I couldn't put it down." - Alan G. Robinson, Co-author of *Ideas Are Free* and *Corporate Creativity*

"From the Suggestion Box to the Toyota Production System--All You Gotta Do Is Ask has a lot of good ideas to save an organization time, effort, and money. It is well worth reading!" - William C. Byham, Ph.D. , Chairman, DDI and author of Zapp!: The Lightning of Empowerment : How to Improve Productivity, Quality, and Employee Satisfaction

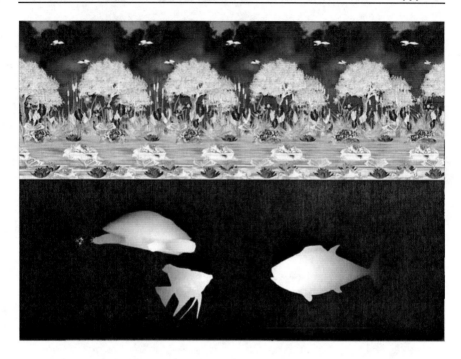

The cover: The picture on the cover is a stereogram. Hidden for your discovery is a three dimensional picture (3 D) by the artist **Gene Levine**. Relax your eyes, focus six inches beyond the book, above or below the picture to see either your reflection or a subtle light. You can also look at the cover cross-eyed by holding your index finger three inches in front of your nose. Or hold the cover right up to your nose, focus as if looking off into the distance and slowly move the page away. With patience and a little practice you will see the magic happen. For help go to: http://www.colorstereo.com/texts_.txt/practice.htm or to: http://www.magiceye.com/faq_example.htm

"Innovation = Imitation (learn from others) + Imagination (think and write)." – *Takashi Harada*

Introduction

Improvement is really everyone's responsibility

Innovation is the lifeblood of every organization. In the past we looked for that powerful new idea, that new product, like the iPhone, to get us a competitive advantage. We looked for the big "ticket item," but often neglected innovation that can pour out of every single worker. Today, we still need the big great idea (Japanese call this Kaikaku[1]) but there is an equally powerful innovation process called Kaizen (continuous improvement,) gathering small ideas from everyone. These ideas can change your company's culture in many wonderful ways: people feel good about themselves and in their ability to participate; also these millions of new ideas translate into millions of dollars of cost savings.

How do you do Kaizen? Easy, you just ask people for their improvement ideas; then listen to them; empower them to implement their own small idea; teach and coach them on the new tools and techniques; help them build new skills; thank and praise them for their efforts; and share their ideas with everyone.

Then watch the magic happen.

In America, a top down management style for decision making has been the primary focus of most managers for the past hundred years. Typically, the senior officer makes a decision and passes

---

[1] Kaikaku means radical change.

down instructions to get the job done. For long periods of time, top-down decisions made corporations very successful and you can't knock success! The thinking was that the most intelligence rested with senior management; they were better educated, more devoted, more committed, had a wider understanding of the overall goals and problems of the corporation and were better equipped to make the kinds of decisions to fulfill the needs of the organization.

However, when we look at General Motors, Chrysler, Bank of America, Citibank, Lehman Brothers, Fannie Mae, SIG, Freddie Mac, and several other billion-dollar companies going bankrupt or close to it, we might begin to think that a top-down decision making strategy doesn't always work. At one time, General Motors was the richest and most successful company in the world. There was an old saying, "As GM goes, so goes the country." As we can see this is no longer the case.

In fact, the person closest to the job and closest to the customer should be strongly involved in the decision making process. There on the factory floor or in the office are people with vast experiences in doing their work. They are most likely aware of the problems and the potential problems but their ideas about possible improvement often lie dormant and untapped. Power is at the top but real knowledge of the work and the processes lies elsewhere. Is there a system that can have both the vision and guidance from the top and an empowered work force to respond to the real needs of the organization's day-to-day problems? Yes, there is a powerful mechanism already in use by many companies and it is our intention to describe it in this book and to help you implement it in your organization.

This movement, which we call Quick and Easy Kaizen, works very well and we will explain in detail how it works, why it works and how you can implement the process. Of course, supervisors and managers' attitudes about workers need to be shifted, but that will come as managers listen to and implement the ideas of their workers. With this new process, managers gain a whole new level

Introduction

of respect for the people that work for them. When you ask people to identify problems in their work area and create new solutions to solve those problems, you will then see the hidden intelligence in those ideas. You become amazed and so much more respectful. With your new awareness about people's hidden talents, you will be able to bring forth a steady stream of creative ideas that will strengthen your company and develop your people to their fullest.

People should be trained to listen to the customer's needs. Workers, especially those trained on Lean principles, have been taught that the next person that receives their work is their customer. We should treat our customers with the highest of respect and never allow, as an example, a defect to be passed to them. The customer is our means to our livelihood and we should always be very open and empathetic and carefully trained to listen and to serve them properly.

To listen to our customers properly, our employees should learn how to remove all of the barriers often placed between the customer and them. Quick and Easy Kaizen is a great tool to allow people, autonomously, to learn from their own ideas to serve customers better.

Stew Leonard's store in Westport, Connecticut, at one time was the country's largest grocery store. It was like buying your weekly food at Disneyland with live animals to pet, music while you shopped and dancing dolls to entertain you. As you walked into the front of the store you would see the large rock shown above.

A few years ago, I was writing a newsletter on customer service, and I interviewed Stew Leonard. I also called Stew Leonard's customer service department and asked their representative, "How is it possible for the customer to be always right?" She said, "Well, when the customer calls with a complaint, we just listen. We let the customer explain their problem. We don't defend[2] the company. Our goal is to always find a way so that the customer feels that they are right, not the company." This is very unusual.

I was told about a woman who shopped at Stew Leonard until nine o'clock at night. She filled her cart with products and was at the counter ready to check out when she realized that she left her purse at home and had no cash, checks or credit cards. "What can I do," she asked the cashier? "No problem, you just take the goods home and come back tomorrow morning and pay us."

The next morning she came back, paid her bill, and since she knew Stew personally she went to talk with him. "Stu, how can you allow your cashier to let me go home without paying?" Stu laughed and said, "I trust her discretion. She is the one talking to our customer, and she is empowered to make the decision. It doesn't mean that she lets everyone shop without paying. Look, I do close to a half billion dollars a year in sales and what does it mean to us if I lose $100? It is more important for us to keep our customers and our employees happy."

---

[2] Almost every time I call to question or to complain about products or charges, immediately the company spokesperson defends the actions of their company. It is as if the company is always right and you the customer are always wrong. How is it possible for a company to stay in business when customers are treated this way?

Introduction

Our employees are filled with wonderful ideas to improve our customer service if we can only trust them, respect their intelligence and let them all become problem solvers.

Circuit City executives decided that they did not need older employees at their stores – employees with the most knowledge to help their customers. They only needed people to help find products for their customers and run the cash registers. How can people without product knowledge be asked for their opinions to help customers make their choices? Very quickly Circuit City went bankrupt.

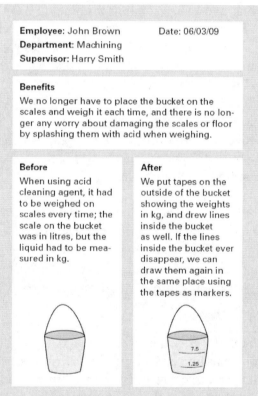

Fig. 1 <John Brown identified a small problem and then used his or her imagination to make his or her job easier. This is Kaizen, whereby we empower all employees to make their work easier, more interesting and to build their skills and capabilities from their own creative ideas.>

Top management is often isolated from the day-to-day problems confronted by the average worker. Even though the top manager does not have all of the detailed knowledge of the actual situation happening every day at the worksite, it doesn't prevent them from making the decisions that affect the way work is done and how employees interact with customers.

Traditional retail stores can only compete with the Internet by giving quicker service and better personal advice. I love shopping in Japan. My favorite store is Bic Camera where I find store employees who are like walking encyclopedias about their products. A year ago, when looking for a new HDTV set, I asked a Circuit City employee's advice about which set I should buy. Immediately, I saw that the Circuit City employee was neither really interested in serving me or knew much about the products on the floor. So, I walked out and didn't buy a set. A few weeks later, I was at Bic Camera in Tokyo and asked the same question to a Bic Camera employee. He advised me to buy a Panasonic plasma HDTV and told me all of the advantages. When I returned to America, I went to the Internet to look for the lowest price at the most reliable outlet and bought the set.

The challenge for American industry is how to educate their workers on their products, to trust their knowledge and to allow them to use that knowledge with the customers. I believe Quick and Easy Kaizen, the heart of this book, is the fastest approach to that aim. I do hope you enjoy the following journey with Bunji and me.

There is real magic, a depth of talent and latent abilities resting with all of your employees waiting for the right kind of leadership to harness their creative ideas. By nature all humans are problem solvers. Industry, in order to be internationally competitive today must learn how to ask, listen, support and harness the problem solving ability from all of those working for them. This book will teach you how.

Fig. 2 <The choice is yours either to continue to carry that heavy weight on your back, doing the same work the same way, over and over again, or you can stop for a few seconds, look around you, change and find better ways of doing things.>

Introduction Part II

Often when I keynote a conference I ask the audience, "What is the best day of the week?" Ninety-nine percent of the audience will answer the question by saying, "Friday." Why is Friday the best day of the week? I think it is because we all look forward to the weekend.. This holds true not only for the bulk of the workers but for management also. Why is the weekend better than the days we spend at work? Maybe it is because on the weekend we can do whatever we want to, but at work we have to do what we are told to do or what we are required to do.

***"The difference between work and play is that work is something we are obliged to do."* - Mark Twain**

Is it possible to make work as enjoyable and as fulfilling as what we do on the weekend and still be productive for our company, our society and for ourselves? What do we have to change at work to make this possible?

We human beings are distinct from the animal kingdom in that we can be creative in the things that we do. We are, by nature, problem solvers and have succeeded tremendously within this evolutionary process. In fact, the universe formed hundreds of billions of years before humans existed and could solve problems. Just go back to the year 1900 and see the differences that have taken place in only a little over 100 years. There were no automobiles, airplanes, radio, television, computers, or millions of other marvelous things that added to the quality of our lives.

For most people, the weekend is a time that provides the opportunity to be creative. Somehow at work this creative spirit for most of us has been dampened. I believe that we all are born to be creative, to solve problems continuously and to make life better for others and for ourselves. There are many companies in the world that have changed drastically to allow their employees to find a multitude of opportunities to be creative at work. When workers are encouraged to be creative, employees have richer lives and the companies are much more financially successful.

In this book, Bunji and I will share with you what other companies are doing to foster creativity with every one of their employees. We will show you how to do it. It is not complicated and if you are willing to experiment and to learn with us, we are sure that after you read this book and apply the knowledge available to you -- you will get up Monday morning and be excited to go to work. You are creative and with out any doubt you can easily apply the magic of creative involvement to your company. By doing so you will reap the benefits and rewards of happier associates, an overall more enjoyable work environement and significant success.

Acknowledgments

I want to thank many people for helping me write this book. First, I wish to express my gratitude to Bunji Tozawa, co-author, for introducing me to Quick and Easy Kaizen and allowing me to participate with him in writing this book. I also want to thank Alan G. Robinson for his preface; Tom Hartman and Jim Ambrey at Autoliv, for their interviews; Gene Levine for his beautiful stereogram cover; Mark Graban, Steven Hatch, Anthony Miriello, Malcolm Jones, for reading the book and recommending changes; and especially Kevin Tame and David Hubbard for their careful and marvelous editing; John Loftus for his translation of Bunji's Japanese material; Lorraine Millard for her work on the figures; Shana O'Brien for her transcriptions; Ryo and Noriko Hosoyamada for their discussion; Rob Clark, Jim O'Hearn, Mike Rempel, Michael Miller, Claudia Washington, Salvador Jesus Cesena for many of the Kaizen examples; Dan O'Malley and the other fabulous workers at Gulfstream, winners of the Shingo Prize, for their participation; Alicia Pollack for her help on Microsoft Word; Rory Bowman for his help with my Apple computer; John Grout for the Poka-yoke slides; and Shigehiro Nakamura for his infinite wisdom keeping me up to date on the latest in Japanese management concepts.

Preface
By Alan G. Robinson

Professor, Department of Finance & Operations Management,
University of Massachusetts
Co-author *Ideas Are Free*

This is a timely book on a topic of great importance to managers in these difficult times. The concepts in it will not only help you to survive the recession, but they will help you to emerge from it stronger. If you implement a high-performing idea system, like those described in this book, you will raise your organization's performance to a new level, one that would have been impossible to reach before.

Here is the opportunity the book addresses. Your front-line employees see many problems and opportunities that their managers don't see. Front-line workers interact with your customers using the processes you have designed, and they are full of ideas on how to improve the customers' experience and how to make your company work better. From hotels and financial services to retail and manufacturing, forward-thinking managers all over the world are waking up to the enormous potential in front-line ideas. Sadly, most organizations still do better at suppressing these ideas than promoting them. They are failing to tap one of the biggest resources available to them.

Why has doing something as obvious as listening to employee ideas always proven so difficult for managers since the beginning? As Norman Bodek and Bunji Tozawa state in the opening pages of this book, and as the research literature is increasingly showing, the ultimate problem is the strong human propensity for top-down management. When a people are put in charge of others, it is easy for them to start believing that they know better than their

subordinates. If this is true, the manager's job is indeed to issue orders and the worker's job is to follow them, as Frederick Taylor advocated a hundred years ago. But the fact is that your front-line workers – the lowest people on your totem pole – actually know a lot more about your company and how to improve it than you do. The first step to running a good idea system is *personal humility* – genuinely believing that your subordinates know many things that you don't.

Once you do believe this – and if you don't I hope this book will convince you to – there is still a lot to learn about how to encourage and implement large numbers of ideas. How did Autoliv and Gulfstream – two of the companies featured in this book – get 63 and 33 implemented ideas per person in 2008? This book will show you.

I have always admired both of the authors of this book, because they have always been just enough ahead of their time to be agents of significant positive change. In the early 1980s, Norman was one of the first Americans to appreciate the significance of the Toyota Production System and to understand what was behind it. But he didn't stop at mere appreciation; he acted on what he saw. He founded Productivity Press and Productivity Inc., where he played the key role in bringing those concepts to the West. He was the right person in the right place at the right time. We will never know what would have happened if he hadn't done what he did, but it is clear to me that he was a huge factor in waking U.S. manufacturers up to the fact that a superior production model had been developed in Japan and they had better pay attention to it.

I first met Bunji Tozawa in 1989 and was immediately impressed by him. As far as I am concerned, Bunji is the leading authority on idea systems in Japan. He knows more about how world-class Japanese companies manage kaizen and employee ideas than anyone on the planet. The Japan Human Relations Association, which he now heads, has almost all of the leading Japanese companies as members, and is the central repository and exchange

for knowledge about how to promote employee ideas in that country. I can still remember when, in 1990, Bunji first sent me a copy of the Japanese national idea statistics at that time. In that year, the average Japanese worker contributed 32 ideas, of which 87 percent were implemented. In the same year, according to the National Association of Suggestion Systems, the average American worker gave in 0.1 ideas, of which only 32 percent were implemented. To me, that single set of numbers – which remained essentially unchanged for fifteen years, goes a long way to explaining the long and inexorable decline of the U.S. automobile and other manufacturing industries. Bunji's organization, and Bunji himself, had a lot to do with creating this astonishing difference.

So when two such accomplished men – who have been at the center of the *kaizen* story – team up to write a book, I pay attention, and I urge you to as well. Only a relative handful of organizations in the world already do what is outlined in this book. In that sense, this book is ahead of its time. But in another sense it is not. When these concepts first came over from Japan in the 1980s, there was perhaps an excuse for being skeptical. I remember many managers thinking the concepts could apply only in Japan. Now, when companies like the ones featured in this book have proved that any company - of any size and in any industry - can do this, there are no excuses any more.

It is time to listen to your people and to act on their ideas.

One final note: for many companies in developed countries, an effective employee idea system may be one of the single biggest weapons against foreign competition. At the time of this writing, I have just returned from Vietnam, a country that is currently perceived as one of the main outsourcing threats to U.S. manufacturing. After moving from Mexico, to Malaysia and Indonesia, then to China, many U.S. companies are now starting to subcontract their manufacturing in Vietnam. My observation at all but one of the companies I was asked to help in that country – the

one exception being Toyota in Hanoi – was that they were relying almost solely on low labor costs, and not involving their workers in daily *kaizen* activities. If labor costs are all that drives business to them, soon their foreign customers will move to Cambodia or Sri Lanka, where wages are half again as much (and this is already starting to happen).

In an increasingly globalized future, it will be *ideas* that generate the competitive advantage which will keep jobs in the developed countries, and in the countries that currently rely on low wages to compete.

Many of those ideas lie untapped in the heads of front-line workers. That is why this book is so important.

Table of Contents

COVER	
INTRODUCTION	V
ACKNOWLEDGMENTS	XV
PREFACE	XVII
TABLE OF CONTENTS	XXI
FIGURES	XXVII

CHAPTER I	**1**
Doing, Documenting & Sharing	**1**
Be Persistent in Helping Others Change.	5
① Just talking about it (and leaving it at that)	8
② Just doing it (and leaving it at that)	8
③ Just documenting it (and leaving it at that)	8
① Just talking about it (and leaving it at that)	8
Be a Driver!	9
② Just doing it (and leaving it at that)	11
Nothing Changes When Things Are 'Left at That'	13
The Role of the Supervisors	18
③ Just documenting them (and leaving it at that)	22
Without Continuity, There Can Be No Results	26
Slow and Steady Kaizen Builds Underlying Strength for Corporate Renewal	29
Slack Times are Exactly When We Need to Push Kaizen Hard	31

CHAPTER II	**33**
'Systems' and 'Mechanisms'	**33**
For Sustaining and Extending the Kaizen Program	34
Reaffirm the Purpose of the Kaizen System	42

CHAPTER III	**49**
Discussion	**49**

The Mistake Board	71
Discussion Continued:	74

CHAPTER IV — 79
Partial Kaizen — 79

Toyota Claims Two Pillars For Their Success: JIT and "Respect for People."	83
Specific Examples are Our Most Powerful Weapon	84
Please do Think About This: as You Raise the Skills of People, You Both Add Value and Lower Costs.	90
How Can We Change All of This, Maybe by Doing More Homework?	90
Anyway, Start Wherever You Can	91

CHAPTER V — 97
Documenting Problems — 97

Documenting Kaizens	98
Why Things that Should Never Have Happened Keep on Happening	99
Kaizen Reports Show What's Going On in the Workplace	100
Praise	101
3-Gen	102
Routine Disclosure	105
Written Kaizen Confessions Are Painless	107
Establishing the Documentation and Sharing of Kaizens Starts with Forming a Habit	111

CHAPTER VI — 115
Real-Life Case Studies — 115

① Teaching Kaizen	116
② Battling with Practical Constraints	116
③ Solution – Compromise - Kaizen	116
④ Principles – Parameters – Set Moves	116
⑤ The Three Rules for Implementing Kaizen	116
Teaching Kaizen	116
Train in Accordance with the Three-Part Definition of Kaizen	116
① Change, Choosing Better Ways of Doing Things, or Changing the Conventional Methods	117
② Progressive Small Changes, Not Big Ones	117
③ Within a Framework of Constraints, Overcoming Resistance to Change	117
Begin by Defining Kaizen Clearly	117
① Change, Choosing Better Ways of Doing Things, or Changing the Conventional Methods	117

② Progressive Small Changes, Not Big Ones 121
There Are Wide Variations in People's Kaizen Abilities 123
③ Within a Framework of Constraints, Overcoming Resistance to Change 124
Kaizen Ability is the Ability to Cope with Reality 124
Why Is Kaizen OJT (On-the-Job Training) Needed? 127
Developing Kaizen Ability While Doing Kaizen 128
Doing Kaizen While Developing Kaizen Ability. 128
  ① Avoiding or Dealing with Constraints 128
  ② Surmounting Constraints 128
  ③ Breaking Through Constraints 128

CHAPTER VII 133
Practical Constraints 133
Doing Kaizen without Resources 134
Don't Just Write People off as 'Unmotivated' 135
Kaizen Power Equals Multiple Ideas 136

CHAPTER VIII 141
Solution–Compromise–Kaizen 141
The Three Approaches to Solving Problems 142
① Confrontation – Threats – Conflict (the Coercive Approach) 142
② Negotiation – Concession – Compromise (the Conciliatory Approach) 142
The Coercive Approach: Using Force 142
The Conciliatory Approach, Using Kind-Heartedness and Consideration 144
③ The Kaizen-Type Approach, Where the Method is Changed 147
Satisfying Both Parties through a Kaizen-Type Approach 149
Start by Thinking How to Change the Method (the way you do things) 150
The Method Decides whether You Stay in Hell or Go to Heaven 152

CHAPTER IX 155
Principles – Rules – Formulas 155
A Simple Kaizen Reveals the Standard Formula 156
A Kaizen for Reducing Inefficiency in a University Student's Part-Time Job 156
Basing Kaizens Based on Fixing Locations and Making Things Visual 157
Kaizens Based on Integration 159
Kaizens Based on Simultaneity and Single-Touch Operation 160
Fix One of the Elements 162
Don't Adjust; Set 163

CHAPTER X — 165
Three Rules for Doing Kaizen — 165
- The Standard Formula for Quick and Easy Kaizen — 166
- ① Attack on Different Levels — 172
- ② Attack from Various Angles — 172
- ③ Attack One Part at a Time — 172
- Use the 'At Least' Concept to Start Where You Can — 175
- If 'Best' is Impossible, Start with 'Better' — 175
- Break through the Limits with a Combination Play — 181
- A 'Combination Play' Kaizen for a PC — 182
- A Small Difference Can Make a Big Difference — 183
- A Kaizen Like That Can Soon Be Done — 184
- Respond Flexibly 'For the Time Being' — 189
- Multiple Causes Have Multiple Solutions — 191
- High-Tech Industry also Uses Successive 'For the Time Being' Solutions — 193
- If at First You Do Succeed... — 195

CHAPTER XI — 199
Real-Life Examples — 199
- ① The Spirit and Technique of Kaizen — 200
- ② Enforced Kaizen — 200
- ③ Anyone Can Do It, Every Day — 200
- ④ Established Formulae and Key Words — 200
- The Spirit and Technique of Kaizen — 200
- ① The Psychological Approach — 200
- ② The Technical Approach — 200
- We Have to Think for Ourselves – No-one Can Do It for Us — 201
- Work Smarter *and* Work Harder — 201
- No-One Can Be Forced to Do Kaizen If They Don't Want To — 210
- Use Concrete Examples to Convince People of Kaizen's Benefits — 211
- Even Pre-Schoolers Can Spot Differences — 213
- Psychological Regression When Faced with Kaizen — 215

CHAPTER XII — 219
Enforced Kaizen — 219
- Kaizen Only Lasts if Self-Directed — 220
- Enforced Kaizens Do Not Last — 221
- Self-directed Kaizens — 223

CHAPTER XIII — 227
Anyone Can Do It, Every Day — 227

Table of Contents

Simple Examples Are Truly the Stars of the Kaizen Program — 228
What and Who Are Case-Study Collections for? — 229
Start by Putting Together a Collection of 'Easy Examples' — 231
Compile These Collections Speedily — 232
The Secret of Keeping Kaizen Going is Speed — 233
Recognize Simple Kaizens Appropriately — 236
Examples and Keywords are the Weapons of Choice for Kaizen Coaching — 239
Can You Write Out Ten Kaizens Your Team Has Done? — 240

CHAPTER XIV — 247
Formulas and Keywords — 247
Words to Help People Notice Problems — 248
Finding Problems in Our Everyday Work — 249
'Stopping' is the Best Kaizen — 250
Stop — 250
Reduce — 250
Change — 250
If You Can't Stop It, Reduce It — 251
Change the Elements or Conditions — 252
Anyone Can Understand a Kaizen Example from Her Own Workplace — 254
Keywords for Rapid Implementation — 256
If at First You Don't Succeed… — 258

CHAPTER XV — 261
The Four Fallacies — 261
A Manual for Annihilating the Four Fallacies — 262
No. 1 If our jobs get easier, they'll give us something else to do — 264
People Make Improvements and the Work Increases — 264
Kaizen Does Not Cause Layoffs — 266
No. 2 Kaizen stresses us and takes away our breathing-space — 269
Use Kaizen to Take the Pressure Off — 269
Kaizen Releases us from what is Useless — 270
No. 3 My work is special, so I can't do Kaizen — 273
There Are Differences, Yes, but There Are also Similarities — 273
No.4 'Mickey Mouse' Kaizens are embarrassing — 279
The Best is the Enemy of Kaizen — 279
Aim for the Best, but Start with the Better — 280

CHAPTER XVI — 283
Simple Kaizen Case Studies — 283
A Collection of Case Studies that 'Tell It Like It Is' — 284

Simple Examples Lead to Sustained Expansion of the Kaizen Program 284
Collect Case Studies Promptly 284
Think We now Know that Top Down Doesn't Always Work. 293
Top Management in Japan Leads the Suggestion System in 48.2% of the Companies Involved. 294

CHAPTER XVII   **297**
SUMMARY   **297**
Interview with Tom Hartman   **301**
Interview with Tim Ambrey   **329**
Kaizens (Before and After)   **341**
Bunji Tozawa - Biography   **359**
Norman Bodek - Biography   **363**
Bibliography   **369**
Index   **379**
Books Previously Published   **381**
If you need help in implementing Kaizen contact me at bodek@pcspress.com   385

Figures

Fig. 1 <John Brown identified a small problem and then used his or her imagination to make his or her job easier. This is Kaizen, whereby we empower all employees to make their work easier, more interesting and to build their skills and capabilities from their own creative ideas.> ix

Fig. 2 <The choice is yours either to continue to carry that heavy weight on your back, doing the same work the same way, over and over again, or you can stop for a few seconds, look around you, change and find better ways of doing things.> .. xi

Fig. 3 <It is easy to see that there are documents in the "out" box.> 5

Fig. 4 <Jim O'Hearn doubled his productivity from his one idea.> 9

Fig. 5 <Autoliv in Ogden, Utah received 63 written implemented ideas per person in 2008 and expects 96, 8 per month, in 2009. Just amazing what people are capable of doing when you ask them to identify problems and solve them.> 14

Fig. 6 <Idea – do it – document it – share it> 15

Fig. 7 <Picture shows a bump on the factory floor.> 20

Fig. 8 <Don't just leave it at that.> 25

Fig. 9 <A Kaizen Memo or Form> 26

Fig. 10 <Michael's idea.> 37

Fig. 11 <The "leave-it-up-to-you-type of suggestion scheme."> . 39

Fig. 12 <How can you improve the shelves?> 45

Fig. 13 <"Tilt the shelves.> 45

Fig. 14 <Michael Tobin and his mistakes. Eight times he knew how to not repeat his mistake, 3 times unknown to him and 3 mistakes are under study.> 72

Fig. 15 <Gulfstream Mistake Board> 73

Fig. 16 <Mistake Board> 73

Fig. 17 <Going to all the trouble of.>	82
Fig. 18 <Citizen Watch saving seconds.>	85
Fig. 19 <Lighten your load.>	87
Fig. 20 <Other companies Kaizen examples.>	89
Fig. 21 <DCI Kaizen display wall.>	93
Fig. 22 <Our own Kaizen examples.>	95
Fig. 23 <Accident Happens>	100
Fig. 24 <Change the line from black to white making it easier to see.>	104
Fig. 25 <Documenting Kaizens>	106
Fig. 26 < A Kaizen Form>	108
Fig. 27 <File cabinet door shows what is inside the cabinet.>	109
Fig. 28 <Kaizen memos tell us what's really going on.>	111
Fig. 29 <Concealing poor working conditions.>	113
Fig. 30 <The three-part definition of Kaizen.>	120
Fig. 31 <Kaizen is not difficult.>	125
Fig. 32 <Kaizen ability – ability to cope with constraints.>	129
Fig. 33 <Eliminated a fire risk.>	131
Fig. 34 <Doing Kaizen – Battling with constraints.>	138
Fig. 35 <Knobs now go on to the next process.">	139
Fig. 36 <Conflict of interests.>	144
Fig. 37 <The coercive approach.>	145
Fig. 38 <The conciliatory approach.>	146
Fig. 39 <Splitting the difference.>	148
Fig. 40 <Mutual satisfaction and sacrifice.>	149
Fig. 41 <This makes is much easier.>	151
Fig. 42 <Satisfying one party does not increase the other's dissatisfaction.>	152
Fig. 43 <The right order of thinking.>	154
Fig. 44 <Scoop the sugar out.>	158
Fig. 45 <Kaizen makes it easy to find things.>	160
Fig. 46 <Integrate.>	162
Fig. 47 <Reduce variable elements and adjustments.>	164
Fig. 48 <The 3 rules.>	167
Fig. 49 <Failure to change is a vice!>	171

Fig. 50 <You can't put a square into a round hole. Picture from John Grout http://csob.berry.edu/faculty/jgrout/pokayoke.shtml>........ 176
Fig. 51 < The plug only goes in one way. http://csob.berry.edu/faculty/jgrout/pokayoke.shtml>........ 176
Fig. 52 <Laser Poka-yoke device - 177
Fig. 53 <Even your sink has a Poka-yoke device. The small hole is used so that water will not overflow. http://csob.berry.edu/faculty/jgrout/pokayoke.shtml>........ 177
Fig. 54 <*Aim for the best but start with 'better.'*> 178
Fig. 55 <Action against quality defects.>.................................. 179
Fig. 56 <Action against quality defects.>.................................. 180
Fig. 57 >The irritating PC.>... 182
Fig. 58 <When you see the hourglass, you don't get annoyed.> 183
Fig. 59 <Relieving the irritation of.>.. 184
Fig. 60 <Problems.>.. 185
Fig. 61 <Relieving the irritation of waiting for a train.> 186
Fig. 62 <Big ideas but small.>.. 190
Fig. 63 <Multiple causes are involved in producing results.>... 192
Fig. 64 <Solutions are the reverse of causes.> 193
Fig. 65 <Computer software development is also a series of Kaizens.> 194
Fig. 66 <In Kaizen, you can take your move back.> 196
Fig. 67 <Changeover time was reduced.> 197
Fig. 68 <A hazard was eliminated.>.. 207
Fig. 69 <Teaching and promoting.> 210
Fig. 70 <Which Way of Doing the Job is Easier?.> 213
Fig. 71 <The cable is held off the floor.> 216
Fig. 72 <It is easier to make notes.> 217
Fig. 73 <Enforced Kaizen.>.. 221
Fig. 74 <Voluntary Kaizen.> 224
Fig. 75 <Easy Kaizen examples.> 230
Fig. 76 <It is much easier to thread wires through the tube.> ... 232
Fig. 77 <Our own Kaizen examples.> 234
Fig. 78 <Presenting high level Kaizens.>................................... 238
Fig. 79 <Key words – Observation.>.. 242

Fig. 80 <Key words Ideation 243
Fig. 81 *<Key words Implementation.>* 244
Fig. 82 <A Kaizen form.> 245
Fig. 83 <Sending windowed envelopes.> 246
Fig. 84 <Here are some clues for Kaizen.> 249
Fig. 85 <Stop – reduce – change.> 252
Fig. 86 <The problem was eliminated without changing the functional part of the roller.> 253
Fig. 87 <There are now fewer latecomers.> 257
Fig. 88 <It is much easier to hide a group of columns.> 259
Fig. 89 <The area looks much tidier.> 260
Fig. 90 <Now we can monitor staff attendance visually.> 263
Fig. 91 <Fewer people, but more work.> 268
Fig. 92 <Leave out.> 270
Fig. 93 <The chain turns much more smoothly.> 271
Fig. 94 <We can learn from others if we focus on commonalities.> 274
Fig. 95 <I no longer forget to make calls.> 276
Fig. 96 <I don't waste time looking for the test stick.> 277
Fig. 97 <Aim for the best but start with better.> 280
Fig. 98 <Reading and understanding case studies.> 286
Fig. 99 <Packing the videos.> 288
Fig. 100 <Hanging up the bubble rack on a stand.> 289
Fig. 101 <Replace the bubble wrap with plain wrapping paper.> 289
Fig. 102 <Bubble wrap shelves are now empty.> 290
Fig. 103 <A pencil.> 291
Fig. 104 < Remember the old pencil sharpener?> 291
Fig. 105 <Pen and ink.> 292
Fig. 106 <A ballpoint pen.> 292
Fig. 107 <Zebra pen with 4 colors and a pencil.> 292
Fig. 108 <Kaizen is about doing the obvious as a matter of course.> 293
Fig. 109 <Autoliv Suggestion Form.> 323
Fig. 110 <No Home for Blue Tape on Wire install> 324
Fig. 111 <Problem: Hard to reach lead wires on top layer of rack for wire install> 324

Figures

Fig. 112 <Problem: Wire on Driver #4 on Do All station. The octiker gun rubbing on wire.> 325
Fig. 113 <Problem: Redbook holder on the side of the bag fold is not longer needed.> 325
Fig. 114 <Problem: On Wire Rack boxes w/wires won't come forward, needs rollers.> 326
Fig. 115 <Problem: Clip mounting hanging tab.> 326
Fig. 116 <Problem: Need more totes of inflators on rack.> 327
Fig. 117 <Problem: Sock holder on right side obstructs walk through.> 327
Fig. 118 <Problem & Solution: Add water to bottom shelf of refrigerator in A/P area. Lean groups seem to want water in the afternoon and they are always running to basement refrigerator.> 328
Fig. 119 <Pokka Corporation Nagoya Factory.> 340

Chapter I
Doing, Documenting & Sharing

① Abolish 'Leaving It At That'

② 'Systems' and 'Mechanisms'

③ Detecting Problems Promptly

2 How to Do Kaizen

Since this is really three books in one:
- Bunji's [3] - principles
- Norman's - application of Kaizen in the West
- Together with the interviews in the back

There might seem to be some inconsistency, but I hope to tie it all together and give you something practical to help you establish or perfect a participative management system. Employees have many opportunities to discover problems and their solutions in the work environment and it is management's responsibility to help foster those creative ideas and bring them to fruition.

I often keynote conferences and run workshops where I talk about my favorite subject Quick and Easy Kaizen. At the end of the presentation, I ask the participants if they liked the subject and if they are willing to go back to their companies and start a Quick and Easy Kaizen process. Everyone stands up, raises their right hand, and makes a commitment and pledge to go back and implement a new Quick and Easy Kaizen process. But, hardly anyone lives up to their commitment. They like the idea of empowering employees to solve small problems around their work area, but virtually everyone is reluctant to do it. Virtually everyone is excessively cautious about doing something new, about bringing change to their worksite.

Why are we willing to change but then become reluctant to do it? Do most of us have a fear of change? If we do fear change, is there a way -- a simple way to overcome that fear and bring positive change to the workplace?

For the moment let us accept the idea that we personally resist change but we can still be a positive force in helping others move

---

[3] Bunji Tozawa, co-author, is the CEO of The Japan HR Association and has been Japan's leading teacher of Quick and Easy Kaizen.

towards change. I do believe that the key role of a manager, supervisor, is to be a coach and to help people with this process.

A great change maker was Taiichi Ohno, vice president of manufacturing at Toyota. Each day he stood on the factory floor getting people to change for the better. He challenged people by demanding they do something different to make the workplace more efficient. He never really told people how to do something he just demanded that it be done. "Reduce costs by 10%!" then workers were required to reduce costs by 10%. Ohno often had no idea if the workers could do it. If he didn't ask then he would never know if they could do it or not.

After World War II, Toyota was known for making "junk" automobiles and now they make the Lexus. How did they do it? One of the keys was getting every employee to participate in problem solving activities.

Ohno was a master of identifying "wastes" (Muda in Japanese) and then challenging people to eliminate those wastes. The art, of course, is for you to be able to see the wastes:

Classic wastes from Mr. Ohno and Dr. Shingo:

- Overproduction
- Waiting
- Transportation
- Excess inventory
- Defects
- Excess motion
- Over-processing

Two other wastes to consider:

- Underutilization of people's talents
- Manager's resistance to change

Your company needs managers who are willing to make demands - not by telling people how to do it, but by demanding that they stretch themselves to do things beyond their current perceptions or capabilities.

Like a teacher at the ideal school, your role is to look for the potential in each student, and guide them to develop themselves to their fullest. You focus and coach them on their strengths not their weakness. You look at them as flowers ready to open to the beauty, wisdom, and potential greatness lying within. You see yourself as a limitation, a possible obstacle for them. You ask yourself how you can help them bring out the best from within and you are there as a guide, a mentor and a coach for them.

In 1970, Toyota received around one idea per employee per year. Then in the 1980s, they were up to 47-implemented ideas per employee per year. You ask, you can get -- you don't ask, you don't get.

The Kaizen Blitz has been very popular in recent years, but this book is not about the Kaizen Blitz. The Blitz, even though very powerful, is normally a weeklong event where teams look to reduce the non-value adding wastes in their processes. Kaizen, on the other hand, starts by asking every employee to look around their work area and begin to identify small problems. Then they bring those problems to the attention of their supervisor, and, if possible, implements a solution that solves the problem. Sometimes, solving the problem is beyond the ability of worker. At this point, others come to help assist in finding an appropriate solution. This book is about this idea of Kaizen, asking everyone to be involved in continuous improvement and opening up to their maximum creative potential.

The average worker might not discover a new product, but they can participate in problem solving activities and collectively help make your organization more competitive. How can you compete with a company like Toyota that received 47-implemented ideas

per worker? A year ago, Subaru received 108 ideas per worker and saved over $5000 per worker, while Gulfstream received 33-implemented ideas per worker and saved millions. How did they do it? **How did they manage so many ideas with ease?**

Two things: if you want continuous improvement then you have to be willing to change and find a way to empower all the employees to be involved in the change process.

How can you overcome this mountainous resistance to change?

Be Persistent in Helping Others Change.

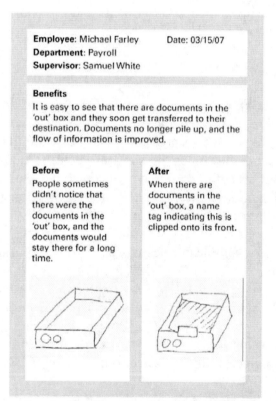

Fig. 3 <It is easy to see that there are documents in the "out" box.>

Surely, one of our major goals is for everyone at work to be involved in continuous improvement activities. We should be always looking to find new ways to make work easier and more interesting, while build skills and capabilities. Of course, you want to help make your organizations become more successful by reducing costs, improving quality, safety and productivity. However, you can get all of this by not demanding the worker focus only on the organization's needs, but by simply asking the worker to look around their own work area to make their own work easier. This is a subtle but very important shift that will get you the results that you want.

I met with Bunji in Japan and asked his advice on how to get people to live up to their commitments and implement a Quick and Easy Kaizen system. He said, "Norman, ask them to go back and identify two small problems, come up with the solutions and send you an email with their ideas."

At a recent BAE Lean conference in Fort Wayne, Indiana, I took Bunji's advice and asked the audience, "Please go back to your work areas, look for two problems and their solutions, implement them and send me an email showing your results." It worked. Three weeks after the conference, at the time of this writing, 46 people had each sent me two ideas, a total of 92 wonderful items that helped their company be more productive.

One of the 92 examples: *Review of cycle time and cost reductions via elimination of the Washing/Baking process for printed circuit boards. We will flow this back to our supply base through our Strategic Sourcing organization. It is believed that most if not all of our suppliers are already doing this. This will eliminate in some cases 24 hours worth of cycle time.* - Sean Cafferty, NH Operations Director of Mfg., Electronic Solutions BAE Systems

Quick and Easy Kaizen simply asks you to stop for a moment and look for opportunities to improve. Now that we got them started, the next problem is how to make sure that the process is sustained?

Doing, Documenting & Sharing 7

According to Bunji, work improvement means doing, documenting and sharing Kaizens. You detect a small problem; you stop, record the problem, think about the solution, implement the solution and share it with others. The sharing is normally done by hanging up your written idea onto a bulletin board or wall, displaying your ideas with other workers.

Kaizen is a Japanese word meaning change or continuous improvement:

- **("kai")** means "change" or "the action to correct."
- **("zen")** means "good."

Be like Mr. Ohno. Ask people to go and make improvements and then listen to their ideas and help them to implement them.

Start off by asking every employee to look around their work area and begin to identify small problems, bring these problems to the attention of their supervisor, and if possible implement a solution that solves the problem. We want employees to be change makers. You, as a manager, must look at people as if there were gold mines of knowledge sitting inside them waiting to be tapped.

Once you get started with a new Kaizen program and people see that they can do it because you listen to and respect their ideas, then you can start to begin to ask every employee to find two problems per month. Kaizen is change for the better; Kaizens are improvement ideas. We want to abolish complacency – to eliminate the 'leave it at that' syndrome. In other words, work improvement consists of getting rid of the following three Leave-It-At-Thats:

How to Do Kaizen

① **Just talking about it (and leaving it at that)**

② **Just doing it (and leaving it at that)**

③ **Just documenting it (and leaving it at that)**

What do these mean? Let's examine each in turn.

① **Just talking about it (and leaving it at that)**

Don't just talk about or appeal to people to do Kaizen and leave it at that; get going and actually start doing whatever you can to make the process work. If you know the process of how to look for a problem, you will always be able to find problems. We will teach you in this book how to look. Dr. Shigeo Shingo's[4] favorite phrase, similar to Nike's, was "Do it!" Chihiro Nakao, a consultant from Taiho Kogyo, a Toyota subsidiary, who brought the Kaizen Blitz to America, once said to me "I was always frightened of Dr. Shingo. He used to come to our company monthly, and then challenge me to do something different. I was always afraid that I couldn't live up to his expectations." However, through learning from Dr. Shingo the process of continuous improvement, Nakao became one of the most successful Lean consultants in the world.

One day, while walking along the factory floor at Clark Metal, I stopped and turned to a worker and asked him to show me one of the ideas he had recently submitted. Jim's job was to attach two metal plates to a fixture, take the fixture to a grinder and polish the plates. Since Kaizen is encouraged at Clark Metal, Jim was excited to show me the new fixture that he designed on his own. The great thing about Jim is he didn't wait for an engineer to think for him; he took the initiative on his own and doubled his productivity without sacrificing any quality. This one small idea saved Clark Metal at least $40,000 a year.

---

[4] Dr. Shingo taught 3000 Toyota engineers on problem solving.

Doing, Documenting & Sharing

Fig. 4 <Jim O'Hearn doubled his productivity from his one idea.>

Jim's example easily shows how important Kaizen is to a company and its financial growth. However, the most puzzling thing to me is, why isn't everyone doing Quick and Easy Kaizen?

Of course, the supervisors and managers must be the "cheerleaders" that inspire people to look for opportunities to implement improvement ideas. Towards the end of the book you will find a list of keywords to use to guide workers to come up with improvement ideas.

A great key is to realize that after every improvement is an opportunity to make another improvement. It is one small step after another.

Be a Driver!

Be a driver! I use the term, "driver" to show that Lean efforts, in order to be successful, must have a leader - a person - who is primarily responsible for moving your Lean efforts forward. Like

an automobile, a company committed to continuous improvement needs a driver that is always looking for improvement opportunities and encouraging others to improve everyday.

Taiichi Ohno was an incredible driver. Ohno knew how to identify waste and see opportunities for improvement. He was relentless in his demands for continuous improvement and required them from every person that he came in contact with. People were afraid of him, not because they would be fired for they all had lifetime employment, but because they were unsure if they could live up to his expectations.

He would challenge them constantly to make improvements, never knowing if they could do it or not. He was always keenly aware of the fact that he did not want to be their limitation to their improvement. He knew that by telling them how to do it he was hindering their growth. He just demanded that improvement be done.

The miracle was that over time and with lots of patience, Ohno was able to drive Lean/JIT throughout Toyota and all of their subsidiaries. He would be able to say to someone, "Look, I would like you to improve productivity by 10% in your area, and they would do it. "I would like to see that waste eliminated," and it would happen. It would happen because he was relentless.

"Just do it!" This was Dr. Shingo's favorite phrase. Like Mr. Ohno, Dr. Shingo would not accept excuses. Both were amazing drivers of continuous improvement.

I think that a driver is what every company needs. Think of it. If you are a manager, isn't it your prime responsibility to drive continuous improvement? You do it by asking and by driving it, by challenging, unendingly. By demanding it -- it begins to happen, and then you learn what's possible and people begin to see what they're capable of doing. Unless you demand, you surely don't know what people are capable of doing.

Doing, Documenting & Sharing

So be a driver. Don't be reckless, but take your foot off the brakes and let people show you what they can do. You will be amazed.

Either you become a driver of continuous improvement or find someone else to do that role, or else you will just continue, "to talk about it and leave at that."

② Just doing it (and leaving it at that)

Don't just go to the trouble of doing Kaizens and leave it at that: document them and keep records of them as simple 'Kaizen memos'.

Of course, many people come up with ideas to make things better but the process is often not systematic, not really sustained, and it doesn't get on the average at least 24 implemented ideas per person per year. It doesn't get everyone excited about doing new things.

A 'Kaizen memo' is a simple document that workers use to write down the problem facing them and to also write down ideas on how to solve the problem. You will see many examples in this book.

I remember a worker at Technicolor showing great resistance in writing his ideas down. He liked the idea of implementing ideas but couldn't understand the need to write them down. If you don't write them down you lose the opportunity to share your ideas with others and to inspire other workers to copy your idea.

We want continuous improvement. We want better quality, lower costs and happier employees. Yes, we want people to be creative, but copying is one important way that we learn and we can be creative as we copy. How does a baby learn? The child copies the

parents and adds to his or her knowledge base. They see daddy use a hammer. They pick up the hammer and smash the furniture.

We want to copy, but part of the Quick and Easy Kaizen system is the safeguards that we do things only for the better and we don't end up smashing the furniture.

I recommend that you allow the worker to also take a picture of the problem and then another picture to show what the improvement looks like. Then display those pictures for the others workers to see and to copy for themselves. Of course, you want the workers to be creative, but even copying and using someone else's idea can lead to other innovative and creative acts.

Many workers also like to draw simple diagrams to show their idea. When writing an idea, try to confine it to just 75 words or less. We don't want Quick and Easy Kaizen to be a new bureaucracy. Gulfstream, with 1000 employees in one of their plants, has only one person keeping the records. The company received over 33,000 ideas last year all administered by their supervisors and managers.

Don't just file the memos away and leave it at that; take every possible opportunity and use all sorts of formats to share the Kaizens around.

Year's back, I visited a Dana plant in Kentucky. Dana is a supplier of frames to Toyota. Up on virtually every wall were ideas submitted by workers. The lunchroom seemed to be the hub of the idea program with Kaizen memos everywhere on display.

It is only when we follow up our talking, doing and documenting that work improvement can be said to be taking place. If even one of the three, just talking, just doing, just documenting is missing, even if some Kaizens are being done, the activity will eventually cool off and the Kaizen program will grind to a halt. Either that, or it will be confined to particular groups of people and will not

develop into a companywide program of work improvement involving everyone.

Nothing Changes When Things Are 'Left at That'

Any company facing hard times in the form of a lengthy recession clamors about the need to reform its business processes and improve the way it works. However, although some companies get solid results from their programs of reform and improvement, others never get beyond the talking stage. The difference between them is that, while the latter type of company does nothing about the three 'leave-it-at-thats,' the former type of company abolishes them by doing, documenting and sharing its Kaizens.

The worst type of company is one that talks about Kaizens but does nothing – the type of company whose senior executives and middle managers spasmodically rant and rave about the need to do Kaizen, saying things like, "We can't go on like this!" "We need to slowly and steadily improve the way we work!" and "Our company won't survive if we don't reform!" Naturally, some improvement takes place whenever they start shouting, but it doesn't continue. As soon as the managers stop talking about it, it's all over. Because the employees know this, they temporarily pretend to be doing Kaizen. But it doesn't last.

Of course, even engaging in Kaizen activity spasmodically is better than standing by and watching the company go under; but the benefits obtained from transitory Kaizen activity like this are insignificant. Everyone must pull their own weight. You want to harness everyone's talent. It is like a tug of war, a wonderful exercise to show the need for everyone to fully participate.

Stored Gas ASH F-Cell

Before: E-check machine is not required for all part numbers. Operators have to take 5 steps around this machine every time they produce a part that does not require E-check.

After: Installed wheels on E-check which allows it to be pushed out of the way and installed sliding rollers to bring the work to the operator when E-check is not required.

Results:
Eliminated 5 steps per part or 2,250,000 steps a year.

Fig. 5 <Autoliv in Ogden, Utah received 63 written implemented ideas per person in 2008 and expects 96, 8 per month, in 2009. Just amazing what people are capable of doing when you ask them to identify problems and solve them.>

Transitory Kaizen activity will not deliver the gains required for companies to get through the tough times they currently face.

Repeated stirring calls to action are all very well, but if they are not followed up, employees will soon recognize them and regard them as merely temporary. In fact, such posturing may even have the opposite of its intended effect. Employees might get sick and tired of hearing it and lose their motivation.

Just talking about Kaizen and leaving it at that is certainly not confined to the upper echelons of management. Middle managers and ordinary employees are just as prone to go around making suggestions and telling people what they should do. They often do

Doing, Documenting & Sharing

not take responsibility for acting on their own ideas and do not

Fig. 6 <Idea – do it – document it – share it>

Make any effort to reform or improve their own ways of working. The upshot is that both management and the workers do nothing but talk, and no one actually tries to get things to change. Even if something is done, it is no more than a temporary display, and no one attempts to carry on with it.

You can tell people what to do and they will do it because you are paying them. However, you can also challenge them to be more creative and make a powerful difference for both themselves and the company.

Just ask yourself, "How did Gulfstream Corporation go from less than one implemented idea in 2005 to over 33 ideas per employee

in 2009, over 33,000 ideas implemented? And how did Autoliv in Ogden, Utah get on the average 63 ideas per employee in 2009?"

I published a book in 1991 titled "40 Years, 20 Million Ideas -- The Toyota Suggestion System." In 1960, Toyota received, on the average, only one idea per person. We hope to give you the knowledge and the power to replicate what Toyota has done to go from one idea per year per employee to 47-implemented ideas. I always feel that if someone else can do something, then I can do it. Simply said, "If there is a will, there is a way."

Yes, most of us are afraid of change, but if we want to succeed in this highly competitive world, we have to break through our resistance to change.

You need a change driver, like Ohno, in your company. Just bite the bullet and become the 'hero' for your organization and for yourself.

I like the saying, "If not me then who?" And, "If not now then when?"

In 1898, Kodak invented the first suggestion system and the first suggestion was, "Clean the windows!" A great idea! Unfortunately, the supervisor would not let the worker implement the idea. The worker was not allowed to leave her/his job. The supervisor had to implement the idea and it became a burden to management and they quickly 'killed' a very powerful employee involvement system. It became a typical suggestion program using the 'I suggest, you implement' type of scheme.'

To make Quick and Easy Kaizen work, the employee who comes up with the idea implements it either by herself, with the help of their work team, or with a support group such as maintenance. The intention is to encourage employees to improve their own ways of working.

Doing, Documenting & Sharing 17

Employees will sometimes come up with ideas that are grand ideas but must be done by others or are out of the range of the budget. For example, a worker once at Technicolor said, "Why can't they put a roof over the parking lot? When it rains I get soaked to the skin." This is a great idea but not necessarily possible to implement easily.

The scope of work improvement is restricted to what individuals can do within the limits of their own authority and capability. When you read the interview in the back of the book with Tom Hartman, you can see how Autoliv has been able to expand this concept to dedicate a cadre of people to assist its workers to help them get their ideas implemented. I saw this both at Aisin Seki and Canon in Japan. They had set up machine shops that build new devices that workers had suggested to improve productivity, safety and quality of the products. While workers will normally focus on small ideas, especially to get started, major changes and reforms that exceed the workers' limits are the responsibility of others who do have the necessary status, authority and capability to implement change.

The more you look at the worker as an integral part of the production process, the better the ideas will become. However, if all anyone has to do is make suggestions, without any responsibility for implementing them, they can say whatever they like. Regardless of how many ideas are suggested if the idea is not implemented it is useless and merely garbage. By having people not only make suggestions but by allowing them to become full partners in the implementation proccess you set up the environment for success.

The Role of the Supervisors

In the past six years, I have taught many companies Quick and Easy Kaizen, some like Gulfstream (33 ideas per employee per year), have been very successful in getting many creative ideas from almost all of their workers while other companies have not been that successful, only getting five to seven ideas per employee per year. Why the difference? Why are some companies able to be so much more successful than others? Surely it is not the workers. It is supervision. You have to ask, listen, praise, be thankful, persistent, and even demanding that people bring out the best from themselves. You have to be like a "bull" knowing that if other companies can do it so can you. Of course, supervisors have to be trained to be coaches, not to beat up on people, but to simply ask and help people come up with ideas and help them implement those ideas.

Yes, supervision either makes or breaks Quick and Easy Kaizen. Often when a company needs a new supervisor, they look at the workforce and select the best worker and makes her/his a supervisor with very little extra training. Unfortunately, what happens is you often take a very good worker and make them into a poor supervisor; you lose both ways.

The new supervisor's role model was his or her last supervisor who came up the same way. Needed is a new way to select, train and develop supervisors to be real coaches. A real coach focuses almost solely on bringing out the best from their workers. They are not there to control people. But how do you do this? Just believe that people are adults and fully capable of controlling them selves. But, they do need leadership, teachers, and coaches to inspire them.

Doing, Documenting & Sharing   19

Toyota has a team leader for every 4 to 8 workers who spends 50% of their time coaching workers to solve problems and 50% of their time substituting for their team members on the line. This allows the team members time away from their jobs to solve problems.

On my first trip to Japan in 1981, I went to Sumitomo Electric and heard a lecture by Dr. Ryuji Fukuda on the topic of "On Error Training." The following are the rules:

1. When a person detects an error he/she stops working, immediately, and calls over their entire group.
2. The person who detected the error leads the discussion.
3. They are looking for the root cause of the problem.
4. The supervisor, at first, is not allowed to speak and must patiently wait and give the person who detected the error the opportunity to discover, on their own, the cause of the problem.
5. All the team members are allowed to participate and ask questions to determine the cause of the problem.
6. The team members use the Five Why's[5] technique to find the root cause of the problem.
7. The supervisors are allowed to speak only after the team has had an opportunity to discover the cause of the problem by themselves.

Toyota's system of stopping the line when a problem occurs is very similar to on error training. It gives workers the opportunity to develop their problem-solving skills while giving the supervisor an opportunity to develop their coaching skills. Sure, you do lose some production time, but you gain enormously in the long run by reducing the repetition of the same errors.

Also, every time the line stops many problems are revealed which are opportunities to add to the Quick and Easy Kaizen system.

---

[5] Five Why's technique asks people when faced with a problem to ask why questions five times, attempting to get to the root cause of a problem.

At the beginning of my workshops, I ask all of the attendees to think about two problems they currently have at work. I tell them that during the class they will write two problems and two solutions. At the end of one of the workshops, Scott got up and walked to the front of the class to give one of his problems.

Scott said, "When I move the glass windows along the floor, sitting on a cart, occasionally, when I go over a bump a window breaks." I thanked Scott for being the first to present the problem to the class and then asked him, "How would you solve that problem?" Scott said, "I would bring the problem to the attention of my supervisor."

Fig. 7<Picture shows a bump on the factory floor.>

This is very typical in most companies when a worker detects a problem they present it to their supervisor and expect the supervisor to solve the problem. However, with Quick and Easy Kaizen we want to develop the skills of the workers and that can be done when the worker takes the initiative to solve their own problems.

Doing, Documenting & Sharing   21

A week later, in a different class with about a dozen supervisors from the same company, I presented Scott's dilemma. I asked the supervisors, "What would you tell Scott when he showed his problem to you." One supervisor said, "I would tell Scott to be more careful." Another supervisor said, "I would tell Scott to move the cart around the bump." A third supervisor said, "We should fix the floor removing the bump, but I don't have the time or the budget to take care of it now."

When I asked Scott how would he fix the problem he responded by saying, "I need to remove the bump. I would have to get an axe and a shovel and chip it. I would then have to make some cement to finish the job." I told Scott, "Great, do it." Then he responded with, "I have never used cement before." Then what could you do now, Scott?" I asked. "I would have to ask maintenance to help me." "Yes," I replied. "And what is even better is to have maintenance teach you how to do it."

A wonderful technique I could have used to identify the root cause with Scott is 5 Why's technique:

Why did the window crack?

> "The cart went over the bump and the window was not secure enough."

Why wasn't the window secure?

> "Someone forgot to tighten it down."

Why do you think it was not tightened down?

> "We didn't use a checklist to remind us."

Why didn't you use a checklist?

"We did not have a checklist for tightening."

Why didn't you have a checklist for tightening?

"We didn't think it was necessary, but now we will make a checklist and make sure that it is used and posted for everyone to see."

The 5 Why's technique is simple but needs to be re-enforced by supervision until all employees get into the habit of using it. It works. It works very well. Try it!

Quick and Easy Kaizen is a new and simple way to improve people's skills. The role of the supervisor is not to do it for the worker but to be a coach and help people build their skills and capabilities.

③ Just documenting them (and leaving it at that)

When companies run less-glamorous, slow-but-steady implementation-type Kaizen systems they are able to exercise their underlying strength and stay the course.

There have also been some companies that have changed their suggestion schemes from conventional types to the implementation types and are still not achieiving meaningful results. This was because, although their employees did worthwhile Kaizens, they just did them and left it at that, so the Kaizens had no staying power. The mechanisms for documenting and sharing them were not working effectively. This is because their employees do worthwhile Kaizens, but they just do them and leave it at that. This causes the Kaizens to have no staying power. The mechanisms for documenting and sharing Kaizen are not working effectively.

Doing, Documenting & Sharing

Just doing Kaizens is not good enough, because if nothing more is done the improvements are not sustained. Even when the Kaizens are recorded and documented at these companies, the records are simply collected and filed away, so the circle does not widen and the Kaizen program fails to continue.

Kaizens should be shared with the rest of the workforce; if this is not done, they remain the property of particular groups of people. In short, mechanisms for documenting and sharing Kaizens are absolutely indispensable in order to evolve and develop them in the following ways:

① Transform Kaizens from short-lived improvements to enduring ones.

② Disseminate the lessons from Kaizens throughout the company, and avoid the problem of benefitting just one group of workers.

③ Allow for planned, organized, systematic Kaizens, instead of unplanned, spontaneous, unsystematic Kaizens.

Sustained Documenting Leads to Sustained Kaizen

Years back, I ran a data processing company in Grenada, West Indies, with about 200 people and received a very difficult assignment from the New York Telephone Company. I was not sure if we were capable of doing this particular job. Many of the employees did not go to high school. By not doing this job, we would not be able to continue in business. I was left with no choice. I had to find a way to do the work with the staff I had.

I gathered the people and told them about our challenge. I explained to them that the work was also being done in New York City and in Jamaica and that if other companies were capable of doing it so were we. We surely did rise to the occasion. The people were wonderful. I learned a great lesson about how I could be the limitation to their success and how I had to get out of the way and allow others to do what they're capable of doing.

I say to you if Autoliv and others like them can do it so can anyone. It is only up to you to envision what is possible and with patience and further understanding you can have the best Quick and Easy Kaizen system in the world.

Why does documenting Kaizens and recording the number implemented become effective in keeping them going? It is because documentation shows us the facts.

Imagine going to a basketball game where there is no scoreboard and all you see is thin "giants" running up and down the court throwing a ball into a basket. How long do you think you can you maintain your interest? How long will you continue to watch the game? Not long I assume. Then how different is it by not keeping score at work? How can you keep people excited when they do not know the score, and they do not know what is expected of them each hour of each day. When you document, write down all of the ideas to share, and keep score of how many ideas were submitted today, this week, this month, people can be constantly reminded that it is their job to submit creative ideas on a regular basis. Believe me, documenting and keeping scores adds to the excitement of what work is all about.

Keeping good records of what has happened makes it more difficult for people to make unwarranted assumptions and enables them to see what is really going on. It is only in companies that do not document and record their Kaizens that one can hear remarks like, "I know we must be doing Kaizen, but…" and "I'm sure everyone's doing Kaizen, but…" When managers are asked a

Doing, Documenting & Sharing

specific question like "What kinds of Kaizens are your people doing?" or "Roughly how many Kaizens have they done?" they cannot give a clear answer. All they can do is to keep on vaguely repeating, "Well, I know they must be doing some."

A Kaizen program cannot be sustained in this way. The managers may sporadically say things like, "Let's do Kaizen" or "Please do some Kaizens," but all that happens is that some people do some for a while and then stop. There is no way that this sort of thing can give a company any underlying strength.

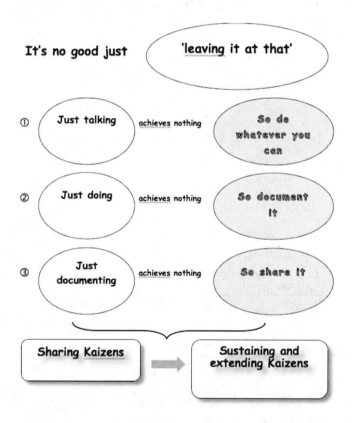

Fig. 8 <Don't just leave it at that.>

Documenting and recording things can free us from fantasies and illusions and help us to grasp reality and see the facts.

Without Continuity, There Can Be No Results

Kaizen has quite a lot in common with things like language learning and health regimes. Doing them is not that difficult, but their results are cumulative, and only become significant if the activities are sustained for long periods of time. For example, it is not difficult to go jogging or do a few physical exercises in the morning. However, it is difficult to do so morning after morning without a break. It is obvious that exercising regularly is in itself the best method of improving one's health, almost regardless of the type of exercise one takes.

Before **After**

There was this kind of problem:	We tried doing this:
And we got this kind of result:	

Fig. 9 <A Kaizen Memo or Form>

Result

Look the Facts Square in the Face
We weren't doing what we obviously should have been doing, documenting the Kaizens and sharing the facts

I am not in love with exercise. I know that exercise is good for me and I do try to do it everyday. At my age my muscles hurt, especially in the morning, but I want to be able to continue to work and I know how important exercise is to keep my body in shape.

I also want to meditate every day. All the great books I was reading were telling me to meditate everyday, but I always found an excuse not to do it. One day, I went over to my teacher Rudi and said, "Rudi, I meditate one day and not the next. What can I do to make sure that I will meditate every day?' Rudi said, "Norman, if you do not meditate everyday you will break the connection with me." From that moment on, I have meditated every day for the past 38 years. Yes, we do have to find a way to practice those things we think are important to us.

What is the secret of not giving up? It is to keep a record of what one has done. My wife to lose weight does her daily exercises, watches her diet carefully and each morning weighs herself on the scale and tracks the results on a chart. Keeping a daily record of what one has done keeps one motivated to start again. If you stop for some reason, looking at the record is like looking at your golf score, seeing what you have achieved so far and wanting to be better and better. This in turn helps the activity to become established and turn into a habit.

I also like the idea of people keeping a copy of all of their ideas in a notebook to show others what they have done. Imagine, when your boss asks you during your annual review, "What have you done this past year?" I don't know about you, but when this happened to me in the past my mind would go blank. Now you have a solution. Take out your Kaizen notebook and say, "Viola!"

In the same way, Kaizen needs to be continued for a certain length of time and an accumulation of activity needs to be built up before significant results are obtained. Just as exercising sporadically in short bursts does hardly anything to improve a person's health and

fitness, so sporadic, short-lived Kaizen activity can never be a source of competitive strength for a company.

Toyota initially just copied the American suggestion system but eventually found out that this did not get every employee involved in the continuous improvement process. Toyota knew that to catch the American automobile companies, it required a different methodology. To me it was like the story of the Tortoise and the Hare. America, the Hare, was so far ahead of Japan that it just went to sleep on the side of the road while Japan, the tortoise, just plodded forward every day until they won the race. How could General Motors lose? I remember in 1963 working on a GM survey and saw that GM had close to 60% market share. They were worried that if they got any bigger the government would perceive that they would be a monopoly and want to break them up to smaller companies. GM was worried about getting too big and it is ironic that in 2009 they went bankrupt. Why? Simply, they didn't get all of their employees involved. They drove everything from the top.

Bottom-up management is one of the significant differences between American and Japanese management practices. Bottom-up management recognizes that the worker, the closest one to the worksite, and the closest one to the customer, really knows best, most of the time and knows how to solve problems that arise. The problem is that the boss at the top of many companies in America thinks, "Look, I am rich, I am smart, I am the leader, therefore those below me should just follow my directions."

A great leader of a successful organization is like a coach of a very successful athletic sport's team. Their sole purpose is to bring out the best of the players. The players are the ones that play and can win the game. The coach can select the plays and determine the training regimen. However, a good coach recognizes that winning can only be done through superior, highly motivated, team players.

Doing, Documenting & Sharing

One can think of Kaizen as a kind of health regimen for boosting a company's strength and vitality. A Kaizen program is not designed to produce fleeting, short-term results but to improve the company's culture and workplace atmosphere (i.e. the way its employees address their work) little by little over time. This cannot be achieved with intermittent rallying cries and shouts of encouragement. The only way to make the activities long lasting is to continually do them, document them and share them.

Once at a Panasonic washing machine plant, I saw a wall showing groups of pictures, four in a row. Once a month a picture was taken of a specific work area for a period of four months. Just by placing these pictures and inspiring the workers to improve their work area motivated workers to change for the better. People do take pride in their work area. It was amazing to see the progress conducted by the workers just by taking a picture at the beginning of every month.

Slow and Steady Kaizen Builds Underlying Strength for Corporate Renewal

Corporate activities are always subject to a host of changes, and companies encounter many peaks and valleys as they conduct their business. Sometimes they are tossed around by the rough seas of an economic recession, and sometimes they stumble as a result of a little internal disharmony. Managing a business means coping with changes like these. Two methods are used to overcome many of these problems. One consists of responding decisively with sweeping reforms (Kaikaku,) and the other consists of doing continual, slow-but-steady improvements (Kaizen.)

It might sound crazy saying that getting all employees involved in daily improvement activities is as important as coming up with that new great innovative idea. But, it is true. Boeing developed the

Dreamliner Airplane, the 787, but they were more then two years late in delivering the plane to their clients. They just couldn't get all of their employees involved in solving those problems and had trouble getting their supplier's employees involved in continuous improvement to meet the schedules set.

Business commentators are always declaiming about the need for 'renewal,' 'reform' and 'restructuring,' because revolutionary changes like these are eye-catching and appeal to the mass media. However, we must not forget about the underlying strength that makes such sweeping changes possible. Sustained Kaizen is the force behind the scenes that supports corporate renewal.

Ritsuo Shingo, Dr. Shingo's[6] son, was the president of Toyota, China. He would spend 50% of his time on the factory floor. He was devoted to making Toyota the best. Relentlessly, he spent time with the employees encouraging them to come up with improvement ideas. He had a favorite phrase "watch my back." He didn't tell people what to do he just hoped that people would follow what he did. When he opened the first Toyota plant in China he went down and bought a used Toyota car for himself and also used furniture for his office. He did not tell the workers to do the same thing as he did; he just hoped that they would follow him and they did.

In difficult times, difficult actions must be taken. But the underlying strength, both tangible and intangible, that enables companies to take action has to be built up by steady and persistent hard work over long periods of time. This is the only way it can be acquired it; it is not simply going to drop into our laps like a gift from the Gods.

---

[6] Dr. Shigeo Shingo was an independent consultant to Toyota and many other Japanese companies, inventor of the SMED and Poka-yoke systems and with Mr. Ohno conceived many of the concepts that created the Toyota Production System. (JIT and Lean)

Doing, Documenting & Sharing 31

Now is exactly time and place where we must begin to develop and promote our Kaizen programs for real.

Slack Times are Exactly When We Need to Push Kaizen Hard

Economic conditions are wintry right now; but now is just the right time to **build the company's underlying strength** and a golden opportunity to **bolster the company's Kaizen culture.**
The depths of winter are the best times to **put down deep Kaizen roots.** When we face a **headwind,** that's when we need to drive our **Kaizen activities** steadily forward.

A strong company is one that continues its Kaizen program **regardless of economic conditions.**

This is the **source** of the company's **underlying strength.**

Now is exactly when we need to develop and promote our Kaizen programs for real.

In the deep winter put down the roots of Kaizen

32　How to Do Kaizen

Chapter II

'Systems' and 'Mechanisms'

For Sustaining and Extending the Kaizen Program

Managers have told me that their employees are always coming up with new ideas and that feel they do not need a new mechanism to further the process. "Just walk out onto the shop floor or into our offices and you can see many ideas that people have implemented on their own."

It might be true what the managers are saying, but work improvement itself is not practiced quite extensively as they think. Autoliv in Ogden, Utah is the world's largest producer of airbags and seat belts, last year they received on the average 63 improvement ideas per employee - that is what continuous improvement is really all about - empowering all employees to be part of the program.

The quantity of Kaizens is important because it is a reflection of the excitement generated from Kaizen activites. However, having quality ideas is equally important to the overall system. You need both quality and quantity.

The American suggestion system is a cost saving system, but it lacks the the employee participation and empowerment system that Quick and Easy Kaizen provides. Cost reduction, higher quality and greater productivity is important, but is not the only aim of the process. We want people that know their job the best to fully contribute with their brains, and use their intelligence to solve the myriad of problems around them. We want the workers to be happy getting up each morning to come to work.

Problems make life interesting. Solving them is equally important. Too often the worker recognizes the problems but has to live with the frustration of not being empowered to solve them.

'Systems' and 'Mechanisms'   35

Read both Tom Hartman's and Tim Ambrey's interviews in the back of the book and see the value of the Kaizen system at Autoliv.

Toyota claims two pillars for their success: JIT/Lean and "Respect for People." The later is opening people to their infinite creative potential and allowing them to take he initiative in solving problems. There are always problems and as soon as you solve one another pops up. For example, I was at a Toyota pant in Toyota City, Japan and saw one worker push a red button and the entire plant stopped.

Toyota initiated this marvelous system, which encourages every employee to stop working whenever they detect a problem. Toyota does not want a single defect to be passed on to the customer. The line might be stopped many times during the day. Even a new worker is empowered to stop the line. Every time the line stopped is an opportunity to do a Kaizen.

This shows incredible respect in Toyota's part because it is to tell a person - even a new worker - that they can stop everyone in the plant to prevent any defects from being passed to the next person. Every worker knows that they will not punished for doing so. The worst thing that might happen is that they will need to work a few minutes of overtime to get all of the products completed. These actions make a very powerful statement that and show Toyota really wants only quality products to be produced.

Most people like to think up ways of bettering their working methods even without suggestion schemes, incentives or special Kaizen programs. However, the concern that all companies have is that this type of Kaizen does not last or spread. If, when an accident or other problem occurs, a manager says to everyone involved, "Please think about how we can stop this from recurring in the future," "Come on everyone, let's do something about this," or "Please do a Kaizen," people will come up with improvement ideas and some of these will be implemented.

People are good at putting out fires and solving problems when they arise but often after the storm has blown over we say, "Whew! Thank goodness we got through that all right," or "Well done. We did a good job there," and that's the end of it. Of course, some people might go on trying to improve the situation even after the commotion has subsided, but what about the others? In my experience of working with top managers, I have come to see that many of them really believe that 'Kaizen' and that sort of thing are unnecessary and that everything will be fine as long as people work hard and do their jobs properly?

Look we in the West have a different mentality from the Japanese. We want the "big bang for our buck!" We want the new iPhone or the latest popular product. We want the new electronic machine that will solve all of our problems. We want the *gadget* that will make us another million dollars. Of course, the Japanese also want the "big bang for the buck (yen)," but they also are aware of the power of getting millions of small ideas from all of their employees.

Of course, workers do come up with new ideas, many of them very practical but coming up with new improvement ideas is not really part of everyone's job. In fact, according to the *Employee Involvement Association*, formerly *National Association of Suggestion Systems*, the average American worker comes up with one new idea every seven years. We want to start off with at least two written ideas per month. We want a system that encourages every worker, literally every day, to look around their work area to identify and solve those small problems that reduce their personal effectiveness.

On my last trip to Japan, Shigehiro Nakamura, consultant and teacher at Japan Management Associations, told me a new powerful concept in Japanese management is to ask everyone in an organization to improve their work .1% per day. That little bit of improvement adds up to 2.5% per month or 30% per year. For example, in three years Canon expects to double its productivity

'Systems' and 'Mechanisms'   37

while having everyone involved in improvement activities and focusing on very small improvements every day when they come to work.

This new effort where everyone has responsibility for small daily improvements makes work very interesting for employees and strengthens the very constitution of the company. Canon makes great cameras and copiers and continues to innovate, but this new focus on all employees being part of the solution will make the total corporation very successful. Just think, .1% a day is just looking around your work area and finding a way to save around 20 seconds a day: move your tools closer, reduce bending, shorten your meetings, stop rewriting things, etc. Once again if Canon can do it so can you and the vehicle to bring this .1% of improvement is Quick and Easy Kaizen.

Michael Miller's job at Technicolor Corporation was to close 8000 video cassette covers each day. Imagine if that was your only job. How excited would you be to go to work and be asked to close 8000 covers a day? Of course, Michael did it for his job because he was paid to do so.

Fig. 10 <Michael's idea.>

I asked Michael to come up with some new ideas to make his work easier and more interesting. Michael thought about my request, looked at his work and put two pieces of cardboard against the

conveyor belt that would push the lid closed while passing. He then stood back and watched the video cassette covers close by themselves. What did Michael do? In a sense he replaced himself. How many of you would do the same thing as Michael? If you came up with a new idea to replace yourself, would you do it?

The problem is that by making this improvement Michael is out of a job. Will his manager find him a new one or is he just out of work? Michael's motivation to improve is predicated on the fact that if he improves does he lose his job or not? If he does he will be hard-pressed to get employees to want to improve.

Japanese industry was very clever for they devised a lifetime employment system which protected the worker from being easily dismissed and at the same time put enormous pressure on management to be creative to grow their companies. Instead of letting go the weakest employee, they took the best workers and made them into problem solvers where they had to find new opportunities for new products or services.

Michael's efforts effect the overall benefits of the company in a small way but greatly have an impact on him. As a consequence, Kaizens done in short bursts, or by limited groups of people, have no significant effect on a company's business capability. The very fact that individual Kaizens have little effect on the overall company means they need to be done continually by every employee. In the past, companies rarely have every employee participating and it led to many of them complaining that their Kaizen efforts were not sustained and failing to expand.

Thy then searched for ways of keeping their activities going and extending them to all employees. Eventually, after much trial and error, they realized that in order to achieve this, they needed a Kaizen system of the 'I suggest, I implement' type and that all Kaizens should be 'done, documented and shared' (for on the walls for all employees to see.)

'Systems' and 'Mechanisms'   39

As mentioned earlier, I give credit to Kodak for implementing the first suggestion system in America back in 1898 and the first idea from the first worker was, "Clean the windows." A very good idea back then for I imagine lighting in plants was not as good as it is today. The problem is as soon as the worker submitted the idea to the supervisor, the supervisor felt that he or she already had enough to do and the worker was only adding to her or his burden.

- Start whatever you can
- Start wherever you can
- Do as much as you can

Fig. 11 <The "leave-it-up-to-you-type of suggestion scheme.">

Kodak started a great participation management system, getting all employees involved in improvement activities, but it quickly became a cost savings system. Supervisors/managers only wanted to look at the big ideas. They were willing to give the worker 10% of the cost savings but only a small number of workers actually submitted any ideas.

The average company with an old-time cost saving suggestion system gets one idea per worker every seven years. The average in Japan is two ideas per month per employee.

When we would start a Quick and Easy Kaizen system, we would ask people to identify problems at their work site and try to get them to implement the solutions to those problems.

Since, the original suggestion system was 'I suggest, you implement' type of suggestion schemes it is recommended that companies introduce an improvement system for the first time as Kaizen system or Quick and Easy Kaizen system.

From 'Suggestion Schemes' to 'Kaizen Systems'

Whether they have kept the old name or not, why is it that so many companies in Japan have in practice ditched their old suggestion schemes in favor of the new-style Kaizen systems?

In 1951, Toyota received 789 suggestions, .01 suggestions per worker with an 8% participation rate and a 23% adoption rate.

In 1969, Toyota received 40,313 suggestions, 1.1 suggestions per worker with a 49% participation rate and a 68% adoption rate.

In 1986, Toyota received 2,648,710 suggestions, 47.7 suggestions per worker with 95% participation rate and 96% adoption rate.
Initially, Toyota copied the American Suggestion System and slowly over 35 years from 1951 to 1986 went from one idea per employee every 10 years to 47.7 ideas per employee per year. Today you don't have to wait 35 years to do what Toyota did. Read this book carefully and within three years you can get 47.7 ideas per employee. Arvin Meritor, in Troy, Michigan did it, over 25 ideas per worker, and if Arvin Meritor did it so can you.

'Systems' and 'Mechanisms' 41

Since most suggestion systems gave 10% of the savings to the employees, the accountants were very careful and slow to give the rewards. They didn't want to overpay the employee; a little funny to me as the company received 90% of the savings. This meant that most suggestions had to be put on hold and marked 'under consideration' forever and a day, so employees lost their motivation. And since the company was looking for cost savings, all of the small, but important improvement ideas, were often neglected. As a result, many companies' suggestion schemes that started off with good intentions to empower their employees and get real involvement just lapsed into a state of being "open for business but having no customers."

The US Navy had one sailor wait nine years before he heard that his suggestion was accepted. The old suggestion system is a cost savings system, carefully evaluated by accountants - we don't want to make a mistake when we give the worker the 10% reward. Funny, some of our accountants and managers worry about the 10% when the company is saving 90%. The old system also was a system whereby the worker came up with the idea, but someone else was responsible for implementing the idea, not the worker who came up with the idea.

It is probably fair to say that there are no longer any companies in Japan where the old type of suggestion scheme is working effectively. Such schemes are totally old-fashioned and behind the times.

Some companies with a Quick and Easy Kaizen system still give 10% of the cost savings to the worker but I don't think this is at all necessary to get started. You might like to give some small rewards, have a few parties, give out some T-shirts or a couple of free meals at the best restaurant in town. One of my past clients gave out two tickets to a professional football game and received the most ideas ever. Just simply tell the workers we want both your body and your brain. We need both to be world-class.

When I owned Productivity Inc. - Press, back in the 1980's, we had a suggestion system and I remember one day when I opened the suggestion box and read, "Get rid of the box; get rid of the system for nobody reads our ideas." Boy, was I embarrassed.

Reaffirm the Purpose of the Kaizen System

A Kaizen system is designed to enlist every single worker in improvement activities. Instead of people waiting for their superiors to tell them what to do, they must be empowered to look around their work area and find things to improve. It is like a game of "tug and war" where only the strongest team wins. You must keep saying to yourself, "if Autoliv and Gulfstream can do it, so can we."

Quick and Easy Kaizen is radically different from the old suggestion system, in that the worker who comes up with the idea implements the idea. Yes, this is the way to get started.

I suggest you read the interview with Tom Hartman at Autoliv, in the back of the book, and see how they have advanced the concept even beyond most Japanese companies. Simply stated, since workers build, assemble and serve your customers – that is where you earn your money – management's role should be to support them. Managers do not build products and yet they expect the workers to serve them. The funnel is upside down. That is why the Japanese call it 'Bottom-up Management' not the 'Top Down Management,' which we have over here.

The power, of course, is always in management's hands but to have a really productive environment all emphasis should be on helping the worker to succeed. Think about this carefully.

Look, it is a good idea to set targets, say two ideas per employee per month, but remember the system is voluntary not compulsory and some employees might never give a suggestion. Of course, a

good manager will work with the employees to help them come up with ideas.

Just ask people to look around their work area and identify problems or potential problems and come up with solutions to make their work easier and more interesting and to build their skills and capabilities. Keep it simple! We only want very small ideas to keep people involved on a daily basis.

Recently, I walked over to a man working at a metal bending machine at Gulfstream. I had seen him work on a recorded video: looking at the specifications, turning 90 degrees and setting the computer dials, turning another 90 degrees to run a test to bend the first part, turning 180 degrees to the table behind him to check the calibration, re-looking at the specifications, turning 90 degrees again to re-set the computer, turning another 90 degrees to bend another part, turning 180 degrees again to re-check the calibration on the second part, and then turning 180 degrees to finish all of the parts.

When I saw the worker, I told him I had seen the video of him working and asked him what he would do to make his work easier. He immediately said the computer should be moved closer to the machine, and a table should be installed next to the press so he wouldn't have to keep turning around. He knew exactly what to do to make his job easier, but no one had ever asked him, so he just continued to do the as he was required to do. How typical is that?

Simply asking this operator could have made his work easier and added to his productivity. I am sure he would be happy and prideful to contribute more of his intelligence into his work.

It may be possible to get people to do simple manual tasks because people need their salaries to live. But, if you want people to use their brains to help solve problems then a more creative style of management is necessary. When even a little personal ingenuity is

required, motivational management is indispensable. This is because our brains do not work effectively unless we try to think for ourselves, and we cannot produce good ideas unless we really want to do so.

Question yourself! Are you allowing people that work for you to use their brains? Do you challenge them to solve the problems around their work area? Do you ask them for innovative ideas to help your company be more competitive? Do you give them the knowledge and tools necessary to solve those problems?

Look at the picture on the next page and think of opportunities for improvement.

This looks like normal shelves found in most factories. What can you suggest that would make-work easier for the workers? What are some problems that the worker might encounter? How about the bending down to the lower shelf? How about reaching to remove the items from the back of the shelf? Could you tilt the top shelves to make it easier to remove the parts?

You could put stoppers to prevent the parts from falling off the shelves. What other things could you suggest?

The trick is to know how to see differently. When you get to the back of the book, Bunji has a marvelous chart with keywords to help you and your employees see many opportunities for improvement.

'Systems' and 'Mechanisms' 45

Fig. 12 <How can you improve the shelves?>

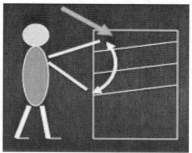

Fig. 13 <"Tilt the shelves.>

Video your workers to identify areas of improvement. When you use video to watch worker's motions, both you and the worker can find numerous opportunities to save time. Industrial engineering and the study of motion were developed in the United States but seem to have become a dying art. Virtually every Japanese

company I visited - and I have been into close to 400 of them - video all of their workers and continue to find and study ways to improve motion so that they can improve their operations.

Last year at Hino Motors, manufacturers of trucks and buses and a partner with Toyota, I saw a supervisor videoing one worker on the line. He filmed the worker for around 10 minutes. He then took the video to a meeting room, and with the worker studied ways to reduce the worker's motion and find new opportunities to reduce the time line it took for him to do his work This video technique is prevalent in Japan, and should be looked at more closely in the West.

I should have mentioned earlier that administering a Quick and Easy Kaizen system does need additional overhead. At Gulfstream with 1000 people only one person was keeping the statistics on Quick and Easy Kaizen. It was not a burden and added very little overhead to monitor the system.

Why Bother Developing a Kaizen Program?

Even if left to their own devices, Kaizen in a casual way does happen. However, if Kaizen is simply left to take its own course, it will only take place as a matter of chance. People have brains, know their job well, and would gladly share their ideas if asked.

All of a company's employees are perfectly capable of doing Kaizen. Having people exercise their ability, deliberately and routinely, as part of their job, is good for both them and their company. This is why top companies bother to develop Kaizen programs.

'Systems' and 'Mechanisms'

It is certainly true that Kaizens will take place. From time to time people do see problems around them and will come up with solutions even if nothing particular is done to encourage them; however, Kaizens like these are no more than accidental. But we work every day, which means that we forget things, make mistakes and create problems. All of these problems are grist to the Kaizen mill. There are always problems occurring daily in every workplace that need improving.

With the right eyes you can find many things to improve and we should try to improve them as much as we can? If we don't, then things away and from where Kaizen points us and time and energy are wasted with people saying things like, "Oops, I got that wrong. I'd better cover it up before anyone notices," and "Drat! I made a mistake; I'll have to think of a good excuse."

Chapter III

Discussion

- Ryo Hosoyamada and Noriko Hosoyamada -

(Ryo is a college student in Vancouver, Canada nephew to my wife Noriko. I met Noriko in 1982 in Japan. She translated my first published book *Managerial Engineering* by Dr. Ryuji Fukuda and often interpreted for Dr. Shigeo Shingo. Noriko is now a doctor of Chinese medicine. The conversation took place while driving from Portland, Oregon to Oregon's beautiful West coast.)

NORMAN: The ninth grade, middle school, was my worst year at school and the other years from grade one to eight weren't much better. I hated school. I can't remember one teacher that liked me. I couldn't do my homework well; I couldn't remember things from my reading and my test scores were terrible.

A fellow student, in the ninth grade, Gary said, "Norman, when I read the history book at home, I jot down the important items; I put a slip of paper into my pocket, and then during the test I look at the sheet of paper."

It sounded like a good idea, and I did it. I read the history assignment at home and I made a small sheet and wrote those points that I thought were important and placed the sheet into my shirt breast pocket.

What Gary was saying is very interesting, because as far as the teachers are concerned, if you read something and you put it in your memory and you can recall it on the test, that's okay. But I couldn't remember things like that. I did not have a good memory from reading books.

The next day during the test, I looked at the sheet; the first time I looked at it, I looked up and the teacher was right there. She saw me look at the sheet of paper.

In the eyes of that teacher I was a criminal. I did not follow her rules. I now feel that she should have recognized that I had a poor memory and given me credit for capturing the important points from the homework. School should be about learning not about rote. Albert Einstein also could not memorize things as a child.

I looked at a sheet of paper instead of relying on my memory. And every teacher in the 9th grade hated me, except the math teacher. But all the others hated me, because I broke their rules, especially the 9th grade English teacher. She really hated me. Told my

friend, "Don't play with Norman because he's going to grow up to be no good."

In the year book, she put the following under my picture, "Norman is the most likely to get 'ahead' because he needs one." But, I think I fooled her. I did not turn out to be a criminal and even though I only read four books from first grade through the 12th, I ended up publishing over 300 books, writing hundreds of articles and even wrote six books, not too shabby for a person without a memory good enough for school.

I never thought of it before, if I go home and study the book and am able to record the key points in my head, and then when the test comes along, I am able to draw on my memory and bring out to the test what I remember is the answer, that's okay. But if I do the same thing and read the book and take out the important points, which shows I have a certain intelligence in taking out the important points, but if I put it on a sheet of paper, instead of keeping it in my memory, then that's considered as dishonest. Isn't that interesting?

When you think of the subject of copying, you don't want to hurt somebody else, but who am I hurting when I'm taking a test and I can't remember, and if I don't do well on the test, what's going to happen? I'm going to flunk, they'll leave me back, my father is going to beat me up, at least verbally -- he didn't beat me physically, but he would beat me verbally which was even worse than the hit.

When you think of it, what is the school system for? To teach you how to memorize or to teach you how to learn and function and build your skills and capabilities so you can live well in life, so you can serve yourself, your family and you can serve society. That's important. But the focal point of the teachers, primarily, at least my teachers, was how good is your memory. Can you remember the facts that they want to jam down into you? Can they mold you

to their image to make sure you don't use any creativity at all? Because they're thinking if you learn all of these facts, then later on you can bring them up and it will serve you in your life. So if you learn when was the Magna Carta -- do you know? Do you know what the Magna Carta is? You don't?

RYO: What is that?

NORMAN: What is the Magna Carta and when was it produced?

NORIKO: I learned something somewhere.

NORMAN: I don't know, but it's something to do with something that was important with history.

NORIKO: I think it is, like, a constitution --

NORMAN: Some kind of thing in Europe, which sort of changed the divine right of kings, maybe, because up to that moment the kings were all powerful.

But it's funny. What does it mean if you can remember those dates? It's funny.

The only real thing about copying is if it takes away from your ability to learn. Then it could be wrong. But I couldn't learn anyway. I mean, I learned from experience. I learned very little by reading, very little. I can read a mystery book, and a year later I can read the same book again and not know who did it.

Look at you Ryo, you just saw a movie for the fourth time, right, and you still enjoyed it. Isn't that funny.

I think what's important is that people are born to be part of this creative evolution that continually takes place. We are continually evolving. If we go back 200 years, there were no automobiles, no

electric lights, no gasoline engines, no airplanes, no refrigerators, and no IPhones.

So over time, we are continuously evolving, and very fast lately, because evolution is exponential. So it might take you ten years to learn something, but the next person can learn that something in five minutes. That's what I mean by exponential.

I want to grow, and growing means evolving. Growing means changing. Growing really is in a true sense a very creative process, because growing is breaking through the constraints that we have, the resistance that we have to change.

So growing is really changing. Not just growing physically, but growing from all the limitations, the perceptions from other people that restrains us from being free at the moment.

There was a study done once of 240,000 Americans to determine how highly creative are we, how highly creative are Americans. And the study showed that almost every child at age three is very creative. Creativity means the ability to learn and the ability to do things differently, the ability to change, the ability to take two different things and something new comes out of it. That's creativity. Creativity helps you overcome a problem while drawing on your knowledge, your resources, your experiences, and you can do something different to solve that problem.

Most people come to work and they do the exact same thing every day.

NORIKO: Okay. So the three year old is creative --

NORMAN: Thank you Noriko for putting me back on course. Almost all three year olds are creative. Just watch children with colors and paints continually doing new things, without inhibitions, until told what not to do. They're learning languages. It's

interesting, too, because normally we teach a child just one language. Ryo, you know three languages: English, French and Japanese; all I know is one language.

Well, they found in the study that at five years, at the end of kindergarten, 90 percent of the children are considered to be creative. At the end of first grade, what do you think it is?

RYO: Does it go lower?

NORMAN: First grade, it drops. It drops.

RYO: Is it, like, 60 percent?

NORMAN: It drops at the end of first grade to only 10 percent of the children are considered to now be highly creative. I use the word highly creative because everybody has some creative flare or you couldn't exist. "10 percent." Something drastic happens in first grade.

At the end of the second grade, it drops to the national average. The national average is only 2 percent of the people are considered to be highly creative. "Only 2 percent." I often ask my audience at a conference, "How many of you consider yourself to be highly creative?" And normally it will run somewhere from 2 to 5 percent, but no higher. It's a rarity if more hands go up.

So something happens in first grade to thwart, strain, restrict people's creativity.

RYO: In the first grade, you're asked to conform to follow everybody else. That's not very good.

NORMAN: You have homework. How would that constrict your creativity?

RYO: You don't get to do, like, your own thing.

Discussion

NORMAN: Very good Ryo. You don't do your own thing at home. I never thought of that. That's very good. You're forced to do what the teacher tells you instead of just doing your own thing. That's very good.

In the first grade, the teachers are a little bit stricter then in kindergarten. You don't have the same playtime; you don't have the same naps.

RYO: You're not allowed to make noise and giggle and carry on.

NORMAN: That's true -- in kindergarten, my vision is that it's not as constrained, not as constricted as you are in first grade. So in kindergarten, you're allowed to be more alive, and then all of a sudden in first grade it's like you're in the army. You're in the first grade army.

NORIKO: Why does that happen?

NORMAN: I don't know. Why does that need to happen?

NORIKO: Because you're expected to finish certain things.

NORMAN: You're expected to follow and conform in the first grade, and conformity is not really creativity. In kindergarten you don't have to conform that much.

NORIKO: How do teachers know whether you're conforming to their expectations?

NORMAN: I've learned recently that the school system is really designed for you to conform and to do what society thinks they will need from you, not what you the individual need. "They" want you to conform to what the corporate, the political system wants from you. This is the divine right of kings, same thing with

politics. We give the power of the king to George Bush, what's the difference?

They want you to conform. They also want you to conform to the mores and the values of big business. Big business is very powerful in America, exercises a great power over our educational system. Big business gives so many jobs to people. Big business today wants people to conform, they want people to come to work, and do those boring, repetitive jobs.

However, most jobs that people have are deadly, truly deadly.

When I run a meeting, I ask everybody, what's your favorite day of the week. What do you think they say, Ryo?

RYO: Friday?

NORMAN: Friday! Of course! Everybody loves Friday. Why do they love Friday?

RYO: It's the last day of work before the weekend.

NORMAN: So the weekend represents a certain sense of nonconformity. Weekend represents a certain sense of freedom, a certain sense of limited freedom.

Actually, you do conform a lot on the weekend, but you have a lot more freedom away from the job than you do on the job. Now, isn't that interesting? We talk about America being a democracy. Democracy represents a society of free people, coming together to live in the best way possible. This is funny. But our political system and our economic industrial system want us really to be like robots.

Let's go back, Ryo, and let's look at first grade. What is the teacher doing that is going to kill your creativity?

Discussion

She wants you to conform. She wants you to learn. Learn what? She wants you to learn what industry wants. Not necessarily what's good for you but what's good for her misperception -- and I say misperception, of what society needs. Because the ultimate that society needs is creative, happy people. But we don't really focus on creative, happy people. Society focuses on pleasure.

You watch this television, the forced comedy, and the things that tickle us under the ribs so we laugh.

Industry wants to sell fine products and deliver excellent services to people but they don't really care at all about the quality of work life. Look at the average factory, which is dirty, and so self-destructive to the creative mind. Look at the cubbyholes given as offices. You sit in the box all day even without a window. It doesn't have to be that way. Just go to Internet and look at the new Volkswagen plant in Dresden, Germany. It is beautiful. It looks like a museum. It looks like a wonderful place for people to work. If Volkswagen can do it so can you.

But back to the school system, I like what we're doing, Ryo, because I'm learning a lot as I'm talking. So what happens in the first grade that causes us to lose a creative spirit from 90 percent to 10 percent in one year?

RYO: We need a different vision, like, towards society?

NORMAN: Well, they want to teach you what society expects from you, that is the truth, much more so in first grade than in kindergarten. You have to dress a lot alike.

RYO: The teacher makes you cynical.

NORMAN: A natural product, byproduct, from losing your creativity would be to become more cynical in life. That's true.

You are less free, you are not allowed or even encouraged to come up with creative ideas. Let's take another step. What else happens in first grade to kill creativity? And it kills it, because it's going from 90 to 10 percent.

RYO: Parents?

NORMAN: Parents have a lot of influence too, but parents are also influencing you in kindergarten, and they're also influencing you in first grade. And parents, unfortunately, because they come from the same educational system and pretty much the same political system, they want you to conform. It's terrible.

RYO: I was just going to say that parents have different expectations regarding the schools.

NORMAN: When you go to grade one, the parents have a different level of expectations for you. Yes. But what? What causes that conformity? What causes that? Come on. We've got to dig deeper. What happens in first grade that causes this drastic change in creativity?

RYO: We are trying to adapt.

NORMAN: Well, we're trying to adapt, that's true. We're trying to adapt, conform more in the first grade to society's norms, right, keeping up with the Jones's.

Yet something happens in first grade that doesn't happen in kindergarten but continues to happen throughout the rest of your school system. What do you think?

Something happens drastically in first grade that I think that we haven't fully addressed yet.

RYO: Different interests?

NORMAN: There was a different interest, that's true. What happens in first grade? We start to teach. We start to teach reading.

Now, the other thing funny about first grade is, not all children are ready to read at the same time. Some can learn to read much earlier and some would be better off learning to read two years later then first grade, and they wouldn't lose out in life. There are schools like the Waldorf system and Rudolph Steiner schools and you don't have to learn to read in the first grade. And by the sixth grade, they're all caught up and they're even superior to those that went to the normal school system.

In first grade, they're going to teach you reading, and writing -- my writing was terrible. I never had good penmanship. Then they start to teach you mathematics. They could be teaching you a foreign language.

NORIKO: China is doing it. English is taught in China at most of their schools.

NORMAN: They're learning English at a very early age. They're very smart, because English is the universal language to communicate, not Chinese, not yet anyway.

So you learn how to read, you learn how to write, you learn a little bit of mathematics. What else do they teach you in first grade?

We know the teacher is teaching. She is teaching. There might be something in the teaching method that could constrain creativity. The teaching method itself, causing you to learn what the teacher wants you to learn, right, instead of you learning what you want to learn.

Prior to you attending school your parents taught you how to speak. You just copied them. Smart parents are reading to the child all the time. Those are very smart parents.

But even the children that are not read to, they also learn how to speak. They learn from television, they learn from the other children, they learn from their parents, et cetera.

So it's true, the teacher is teaching you things like English, like reading, like writing. In the early years, they let you draw a lot, so you have art. You might have some music appreciation courses.

The teacher has an idea in their head of what you should be learning in first grade. But what does the teacher do in the first grade, not in kindergarten, that could cause your creativity to wane?

What do you go through in your average day when you're at school?

RYO: You have to listen to the teacher.

NORMAN: You have to listen to the teacher. She's going to ask you questions?

RYO: She's lecturing you. It's usually boring. So you lose interest. And you don't even care about what's going on. You just wander in your mind about…

NORMAN: The mind is wandering all over the place, and the teacher just loves to catch you when your mind is wandering and just when you are not listening they will surely ask you a question to see if you're attentive.

RYO: And you're lost and…

NORMAN: And you're lost and you get embarrassed, so you close a little bit, often intentionally not listening to the teacher, but she's

boring or you just can't understand what she wants from you. I could never figure out what the teacher wanted me to say.

RYO: Very boring.

NORMAN: Very boring. Hence learning is not easy. And I'm not sure -- I'm sure at least 90 percent of what they gave me is useless in my life, especially when you end up going to a factory and tighten eight bolts and that's all you do all day long is tighten eight bolts on every car.

RYO: Then, like, high school, you do this calculus and all this.

NORMAN: You do this, right.

RYO: And then you ask yourself, like, when am I even going to apply this thing?

And unless you're given, like, a specific job field, like a researcher, you're not going to use it.

NORMAN: They don't put you on a path quick enough. Other countries do. I think it is a crime that children can graduate high school without having the necessary skill to make a living.

When you go back in time, if your father was a carpenter, you're going to be a carpenter. So pretty early in life, you know what you need to be a carpenter, and you would learn those things from your father and you might become an apprentice early in your life. I don't know how old you are when you apprentice to become a carpenter.
But then you go and work with a master carpenter, and that carpenter would teach you. You would learn the hard way. You pretty much learned everything about carpentry from the carpenter. You become a journeyman, which means you would go out with the carpenter and you help him build houses or furniture. And then

at one moment, you can become certified to become a master carpenter, where you can go out on your own. That's a good system. We don't do enough of that in our society.

NORIKO: Germany does it.

NORMAN: Germany does it very early too.

But Ryo, something else happens in school that we haven't addressed yet. So let's keep going.

RYO: What else?

NORMAN: What else happens? Your teacher is teaching you. Teacher is talking to you, lecturing to you, writing things on the blackboard. Today they use Power Point slides and movies. And then what does she do?

RYO: Try to catch your interest?

NORMAN: She wants to attract your interest, which is true, interest in the subjects that she thinks you should learn. And how does she know that you are learning, because that's the reason we go to school, is to learn.

RYO: By asking you questions.

NORMAN: By asking you questions. What else?

RYO: They tell you to write what you think about the topic.

NORMAN: They ask you to think and write about what you think about the topic. And most of the time, unfortunately, they're looking for you to come up with an answer that they already know, right?

RYO: Yes.

Discussion

NORMAN: So how do they know that you're learning?

RYO: By testing you.

NORMAN: By testing you. Congratulations! Tell me about the tests.

RYO: They try to make you memorize after you read or listen.

NORMAN: Did you learn what the teacher was lecturing you and they asked you to write about it? They want to know if your memory is working right, because they think that learning is regurgitating and giving back to them what they told you or being able to recall what you read.

I did not have that ability. I did not have that good a memory. But I ended up publishing about 300-400 books, I'm writing my sixth book right now, and I could not bring back to the teacher what the teacher wanted.

Now, we're missing one point in the test. How does the teacher know if you are learning and what does the teacher do with that test?

RYO: She marks it. She grades you. She judges you. You try to improve yourself to get liked by the teacher.

NORMAN: Yes, Ryo she grades you. Funny, I never got an "A" on any course from the first grade through the 9th grade. Not one single outstanding grade. I wanted the teachers to like me, so I wanted to get high grades, but I couldn't do it. And, if you don't get high grades?

RYO: The teacher doesn't like you, and your parents will get mad.
NORMAN: That's the thing I worried about. I worried about my parents more than that teacher.

So I think, Ryo, that grades are the prime fault for killing creativity.

Now, let's go to the next step. What do you do to get a bad grade?

RYO: Don't study.

NORMAN: Don't study. Okay. What do you do to get a bad grade? You take the test and what happens?

RYO: You don't write anything.

NORMAN: The teacher asks you a specific question, right, who discovered America, and what do you do to get a good grade and what do you do to get a poor grade?

RYO: You write the right answer?

NORMAN: You write the right answer and that gives you a good grade. And what is the other thing that you do to get a bad grade?

RYO: You write the wrong answer. Answer incorrectly.

NORMAN: Incorrectly, which means you made what?

RYO: A mistake.
(APPLAUSE)

NORMAN: The irony of this, Ryo, is how do you learn?
RYO: By making mistakes.

NORMAN: By making mistakes! Noriko?
(APPLAUSE)
NORMAN: You learn by making mistakes, but every time you make a mistake, your grade goes down. There is something screwy in the mechanism. Something is crazy. You learn from your mistakes, but when you make a mistake you're criticized and

you get bad grades. As children and as adults we learn from trial and error.

NORIKO: So what are you saying? The school system -- come to school?

NORMAN: Come to school. Right. What are they saying to you? Come to school and what? Come to school but don't make mistakes. So they're really saying come to school and what? If you learn from your mistakes, and they don't want you to make mistakes --

RYO: Don't learn.

NORMAN: Don't learn. Noriko?

(APPLAUSE)

NORMAN: It's true. I knew in advance what the final answer was that I was looking for, but look at all the wonderful things that came out of our conversation. I have so many new things to write about now. And since I have such a poor memory, I'm lucky I have it all on a tape recorder.
Noriko is right. I think the fear of making a mistake is the prime cause of restraining creativity from people.

NORIKO: You want to please the teacher. Rather than make up your own mind.
NORMAN: Right. Instead of coming up with your own answers, you want to give the teacher what the teacher wants and already knows. And so by coming back and giving what the teacher wants, you're not being creative. If the teaching mechanism was such – instead of asking you to come back with facts – they wanted you to be creative and taught you how to solve problems.

NORIKO: I think there was a story, there was a chemist – I think I remember right –given a chemistry test. The question was; how do you write the process of converting coal to oil? How to create oil from coal? The chemist was expected to come up with the right formula. There was a right answer, of course, for the chemical formula. One student didn't remember the process, so the answer he gave was sell the coal and buy the oil. And to the credit of the teacher, he gave half credit.

NORMAN: It's a very good question. How do you convert coal to oil, and the teacher, the chemistry teacher, was looking for some chemical process to do it. And the students said, well, you could sell the coal and buy the oil.

NORIKO: I think he got full credit.

NORMAN: He should get full credit, because he gave a creative answer.

NORIKO: Because that is certainly one of the options, right?

NORMAN: When we go out into life and get a job, they don't want you to make mistakes when you go to work. And so the boss is saying, come to work and don't –

NORIKO: Learn.

NORMAN: Don't learn. And most companies carry that environment, totally unlearning. People are given such terrible jobs.

I just read about Germany and Saxony and because of the cheap labor in the orient, Poland has such cheap labor, Germany cannot compete with cheap labor. The only way they can compete in the world is with their creative spirit, which is their intellect. So they are insisting that the Saxony government invest with companies more and more to educate the worker, to build their skills, so that

Discussion

the worker can be more creative, so they can compete in the world. In this area of Germany they compete by making chips. Everything has chips today, used for almost everything. You take a car today; so much of a car is computerized.

We covered a lot of the things, the whole idea of conformity and the teacher teaching what they want to teach you.

NORIKO: The fear of making a mistake.

NORMAN: The fear of making a mistake is very big with people. I saw something at Hino Motors, the Toyota truck and bus manufacturer. Noriko and I went there last year. Toyota owns about 50 percent of the company. And as we're walking through the factory I see a big display, a big board. And on that board they had pictures of workers, and then things written in Japanese.

We looked at this board, Ryo, and I asked the plant manager, what is that board? He said, "It is a mistake board." I saw about 24 sheets of paper in plastic sleeves. And if you looked at each sheet carefully, you would see the picture of a person, some writing in Japanese, and then a sticker. They either had a yellow sticker or a blue sticker. The yellow sticker had a smiley face and the blue sticker had a sad face.

Powerful to have people, every time they make a mistake, to write it up to admit their mistake and to share it with their fellow workers. Most companies, when people make a mistake, they're afraid to tell their boss. They hide it. They live with fear about making mistakes. They are afraid they might be fired when they make repeated mistakes.

68   How to Do Kaizen

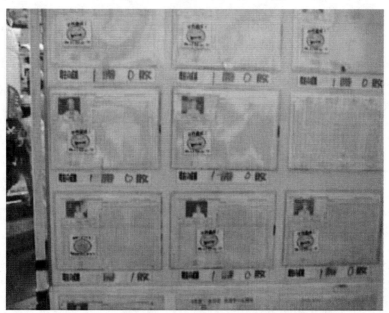

Fig. 14. <Hino Motors Mistake Board>

NORIKO: And it is not solved.

NORMAN: It's hidden. And the customer gets a bad product. Because if you make a mistake and that mistake travels down the line through the production process, it gets bigger and bigger and costs you more and more money.
This Mistake Board could be the catalyst to change your culture.

We're taking about the mistake board, and the smiley face is what?
RYO: Maybe on their board they're expressing that they're learning from their mistake. That would be very good.

NORMAN: I never thought of that, Ryo.

RYO: If we ask the worker, write your mistake and tell me what you learned from it, that's very powerful.

Discussion

NORMAN: Very good. Because we're learning as we're talking. I never thought of that before.

But what else, Ryo? What does the smiley face mean?

RYO: Apologize for it?

NORMAN: Apologize. That's excellent too. That's good. But I'm not so interested in the apology, because we want them to learn from their mistake.

RYO: They apply it.

NORMAN: They're applying it. You're getting very close. The smiling face means what?

RYO: It didn't cost too much.

NORIKO: We don't encourage mistakes.

NORMAN: We don't encourage mistakes, but we want people to learn from mistakes. Mistakes cost money. So the company says, okay, you made a mistake. That's okay. But –
RYO: Make sure you don't do it again.

NORMAN: Make sure you don't do it again. So a smiley face means –

RYO: They acknowledge it, and learn from it? And they teach it to others?

NORMAN: That's excellent, Ryo.

NORIKO: What do they teach others?

RYO: The way to not make the same mistakes?

NORMAN: Very good.

(APPLAUSE)

NORMAN: Very good, Ryo. You're very good. The smiley face means we learn from our mistakes and I'm not going to make it again, because this is what I did wrong, and so now I know what not to do wrong, again.

The blue face means I haven't figured it out, and it also tells all the other workers what?

RYO: That they need their contribution as well.

NORMAN: That's it. They want all the other workers to help me. Help me. That's the wonderful Japanese spirit; it's a team spirit. Help me. Help me solve this problem so I don't make this mistake again.

Go ahead, Noriko, what were you going to say?

NORIKO: I think it is a wonderful environment to work in.
NORMAN: Yes, it's a wonderful environment to work in.

NORIKO: I think that management is allowing the people to make mistakes and share, and making mistakes does not punish them. And by itself that's wonderful. And by sharing the mistake, then you, as an organization, are learning and can make it better.
NORMAN: That's right. The organization is learning together.

NORIKO: That is very, very powerful.

NORMAN: A very powerful system.

NORIKO: But to get to that point itself, the management has to be really good.

NORMAN: Yes. You have to be very good management to put up a board like that. That is one of the most brilliant discoveries that I made in Japan, and I haven't until now exploited it enough. But you've helped me tremendously today.

The Mistake Board by itself, being displayed and encouraging all workers to participate by revealing their mistakes to share with others, will change in a very positive way the culture of your organization.

The Mistake Board

It is an enigma, puzzlement, and a conundrum, that in industry we don't want people to make mistakes, for mistakes can be very costly, but in truth people learn best from their own mistakes. So how can you let people learn from mistakes and yet at the same time eliminate the cost of those mistakes? I think; you must set priorities. I think; the first priority is to please your customers and secondly is to develop people to learn new skills and to use their creative problem solving abilities.

Dr. Shingo early on recognized that you couldn't get zero defects by shouting at people to "not make mistakes." No one really wants to make mistakes. So, he invented a very powerful process called "Poka-yoke[7]," asking all employees to make simple devices that prevent defects from occurring. Poka-yoke recognizes that people make mistakes, but they are prevented from going on to the next person, your customer or a Poka-yoke device will prevent you from making a defect. Gulfstream in Mexicali was taught the Poka-yoke system and in the last two years received from their workers over 4000 devices.

---

[7] Poka-yoke is a Japanese word meaning "mis-proofing."

Imagine workers are asked to share their mistakes with their fellow workers as a learning device. They do not hide them as is often done in the West.

The mistake board is a very simple but very powerful instrument to change your culture. Most people will hide their mistakes. This is what we learned when we went to school for every time we made a mistake we were punished in one form or another. Our grades went down whenever we made a mistake. But, one of the few ways we learn is from our mistakes. So what was the school system telling us, don't make mistakes and come to school and don't learn? Many people are afraid that when they make a mistake they will be fired. It is ironic for all of us learn primarily from our mistakes. Telling people to not make mistakes is like telling them to come to work but don't learn. Surely, we want to learn from our mistakes and not to repeat them and we want to minimize the damage caused by the mistakes.

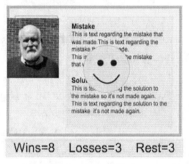

Fig. 14 <Michael Tobin and his mistakes. Eight times he knew how to not repeat his mistake, 3 times unknown to him and 3 mistakes are under study.>

Discussion

Fig. 15 <Gulfstream Mistake Board>

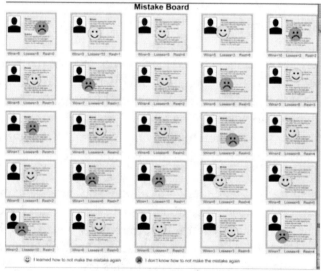

Fig. 16 <Mistake Board>

When a machine makes a mistake we fix the machine. We don't punish the machine! When a worker makes a mistake we often

punish them. For some inane reason we think that people are consciously making mistakes. We must eliminate "fear" from the workplace and recognize that everyone makes mistakes, except maybe my wife.

When mistakes are made it is a great learning opportunity.

This mistake board is so simple but it is one of the most powerful devices I have ever seen to root out fear from the workplace. Please set up a mistake board, test it out and let me know about your results. (send a note to bodek@pcspress.com)

There is nothing more wasteful than hiding mistakes, and this is why companies go to the trouble of developing Kaizen programs and strive to orient the culture toward solving problems and making improvements rather than hiding the facts and dreaming up excuses.

Discussion Continued:

NORMAN: You really want to teach people that want to learn. If they want, then they are open, and then you can teach them. How do we set up the school system where children really want, where they really want to learn? What can we do to entice them, in our school system, so that they really want to learn? Then they'll be open. Then it can be really fun and it could be a mutual exchange.

The other thing is, a teacher has to learn. So when a teacher gets in front of children, the teacher doesn't just want to impart their wisdom, because in a certain sense, much of what the teacher is teaching is their ignorance. Sure, children can learn how to read and learn how to spell, but so many things are not taught well at all. So the trick is to entice children to want to learn?
That's the question I ask the two of you.

Discussion

NORIKO: Let the children talk. And then I will listen and then there is something that sparkles, and then I will try to foster it.

NORMAN: You can say to children, "would you like to learn about the stars, the moon; would you like to learn about how to make a pie? Would you like to learn how to make French fried potatoes?" To entice the children is to ask them, what would you like to learn, see if you can get them interested.

NORIKO: Or you can just let them talk and if you listen to them talk, you can find the seed to guide them.

NORMAN: Yes. So let them talk. See then what their interests are. It's not so easy when they don't know certain things to have an interest in them. But they know so much more just from the environment.

NORIKO: Yes. They notice things. The way to create a sort of a teaching point around it, I think that is also the true meaning of education, I believe, is to draw out what is already there.

NORMAN: Right. Educare is the Latin word meaning "to educate." It means draw out, take out, as if the intelligence is already in the child and the teacher brings it out. Like Michelangelo said when he was carving David, "David was already in the stone. My job was to bring it out."

In a certain sense, draw out of them their curiosity to want to learn. So the trick is for teachers very early to try to inspire people to pick something in their life to succeed at. Early on, I never knew what I wanted. Most kids say they don't know what they want. So if you don't know what you want, how can you be motivated to learn?

NORIKO: The teachers themselves wanting to learn, they have to have interest in what they teach.

NORMAN: That's very good, Noriko. We need a system that teachers will continue to learn. This is also very true for coaches, supervisors, managers, team leaders and others that teach in industry - they have to be passionate about their subject and the desire to help others to learn.

It's true. You have to be passionate about it, and it has to be something that you can continue to learn as you are learning with the children. It has to be learning for both.

NORIKO: There is a famous teacher; I think it was in Japan. She will never teach the same material, ever.

NORMAN: Isn't that wonderful.

NORIKO: Each class, in the same curriculum, every time she will teach something new, every year. If it were the reading assignment, then she would pick another topic. She would talk around it.

NORMAN: She can learn from the children.

NORIKO: So for her, it's new too.

NORMAN: Very good. Ryo, I hope you're taking all this in.

RYO: Uh-huh. I am.

NORMAN: When we talk about a learning corporation, everybody should be learning. The problem with so many teachers is, they stop learning. What we do is we give them a degree. We give them a master's degree, a doctorate degree. We certify them in certain things. We give them tenure.

RYO: Maybe we shouldn't call them teachers. Maybe we should call them leaders.

NORMAN: Yeah. They're coaches. The best word is coach. The goal of a coach in a good sports team is to bring out the best of every player on the team. They want every player to be a superstar, so that they can win.

Virtually every child is born with infinite creative potential dampened by the school system but every person still has the potential to be creative. Quick and Easy Kaizen is a simple and an amazing vehicle to foster the creative spirit at work. Autoliv's plant in Utah has set a goal next year for 96 ideas per person. Imagine the advancements for the company and the excitement generated for every single employee.

I do thank you Ryo and Noriko for participating with me.

Chapter IV

Partial Kaizen to Companywide Kaizen

The jobs people do in a company are all interconnected, forming a chain of processes, so Kaizen delivers significant results if done in every workplace. This is because, just as a chain is only as strong as its weakest link, so a company is only as efficient as its weakest part.

> There is therefore no point in strengthening only a part of the workflow; we need to get everyone to look at his or her own work and try to improve it.

In the late 1980s, I led a study mission to Japan; I visited Toyota Gosei and received a lecture from Taiichi Ohno. He loved to use the example of a river representing inventory covering all of the manufacturing wastes. (Visualize inventory as water covering all of the problems in the plant. For example, if you had a machine problem and was forced to stop the machine, you always had extra inventory to draw upon to keep the process going. Inventory to Ohno was an 'evil,' and to him excess inventory was the biggest waste. To reduce the inventory, he asked people to reduce the batch size (lowering the river.)

At the end of the lecture Mr. Iwata, an assistant to Mr. Ohno, told me he intended to leave Toyota Gosei and start his own consulting company and asked me to help him come to America and teach. I agreed. Some months later Iwata and Chihiro Nakao, from Taiho Kogyo, ran a five-day workshop at Jake Brake - this was the birth of the Kaizen blitz in America.

The Kaizen Blitz has probably been the most explosive and dynamic manufacturing training event of all time. During the first week of training at Jake Brake 50 people moved 50 machines into

Partial Kaizen

manufacturing cells[8] literally creating chaos but bringing enormous improvements to the plant. Hundreds of improvement ideas came out to be solved in the future. The Kaizen Blitz is a marvelous tool if used properly but one main problem is that it does not involve all the employees. ATK, a supplier of rocket propeller systems to NASA, plans to run at least 10,000 Kaizen Blitzes in the coming year. I hope they involve all employees and find a way not to lay off people after all of the improvements are made. It is hard to ask people to be creative when the result for them is unemployment.

When I first went to Japan and met Dr. Shingo and Mr. Ohno, I came back enthusiastically to share the Toyota Production System (JIT) with other American companies. Most people responded to my excitement with, "It might work in Japan, but not here. It might work for the automotive industry but surely it is not for the food industry, the paper industry, the electronics industry, and absolutely it does not apply to hospitals." Now almost 30 years later, we can see the Toyota principles applying to almost every kind of organization. Unfortunately, General Motors, Chrysler and Ford thought it didn't apply to them or they just didn't fully understand how to apply it in their environment.

Ironically, Toyota in the early 1980's wanted to assemble automobiles in America but didn't want to alienate General Motors so they convinced General Motors to allow them to run a joint venture, NUMMI, in Freemont, California. Toyota completely turned around the worst GM plant, in one year, to make it the best but GM said in 2009 that they are not interested in participating further in NUMMI. Go figure?

---

[8] In the past, in plants, often one worker was assigned to work on one machine, spending most of their time just watching, waiting for the machine to stop. Toyota and other Japanese companies realized that placing machines in a U-shaped cell allowed one worker to run several machines at the same time. In America, we focused on keeping the machine working while in Japan Toyota focused on keeping the worker working in takt time – delivering to the customer only what the customer ordered and not creating excess inventory.

Why bother *going to all the trouble of* setting up systems and promoting Kaizen?
What's the point of rolling out a Kaizen program?

1. To do Kaizen deliberately
2. To do Kaizen in a sustained way
3. To do Kaizen systematically

Fig. 17 <Going to all the trouble of.>

Many people still imagine that Kaizen is something done on the production floor and that it has nothing to do with their own particular job. But strong companies declare that Kaizen applies to every kind of job, and extend their Kaizen activities to offices, sales departments and every other workplace, regardless of the type of work being done there.

I was on a Northwest Airlines Flight on business class from Tokyo to Portland, Oregon and they served *terrible* eggs. I told the flight attendant about the eggs, but she felt helpless to do anything about it. "Write to the airline. they will not listen me," she told me. She felt powerless to get the airlines to give better quality to the passengers. *It is a sad story that senior management has not found a mechanism to listen to their own employees.* How can the flight attendant really do a good job and feel good about herself when her own company does not listen to her. The CEOs of the large

Partial Kaizen 83

American airlines blame their loses on the high price of oil and the non-cooperation of unions. If this is true then how does Southwest Airlines continuously make money? In the past, I interviewed the president of Southwest Airlines and she told me that they do listen to both their employees and their customers!

Imagine if all of the airlines had a Kaizen system. Flying might again be fun.[9]

But just calling for Kaizen doesn't lead anywhere. However much we talk about Kaizen and explain the need for it, some people will still find ways of objecting to it rather than doing it, saying things like, "Well, that's what you say, but…," "It might work in other people's jobs, but…" and "Kaizen isn't really appropriate for our work."

Simply appealing to such people to do Kaizen is not enough to get them involved. The company's approach has to be systematized, and to some extent made compulsory, but with patience for some people will take time a lot of time to trust you.

At a Gulfstream plant, on December 31, 2006, with lots of urging and care and respect they had 99.9% of the people submitting at least one idea. Only the controller did not submit an idea. A team went to the comptroller's office and demanded that he come up with one improvement idea. He did and he is truly a great guy.

Toyota Claims Two Pillars For Their Success: JIT and "Respect for People."

How do you really give people respect?

---

[9] On one Continental flight from Houston to Portland, the flight attendants performed a skit for us. It was a lot of fun for the passengers and made the attendants job much more interesting.

The dictionary definition of "respect," is "esteem for or a sense of the worth or excellence of a person, a personal quality or ability, or something considered as a manifestation of a personal quality or ability: I have great respect for her judgment."

To me the highest respect given to a person is to allow them to participate their ideas at work, to ask them to identify problems and come up with creative solutions to those problems. The highest respect is to challenge people to use their brains, to listen to their ideas and to empower them to implement their ideas or to help them implement their improvement ideas. To applaud and praise people for doing a good job is nice but to recognize their uniqueness in solving problems is so much greater.

Hiroshi Okuda, former CEO of Toyota said, "Failure to change is a vice! I want everyone at Toyota to change and at least do not be an obstacle for someone else who wants to change." A great concept, but how do you get everyone to change? You empower them to change their own work area, to identify problems and find solutions. As a manager, you recognize it is your prime duty to help people change and make improvements.
In truth, there are always problems. The challenge is to identify them before they become harmful.

Specific Examples are Our Most Powerful Weapon

Of course, it is not necessary to directly involve all employees in the decision process when making large changes and sweeping reforms. Revolutionary changes should be directed from the top, and it is only necessary to involve motivated and capable people in them.

But Kaizen is all about small changes, and it has to come from the bottom up. In fact, the smaller the problem the better, for it is easier for workers to identify small problems then large ones. If a person can save a second when working on a product, it is great,

for those seconds add up. Even supposedly hopeless, awkward people have to be coaxed and wheedled into getting involved. This is what managing an organization means.

Fig. 18 <Citizen Watch saving seconds.>

I was once at Citizen Watch and saw a series of two sets of pictures side-by-side. They were primarily showing changeovers and you could see where they went from 45 seconds to 37 seconds, 32 seconds to 22 seconds, etc.

This gave workers a wonderful new perspective of how important it is to just save a few seconds.

If I have to reach across my desk for a tool, and can suggest to move the tool closer to reduce my reaching, and even though saves me only a second, it is a good idea. And those seconds surely add up.

If we want to truly be internationally competitive then every human being at work should understand that wasting time is wrong. If you watch a track meet and see people running the hundred-yard dash, you can see the importance of even 1/10th of a second. Should it be any different at work?

It is important for people to recognize that Kaizen activities are part of a person's job not something extra. You are paid to use both your body and your brain. Some companies do give small rewards for ideas that save the company money. As we already mentioned some companies give 10% of the cost savings to workers. Nice, but not at all necessary to get started. You will see that people will just be happy to be more involved and listened to at work.

It is possible to force a Kaizen program through and compel such people and workplaces to show that they have already done large numbers of Kaizens. By showing them specific examples, even those slow on the uptake can be made to see that Kaizen applies to all kinds of work and that it is advantageous to do it. By doing this, we can get even those who seem to be moving backwards and carping against Kaizen to become involved, little by little.

Even some people who do a fine job of managing their family and household at home can get lost when they go to work in a big company, and lapse into an infantile way of thinking. To run an organization, we have to motivate these people.

Partial Kaizen   87

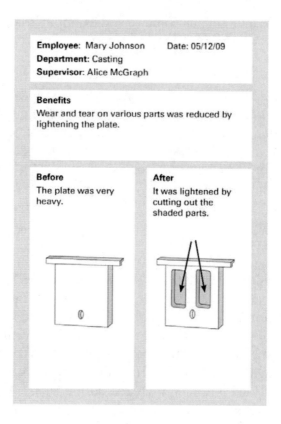

Fig. 19 <Lighten your load.>

There are also people in every company with whom logic does not work. Trying to reason with them is a waste of time, because they just don't understand theory. The only way of explaining Kaizen to such people is by using concrete examples. However, even people like this are forced to accept it if shown a specific, real-life example of how their own job has been improved. And in Kaizen, there is any number of such examples. This is Kaizen's biggest strength. We can teach it and promote it using our own in-house training materials.[10]

---

[10] Contact me at bodek@pcspress.com and I will be happy to send you a set of slides.

With patience and guidance and lots of examples people will begin to see many opportunities for them to make similar improvements.

It is funny. We go to school normally for at least 13 years through high school and we have to study to grow each day. Then many people think that after we graduate high school and go to work the intense routine of learning can stop. I remember when I graduated high school my favorite song was "No more pencils, no more books, no more teachers dirty looks." Boy was I wrong! There is no end to studying. The more you perfect your skills, the more fulfilled life you will have. Everyone must be given the opportunity at work to continuously learn and build his or her or her skills and capabilities.

In the 19th century a craftsman was responsible for knowing every aspect of their job. A carpenter[11] knew how to measure exactly what the customer needed, select and cut the wood, sanded, glued, nailed, assembled, polished and was able to put together the entire product by themselves. Then comes along the 20th century with Frederick Taylor and Henry Ford with scientific management and work is simplified into repetitive and boring tasks. We might have a lot more creature comforts with our cars, automatic washing machines, and thousands of other gadgets and devices. But, the quality of work life was devastated. The result was much higher productivity and products were produced in abundance much more cheaply than in the past, but the worker suffered. We can really change all of that with Quick and Easy Kaizen.

---

[11] Some carpenters can still do many different things but when they end of working for large corporations they are often relegated to doing simple repetitive tasks.

Partial Kaizen 89

Fig. 20 <Other companies Kaizen examples.>

Whenever I go to a manufacturing plant I see people doing the same simple tasks over and over again. My heartbreaks and I look with such confusion. Why can't we create a work environment where people have dignified work that stimulates and challenges them? They might be able at the end of the day find richer and better things to do than to "come home exhausted, filled with tensions, have a can of beer and fall asleep in front of the television set." When the energy is moving inside, I can work for hours on end without getting tired. But if I do boring repetitive work, it is very hard for me to keep my eyes open.

My computer technician, Rory Bowman, a very bright and highly skilled person, gave me a very insightful thought. He said," Our school systems are designed to give us the knowledge we need to do the kinds of jobs that industry provides for us. It is sad. Sure when people only do the work found in industry, most of it very boring and repetitive, it becomes so easy to send jobs to China and India. What do you lose? But, if people were trained to be like the artisans of the past, you could never outsource the work.

Please do Think About This: as You Raise the Skills of People, You Both Add Value and Lower Costs.

When you go to a fine museum and look at a painting or at the antique furniture you can feel the quality, the enormous energy of the master. People pay, today, millions of dollars for the fine artwork from the artisans of the past. Sure, we pay for antiques because they are rare but lots of things are rare and old but do not have the energy, ingenuity and craftsmanship found in these masterpieces. In the past the average person lived surrounded by works of art. You can just look at the old furniture and feel the energy that was put into each piece. Today, most of us have so many more things than our ancestors had but I feel we miss a lot by not having that fine art, from craftspeople, around us.

How Can We Change All of This, Maybe by Doing More Homework?

I was not a very good student and I did hate homework for I believe I was not taught properly. But now I can see the real value of homework. To compete in the 21st century with China, India, and the other Far East countries every place where we work must become a learning organization. That means everyone is learning something new everyday so that they can grow to become a master at whatever they do and to help the company where they work be internationally competitive.

I laugh when I am told that a company explains with pride that they give their workers two hours a month of training. It is a joke! Imagine when you were younger only going to school for two hours a month. Like Pinocchio we would all end up as donkeys living in play land. No, to be internationally competitive every one of us almost without exception must continue to grow and learn something new every single day. Quick and Easy Kaizen is a

great process to help people learn on the job, learning from their own ideas.

I recommend strongly that a minimum of one hour be provided every day to teach workers new skills and widen their depth of knowledge. If you can't do one hour a day, try to train at least one hour a week. Make your company a true learning organization. Our companies must be dedicated to not only producing fine products and giving excellent service but also dedicated to building superb human beings. God forgive me, but everyone should be given at least one hour of homework, every single night. This can be done so easily by asking your most experienced and talented workers to become teachers to teach what they know best.

When we come to work we should be given tests to see that we are building our skills and capabilities and also we must be given opportunities to do new things that are both fulfilling and creative.

Anyway, Start Wherever You Can

A home run scores a point with a big blow. But Kaizens are not home runs; they are singles, and single hits only stand a chance of scoring if there are runners on base. Likewise, Kaizens must be done continually, one after the other, in order to have significant effect. While each is small individually, the combined effect of large numbers of them is great.

This means that the most important part of teaching and promoting Kaizen is about keeping it going. That is why a Kaizen program is sometimes referred to as a 'battle against becoming stereotyped or stuck.'

Kaizen training is clearly not about academic study; it is about developing people's Kaizen wisdom through dealing with reality.

This is the biggest difference between Kaizen OJT and the usual abstract type of training and development.

Dionicio Alvarez Mendez, a worker at Gulfstream, as of November 1, 2009, implemented 760 Kaizens for the year. Sounds crazy! How in the world is it possible to do your job and also find the time to implement 760 ideas? To find out I went over to him and asked him to show me some of his ideas. They were great. On one Kaizen he painted color on interchangeable machine tools to quickly identify them. He set up sub-part stations to reduce walking. He understands the game of Kaizen and plays it very well by looking around the plant and seeing what will make-work easier and more interesting.

Fig. 21 <Dionicio placed a strip of metal on the bottom of the board to prevent the drill from penetrating beyond surface.

In business, the standard for deciding whether or not to do something is whether it is beneficial or not. Companies operate on

the principle of doing as much as possible of what is good for them and as little as possible of what is bad for them. So the quickest and easiest way of persuading employees to do Kaizen is to explain how it will benefit them – and this is where we need examples that directly relate to their own experience. They will understand and accept the need for Kaizen when they see examples that would be of direct benefit to them, or that they are glad they had implemented. This is because one of our most basic motivating factors is whether something is advantageous to us or not.

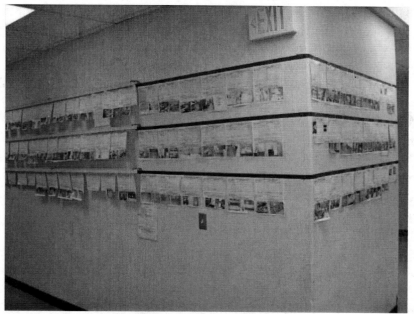

Fig. 21 <DCI Kaizen display wall.>

At the beginning of my class, I ask all of the students to think about the problems they have and try to come up with solutions or I ask them to think about problems they had in the past and the solutions they came up with. At the end of the class I ask them to write two problems and two solutions. I then ask them to stand up and present at least one of their ideas. This process lets everyone in the class learn quickly that Kaizen is easy to do.

It is also important for the supervisors and managers to recognize the workers ideas. They are adding to the company's wealth of knowledge and efficiency and they should be thanked continually for their efforts.

Quick and Easy Kaizen's biggest problem is management's resistance to change. Quick and Easy Kaizen works. It works very well and is not complicated to get started. I know that almost everyone resists change. People are just afraid of making mistakes. I don't minimize this at all. Managers become comfortable when something was tried and succeeded somewhere else. When Six Sigma worked well at General Electric many companies invested heavily to get people trained as "black belts." I feel that Quick and Easy Kaizen works very well and can be used in addition to Six Sigma and is easier to start and maintain it. Not only will all of your employees be engaged in continuous improvement and feel better about themselves, but the Quick and Easy process can save you millions of dollars.

Believe me, with all the things I discovered in Japan, since 1980, including SMED, TPM, 5S, Hoshin Kanri, Poka-yoke, etc., Quick and Easy Kaizen is the most important or at least equally important.

Quick and Easy Kaizen develops people's skills. As people skills grow, costs are reduced and more value is added to your products and services. Yes, improving and expanding value added activities are the real key to the success with Lean or Just-in-time. When workers identify problems and solve them, the result is eliminating wastes and adding value.

Partial Kaizen

Fig. 22 <Our own Kaizen examples.>

Chapter V

Documenting Problems

Documenting Kaizens

When younger, I was convinced that I could not write. All of my past English teachers will attest to my inability to write. I can remember tears of embarrassment coming over me when I would read over the things I had written. I would have never won any prizes for penmanship. My scribbles were not only unreadable to others but were often not readable to me. I was very grateful when the IBM electric typewriter was invented for it allowed me to begin to write things that others and I could read.

It was not until the computer came along with spell check and the other correction features that I felt somewhat comfortable communicating and putting my thoughts down on paper. Now, I teach Quick and Easy Kaizen and I know that many people, like I was, could be embarrassed to write down their ideas on paper.

Bunji has taught me, we can just put down very simple sentences, draw things or take pictures of the before and after, and the supervisor/manager should recognize the need and help people write down their ideas. Many workers can't write English but fellow workers or supervisors can help them write their Kaizens. We are not writing our Kaizens for publication to the outside world. We only want to communicate to our fellow workers what our problems are and what our ideas are to solve those problems.

The Kaizen program brings potential problems to light. But this is not a bad thing; it should be regarded as a good thing. In fact, many small problems that could have developed into critical ones have been exposed and nipped in the bud.

Documenting Problems

If the truth were told, most of us do our jobs in a pretty slipshod fashion. We do a lot of rather strange things at work. However, these normally do not become apparent, and our odd ways of getting the job done, or even our breaches of the rules, remain concealed beneath the surface. They only get found out when a problem like an accident or some damage occurs, and we are told that it happened because we were doing things wrongly or not carrying out the proper checks.

Why Things that Should Never Have Happened Keep on Happening

Undoubtedly some very small things that lead to bigger problems are done in most workplaces, but they usually don't become an issue until some sort of trouble occurs. They are normally hidden under the surface. The problem is, by the time they do surface it is usually already too late, because considerable loss and damage has already occurred. This is what goes on in most workplaces, isn't it?

Then, when these odd practices are exposed, all the people do is keep on repeating timeworn mantras like "This should never have happened." and "This must never be allowed to repeat itself." Stringent checks are carried out for a while, but the tension cannot be maintained. Eventually, as the people in charge move on and memories of the accident fade, discipline becomes lax and the accident is likely to happen again.

You might know the phrase "flavor of the month" whereby managers learn something new like Six Sigma, pay $20,000 to get a black belt and go out and make some improvements. But even though Six Sigma can be very good it does not involve all of the employees and very often is not sustained. Kaizen means continuous improvement – to always look to identify problems and solve them. Toyota has been doing Kaizen for over 59 years.

The fact of the matter is that people are pressed for time every day. They deal with one problem after another, and cannot possibly keep on carrying out detailed checks while continually monitoring the situation. This is a fact of life in most workplaces, and it is why the same types of accidents and scandals keep on recurring and why we keep on hearing the words, "Oh, no! Not again!" It really is a case of history being doomed to repeat itself.

Fig. 23 <Accident Happens>

Kaizen Reports Show What's Going On in the Workplace

I know one plant manager, Dan O'Malley with Gulfstream, who with his senior team, goes on a walk of the plant every Wednesday, and stops and talks to five to ten of his employees. He asks each of them to show him one of their recent Kaizens. He looks at the

Kaizen, listens to the worker, discusses the meaning of the idea with the worker and of course, thanks and praises the worker for helping the plant continuously improve. It is a very powerful learning moment because he gets the opportunity to personally meet around 350 employees a year from these walks. It is also important for the employees to have that one-on-one moment with their senior manager.

Praise

I can't remember ever being praised by my father. I can only remember being criticized by him and all of my teachers. When I grew older, I unfortunately copied from my father and my teachers and was never able to praise my employees. Not one. At one time, I was a vice president of a data processing company with around 35 employees. Since I was a new manager, I read about the importance of praising one's employees. Okay, I was now challenged to find someone to praise, "to break the ice with."

I went into the data entry room and looked around. The previous week, we had a Christmas party, and I danced with a data entry operator. I noticed her and went over to her, looked at her, and said, "I want to thank you for doing such a great work on the Budweiser job." It was very hard for me to praise her, for I had done it before.

The operator looked up at me and I felt for the first time in my life this amazing love that poured out of her into me just from praising her. This rarely happens but tears came into my eyes and I realized for the first time in my life, what not only the worker, but I was missing by not praising. I knew, intellectually, the importance of praising but I didn't want to be insincere and just praise for the sake of praising.

Yes, praising people who deserve this praise is a vital part of the manager's job. People need this simple recognition. It can inspire people at work to be much happier with themselves and the company they work for. I suggest you try it! Find some small thing to praise people. It is very powerful.

Taiichi Ohno's great power came because he spent almost all of his time on the factory floor, observing people and the process. There are many stories of Ohno drawing a circle on the factory floor and insisting that a senior manager just stand there all day and look and learn from just observing what is going on around him. You can learn a little from reading books, manuals and reports but you really learn the most from your experiences. If you go out and talk to the people doing the work and look at their Kaizens you will get a great education from them, and you can spread the ideas by talking to others about them.

3-Gen

One day a senior manager came over to Mr. Toyoda, who at the time was chairman of Toyota, and told him about an incident that had happened in one of their plants. Instead of just listening to the report, Mr. Toyoda got up and went to the plant to see for himself. It is not that he did not trust the senior manager. They know at Toyota in order to move continuous improvement forward all managers, including the senior man at the top should whenever possible go to the exact place, the Gemba, look at the real thing, Gembutsu, and collect the real data, Genjitsu. This is what we mean by 3-Gen.

I don't know about you but I learn from experience. You can delegate many things and I'm sure you can learn but it is not nearly as powerful as when you experience it for yourself. And when the top person, who really has the power to change, goes to the plant

floor positive change can happen quickly. Believe me, there are things you must see for yourself.

Documenting and sharing Kaizen is the best way to learn what is going on in the company, because Kaizen reports and memos are actually reports of what is happening in the workplace. And, what's more, they are not boring, static reports. They are dynamic reports, describing what has been tried, and what has been changed. This makes them very interesting to read. Neither are they long-winded, dressed-up reports. Since, as the name 'Kaizen memo' implies, they are concise, specific accounts of what was done, how it was done, and what happened as a result, they give an accurate picture of the state of the workplace.

Bunji recommends we use only around 75 words maximum to write a Kaizen.

A certain factory general manager said, "I don't really trust the reports my department managers send me. They're basically a whitewash job, glossing over what they don't want me to know. I trust our operators' Kaizen reports much more. Those reports might not look so pretty, but they don't lie. If you read them every day, you get a very good idea of what the shop floor is like. They clearly show where the problems are and gets people to think about acting on their own."

Kaizen memos and reports are the workplace's 'raw data'. Since they are not 'sexed up' or worked over cleverly to make them look nice, they show the workplace in its true colors. This is because Kaizens are a good thing, so even though a Kaizen itself may not be perfect, it does report at least something good. These reports are required to be written concisely and submitted daily, which means that they are written quite frankly.

Kaizen reports really allow the workers to share their intellectual abilities with their company. These Kaizens are not complaints;

complaints; they are what are needed to improve. We talk about continuous improvement but Kaizens by workers are one of the only ways that the workers have the ability to continuously express them selves at work. Look at the many Kaizens displayed throughout this book and even if you have absolutely no knowledge of the companies concerned, you will get a clear idea of what sort of work they are doing by reading the reports.

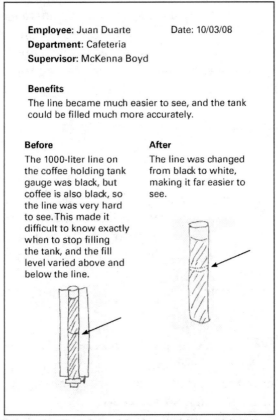

Fig. 24 <Change the line from black to white making it easier to see.>

Documenting Kaizens is like holding a mirror up to the workplace and seeing it in its true light. Kaizen reports reflect everything that is going on, including odd ways of doing things, breaches of the rules, and employees' misperceptions and knowledge gaps. They

are the best possible source of information for preventing accidents and harmful incidents. They are like sonar devices, able to detect problems lurking under the surface.

Routine Disclosure

Seen from this viewpoint, documenting and reporting on Kaizens are clearly nothing less than a routine disclosure system. Kaizen lets you know what the workers are thinking about. And as you teach the workers more and give them move tools and techniques to use, the Kaizens will start to reveal that new learning.

In other words, a Kaizen system is an information disclosure system that all employees can use all the time. The use of a simple system like this for disclosing and sharing information gradually changes the atmosphere of the workplace and the culture of the company. Documenting and sharing Kaizens not only reveals the quality of the work being done but also shows everyone each other's fallibility. If everything had been done perfectly, there would have been no need for a Kaizen, and in fact there would have been no opportunity to do one.

Doing a Kaizen is like acknowledging that the previous method of doing a job had not been the best possible one.

In the early stages of a Kaizen program, you must exercise care and patience because people have not been allowed, in most places, to tell the truth about making mistakes. You have to overcome that natural fear and build some trust by listening to people, allowing them to talk about their problems and solutions without criticism, at all. When a worker submits an idea; you look at it and thank them for their idea – no matter how crazy the idea is, you thank them and praise them.

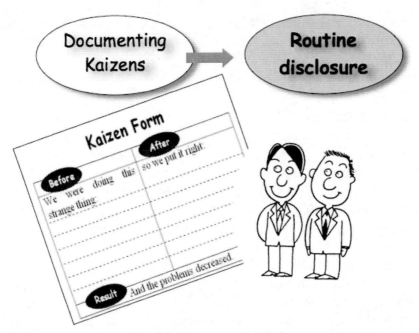

Fig. 25 <Documenting Kaizens>

For example, let us take an idea a worker submits an idea. "I want to blow up the plant!" You read the idea. You thank the worker for the idea. You do not criticize. At first you think the worker might be crazy but you do not say, "Why do you want to blow up the plant?" You don't want to sound as if you are accusing the worker. You just ask them to explain the problem with a little bit more detail. You might discover that the plant "smells" and it is difficult for the worker to properly express them selves. With care you will develop a bright new relationship with the worker. You want to get to the root cause of the problem. You want to allow the worker to express them selves and to trust you. You want to make it a win – win situation.

If you ask and listen you will be amazed at what comes out of workers. In time they will learn to trust you and tell you everything you need to know about the workplace to make improvements.

Documenting Problems 107

Once, I was a soldier, an Army auditor, assigned to audit the Detroit Ordinance Depot in Detroit, Michigan. My supervisor was a civilian auditor. He told me at the start, "Norman we have a very difficult job ahead of us. We have to do two weeks worth of work in three months." I was confused. But, working with him was a lot of fun as we tried to fill the day with our coffee breaks and find things to keep us occupied. I learned many things from him. One was to gain the trust of the employees, each with a file cabinet of things going wrong at the Depot. In time, they told us all things that needed to be improved. Our report, after the three-month period, received praise from our leaders and I made a lead auditor. Go figure!

Disclosures by employees at the beginning can be an obstacle to the Kaizen system. This is particularly true in workplaces that operate on a demerit system, or in high-level government offices where everyone adopts the official position that they are always doing the best possible job, and wild horses would not get them to admit that they had actually anything to improve. The problem with this is that, since what they profess to be doing is so far from reality, they end up working in some preposterous ways, tangled in a web of lies about it.

Written Kaizen Confessions Are Painless

In contrast to this, workplaces where Kaizens are documented and shared do not maintain a façade of correctness; they accept that they are all in the same boat, making mistakes and acting foolishly. Disclosing Kaizens helps to build a culture in which people are willing to share their ideas on how to learn from their mistakes and not to repeat them again.

This is important, for we only feel like doing Kaizens and accept the need for them once we become aware that we have been doing something silly. In workplaces where everyone has to hide their

foolish mistakes from each other, there is no way that anyone is going to feel like doing Kaizen, because doing a Kaizen would be the same as admitting that one had been acting stupidly. Not really, a little over exaggerated for almost everything we do can be improved. However, notice acting stupidly is not the same as being stupid. We can do foolish things doesn't mean we are foolish.

When people hear that they should be doing a certain number of Kaizens, this naturally prompts them to ask, "Well, how many, then?" It is impossible to answer this question definitively, because it depends on the type of work being done and how mature the Kaizen program is. Nevertheless, as a general guideline, it is recommended that a target of one to two per month be set as a

Fig. 26 < A Kaizen Form>

minimum for each person, regardless of the industry or type of work. In other words, each person should review their working methods at least once a month and do, document and share at least one Kaizen.

Documenting Problems

I initially ask the workers to come up with two per month but as the system matures you could ask for three. Just remember at Autoliv they are going to ask for eight per month. Once again if Autoliv can do it, with patience and a little bit of experience, so can you.

At one company, the managers tell people that, even if they do nothing more, they should at least **write out a Kaizen every month on payday**. Another company designates the 19th of every month as 'Idea Day' and sets aside a special time for its employees to document and share their Kaizens. The idea of this is to get everyone into the habit of doing at least one Kaizen a month and thereby make it customary for employees to carry out a periodic inspection of their work practices.

At a plant in Mexico where I taught Quick and Easy Kaizen, several workers submitted and implemented, on their own, over 300 ideas last year. One idea was to put a picture of what was inside a file cabinet on the door of the file cabinet. This picture allows you to know what is inside the file cabinet without having to open it up. It saves people seconds. If you can save just one second doing something, it is wonderful. Imagine if everyone can save one second several times a day – it all adds up and it gives people an opportunity to really do continuous improvement.

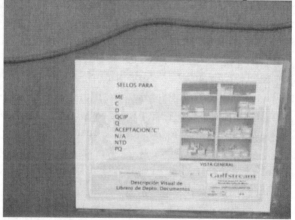

Fig. 27 <File cabinet door shows what is inside the cabinet.>

I know many hospitals that are doing Quick and Easy Kaizen. I like to tell the story about the Baptist Healthcare System in Pensacola, Florida that went from the worst hospital system in Florida to the best. In fact they won the Baldrige Prize.[12] When I interviewed the chairman of the hospital, he said, "It was getting the employees involved with their improvement suggestions that turned the system around."

Last year, I broke my hip and spent three days in the hospital. Twenty-two incidents happened to me in those three days. The doctor, the nurses in the hospital facility itself were great but I was lucky to survive because the communication processes in the hospital were dysfunctional. It was not the operation that would kill me it was the way that people could not communicate properly with each other. The hospital was filled with "smokestacks." Each person was an expert but unable to function in the total benefit of the patient. 15 minutes before the operation, I asked the doctor to tell me what kind of anesthesia I should take. He told me I had to speak to the anesthesiologist. There was "turf" to protect throughout the hospital. I was given the wrong prescription, food I was allergic to, banged up finger, a stiff neck, and a host of other surprises. When we begin to use Quick and Easy Kaizen people learn a whole new way of communicating with each other.

Recently, a certain well-known Japanese company placed large advertisements in all the national papers apologizing for a fault with one of its products and informing purchasers of the recall procedure, but its reputation did not suffer as a result. In fact, the company probably increased people's confidence in it by being so open about the problem and taking such prompt and effective action. Yes, no matter how careful, we all make mistakes but being truthful and being responsible will always win for you.

---

[12] Baldrige Prize is a quality prize awarded annually.

Fig. 28 <Kaizen memos tell us what's really going on.>

Establishing the Documentation and Sharing of Kaizens Starts with Forming a Habit

We tend to react to crises with the ideas and thought patterns that have become ingrained in us. The fact that a punch-drunk boxer, for example, can still respond to his opponent's blows with counter-punches, is the result of the constant training that has embedded that faculty into his physique.

The same thing can be said about our jobs. When we face a crisis, the last thing we tend to think is, "Right, let's tell everyone about it." When a major problem arises in a workplace that is accustomed to hiding small problems, the first thing people think about is how to cover it up – and the bigger the problem, the more energy they devote to doing so. This is because, in emergencies, our habitual thought patterns and modes of behavior come to the forefront. It is only if we are used to disclosing small problems and being open about poor practices that we will not panic when a

serious accident happens. However, in a workplace that does not carry out any training in this kind of thing and is not used to disclosing its problems, people will fall into the same pattern of behavior when a serious problem occurs, and the first thing they will think of is to hide it, at least for the time being.

Often, I hear that the Japanese are able to do Quick and Easy Kaizen for their culture is different from ours. From all of my trips to Japan, 75 to date, I have found very few things that prevent us implementing JIT, 5S, Kaizen Blitz, TPM or many of the other wonderful tools being applied there. Somehow we live with a "myth" that we are rugged individualists and our culture prevents us from getting many ideas from our workers. Maybe in 1875, when we lived on the "range" we were rugged individualists, but today we live in cities, go to schools together, and play on sports teams. We can surely learn to share our ideas with our fellow workers. I see nothing in our culture that prevents us from asking people to look around their work area and find problems to solve.

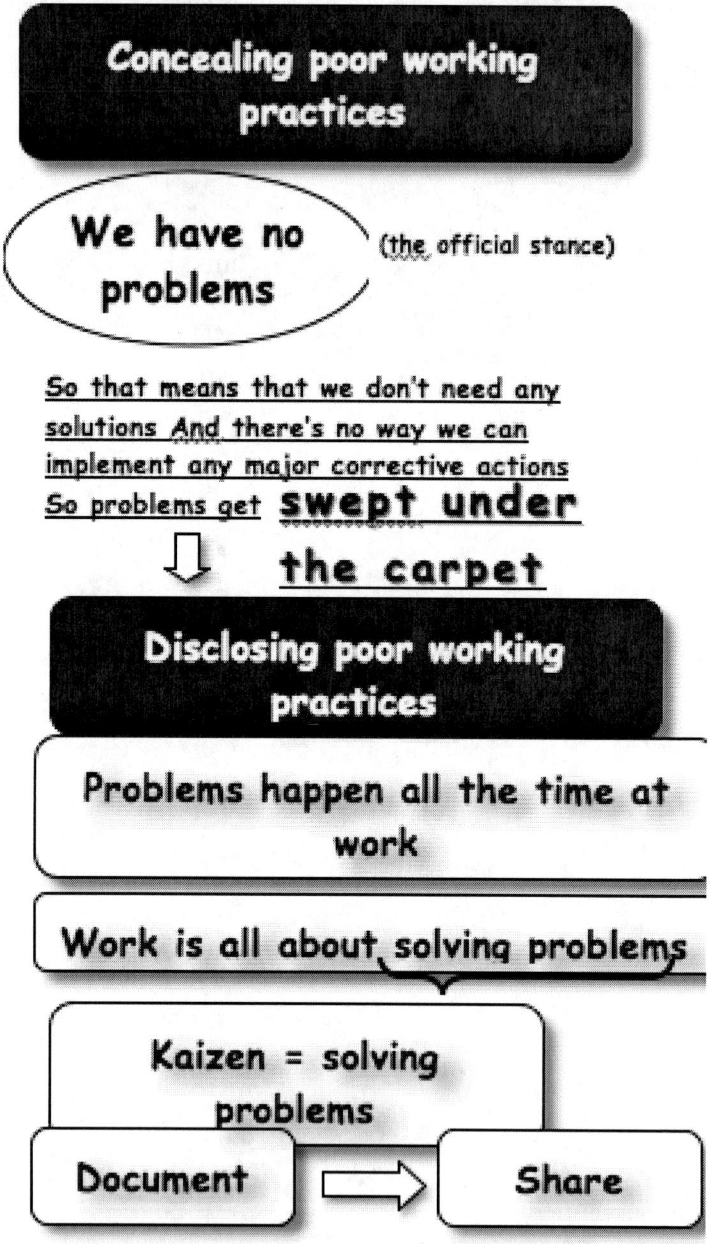

Documenting Problems 113

Concealing poor working practices

We have no problems (the official stance)

So that means that we don't need any solutions. And there's no way we can implement any major corrective actions. So problems get **swept under the carpet**

Disclosing poor working practices

Problems happen all the time at work

Work is all about solving problems

Kaizen = solving problems

Document ⟹ Share

Fig. 29 <Concealing poor working conditions.>

Chapter VI

Real-Life Case Studies

① Teaching Kaizen

② Battling with Practical Constraints

③ Solution – Compromise - Kaizen

④ Principles – Parameters – Set Moves

⑤ The Three Rules for Implementing Kaizen

Teaching Kaizen

Train in Accordance with the Three-Part Definition of Kaizen

Once a system for identifying, documenting, implementing, and sharing Kaizens has been set up, to sustain and expand the organization's Kaizen program, the next thing needed is a mechanism for operating the system; i.e. for teaching and promoting it.

☆

How should we go about doing these things? Kaizen coaching based on the Three-Part Definition of Kaizen is recommended as being the most easily understood method.

Work improvement, Kaizen, is clearly defined by the following three items:

① **Change, Choosing Better Ways of Doing Things, or Changing the Conventional Methods**

② **Progressive Small Changes, Not Big Ones**

③ **Within a Framework of Constraints, Overcoming Resistance to Change**

Begin by Defining Kaizen Clearly

When people are asked what Kaizen is, they may reply that it is 'continuous improvement,' a straightforward definition that is perfectly adequate under normal circumstances. But if an organization is going to the trouble of setting up and operating a system of work improvement, it needs a rather clearer definition than this.

① **Change, Choosing Better Ways of Doing Things, or Changing the Conventional Methods**

Kaizen is changing methods for the better. Kaizen asks all workers to be responsible for improving their own work area. With Kaizen

we are empowering people to do it. Instead of waiting to be told what to do to improve the work environment; we want all workers to be empowered to it on their own. "If there is a better way to build a mouse trap then do it." Don't wait for the supervisor or manager to come by and tell you what to do. Just simply look around your worker area and find a way to make the work environment better. If there is a piece of paper on the floor then pick it up. Better still:

1. Put another basket near places were paper accumulates.
2. Give people a "nickel" for every paper they pick up.
3. Put a paper shredder in the room.
4. Convert all paper to digital files.
5. Put glue on the paper so it sticks to the owner.
6. Teach everyone to make paper planes to bring home to their children.
7. Put a sign up to "save our trees - please reuse your old paper."

When people recognize that creativity and innovation are unlimited then tons of ideas can come forward. Now, some of the ideas maybe foolish and not usable but you don't want to stop the stream of ideas. You just discard the ones you don't want to use and test the ones that might make sense to you.

Kaizen is a methodology to get streams of ideas from everyone.

Maybe in the past, you could succeed with only the managers using their brains and solving problems, but not today. We need innovation, new ideas from everyone to compete internationally. We can't compete with China and other Asian companies on the basis of low cost labor.

I know of many companies running Kaizen Blitz events and doing six sigma but all employees are not involved and improvement is not sustained on a daily basis.

Real-Life Case Studies

When I first discovered Japanese management practices in 1980, I was introduced to Quality Control Circles, whereby small groups of workers, normally less then 10 people, would select a common quality problem. On their breaks and spare time workers would work together solving the problem. They were taught to use initially seven quality tools[13], and would on the average solve two or three problems a year.

While talking with Japanese managers, I would often hear them tell me that they had a bottom-up management system as opposed to the top-down management system like many companies in the West. As I have travelled through Japan, 75 trips to date, I accepted this idea of bottom-up management, but did not really understand it. I did not see the average worker making decisions that would lead their organization. I would see the quality control circles, watched many team presentations of their accomplishments, but never really thought that the workers were having a great influence on top management.

However, what the term bottom-up really implied was that the worker could make the decisions that affects their work and that management would respect their decisions.

Bunji says that the first thing to do is to have everyone clearly understand the definition of Kaizen and know exactly what it means. Kaizen is the worker doing things that makes his or her job easier, more interesting and builds their skills and capabilities. When workers focus on improving themselves, the result is happier workers and lower costs, higher quality, greater safely and higher productivity. When the focus is solely on the workplace, not the worker, people rarely understand what they can do to give you what you want. It is a subtle but powerful shift that takes place.

---

[13] Seven basic quality tools: pareto diagram, histogram, cause and effect diagram, control charts, check sheets, scatter diagram, and graphs.

It is recommended that Kaizen training be based on this Three-Part Definition: changing method for the better, small changes and overcoming these constraints (resistance.) By doing this, you can start getting people to understand the 'What' (what Kaizen is). In parallel with this, you can get them to understand the 'Why' (why we need Kaizen) and even the 'How' (how we can do Kaizen quickly and easily).

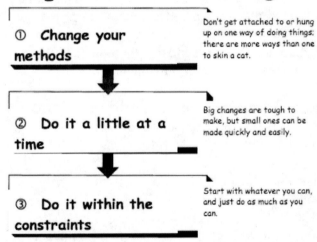

Fig. 30 <The three-part definition of Kaizen.>

When training beginners on work improvement, you need to start by teaching them the most basic thing; that is, the first part of the Kaizen definition ('Kaizen means changing the way we do things; it means changing the way we do our work, for the better, of course.') Then move on to encourage people not to get hung up on one way of doing things but to change their methods in accordance with the situation.

Real-Life Case Studies

You may find it helpful to use persuasive slogans such as 'Yesterday's best is not always today's best,' 'The best method depends on the situation,' and 'Adapt to changing circumstances and find better ways of doing things.' By explaining things in this way, you can break down the outdated view of work that some people hold, namely that all they need to do is keep their heads down and do what they are told and do it in the same way as they did in the past.

Unfortunately, simply understanding the need for Kaizen does not instantly make people able to do it. They will almost certainly say that they understand why they need to do Kaizen but that it is too difficult for them to change the way they do their jobs. Remember we are all "creatures of habit and it is difficult to do anything new without some outer force to persuade us to change.

☆

Standardized work developed at Toyota is marvelous concepts whereby you develop precise procedures based on the best way to do a job and have everybody follow that standard precisely, but you always have the right to improve it. In fact, you are expected to improve it with your Kaizens.

Remember the first part is change but change for the better. This is when you have to explain the second part of the Kaizen definition, i.e.:

② Progressive Small Changes, Not Big Ones

As we said earlier in the book, the confusion with the word Kaizen in America is that someone renamed a workshop from "Five Days and One Night" to "Kaizen Blitz." The Kaizen Blitz is a three day to one week event making radical change where by you do Value

Stream Mapping[14] (VSM,) set takt[15] time, often re-arrange work into cells and make a lot of big changes. It can be a powerful learning experience but it does not involve all employees in continuous improvement.

One day many years ago, I asked Bunji to let my study group visit a company in Japan who had the most suggestions per employee. The company was Oki Denki, an electronic company. They were receiving over 500 suggestions per employee per year. Prior to developing their suggestion system they were very close to going bankrupt. When at the plant, I asked to meet the person who submitted the most suggestions. He, believe it or not, submitted over 5000 suggestions in the previous year. He joyfully took me to his part of the plant and showed me a machine that was totally operating without him.

Every night he would go home and sit with his wife and write down 20 suggestions, each with very slight steps or variations to solve the myriad of problems he faced. Through his suggestions he was able to totally automate his work.

I remember visiting Oki Denki's lunchroom and seeing thousands of suggestions pilled up on tables. Now I am not telling you to have a system like Oki Denki getting hundreds of ideas per employee, but I am just showing you that when people understand Kaizen fully they are capable of doing phenomenal things. We just have to learn how to see differently what's possible with people if they became inspired. Once again, if Autoliv can get 63 ideas per worker per year so can you.

---

[14] VSM is a process to look at the value stream, production process, and make the process more efficient by eliminating the non-value adding wastes.
[15] Takt is a German word meaning baton, used by the symphony conductor, to keep all of the musicians playing music precisely to the beat. Thus takt time keeps the production in the plant exactly on schedule. Everyone should know the takt time.

Real-Life Case Studies

We use the word Kaizen to mean small changes. It is certainly difficult to make drastic changes to the way one works, but that is not Kaizen. On the contrary, Kaizen consists of nothing more than making small changes to the conventional ways of getting the job done. Since small changes are fine, all that anyone needs to do is change whatever they can. If you can save one second of your time, it is great! If you can save the company one dollar, it is great! For everything adds up and most importantly, we want every worker to be highly motivated at work looking for opportunities to improve.

Kaizen doesn't mean making massive changes beyond one's ability or outside one's authority; it means making minor changes and doing things that one has the ability and authority to make. It can therefore be done comfortably, easily and quickly, on a daily basis. It is definitely not something that requires a lot of effort and tension. All you need is to "break the ice" and get started, then you will see magic happen as workers learn to do Kaizen.

There Are Wide Variations in People's Kaizen Abilities

Once the trainees have understood that Kaizen means doing whatever they can to improve things, does this then mean that they will all set about doing it with gusto? Unfortunately not, because there are wide variations in people's ability to go from 'understanding' something to actually doing it; in other words, there are big individual differences between people's ability to actually do Kaizen.

Everyone has the ability to come up with her/his or her own ideas, so anyone should be able to do something as simple as Kaizen without any special training. However, because they have not received any standardized form of training in it, there are wide individual variations in their ability to exercise that faculty. Why

is one person able to implement over 300 ideas when another cannot even find just one?

③ Within a Framework of Constraints, Overcoming Resistance to Change

People who say, "I understand Kaizen, but I can't do it" lack the ability to cope with constraints. They therefore need to be taught the third part of the definition of Kaizen – that it is a battle against practical constraints. Our work is hedged about by rafts of restrictions and constraints ranging from lack of time, money, bosses and human resources through to confining laws and customs, but everyone manages to get their job done within that framework. Work improvement also has to be done within the same constraints.

Isaac Newton's third law of motion states: "For every action there is an equal and opposite reaction."

Every time you attempt to change and do something new your "head" is going to come back and say, "Don't do it." It is resistance! It is just plain fear that you will make a mistake! You tell yourself, "I got through yesterday, why muddy the waters by doing something different today!"

However, we can overcome this inertia. Simply take a deep breath and as Dr. Shingo would always say, "Do it!"

Kaizen Ability is the Ability to Cope with Reality

General Electric used to say, "Progress is our most important product."

Believe me, most managers I meet have a thousand and one good excuses to not do something new. Many like to play "devil's

Real-Life Case Studies

advocate," and they are very good at playing that game. They can always find faults with your ideas. These "Naysayers" are masters at shooting down new ideas. When you meet these people just tell them "Nothing is perfect." Since it is very hard to find perfection, you select the best idea and move forward.

I think it is the primary role of every supervisor and manager to help his or her subordinates to change.

Taiichi Ohno, former VP of manufacturing at Toyota, was a master of getting other people to change.

One day when Ohno became the Chairman of Toyota Gosei, surrounded by a group of managers and looking at a warehouse, he said, "At Toyota we do not need warehouses. I want you to convert this building into a machine shop, retrain everyone and I will give you one year to do it." And, he simply walked away. Of course, everyone was petrified but they did it.

Kaizen Is Not Difficult

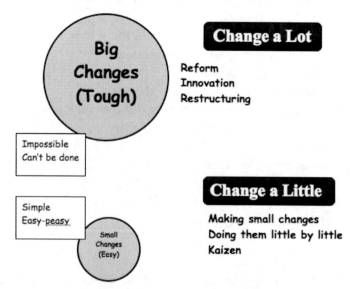

Fig. 31 <Kaizen is not difficult.>

One day, Ohno went over to Dr. Shigeo Shingo, a consultant to Toyota, and said. "I want you to reduce the set up time on this punch press from four hours to two hours." Shingo said, "Okay." A few days later Ohno came back and said to Shingo, "Two hours is no good, we have to do it in less then ten minutes." And Shingo again said, "Okay." Shingo studied carefully the set-up process and was able to develop his SMED[16] system and virtually every set-up at Toyota is now done in less than ten minutes; most of them can now be done with one-touch. This alone has saved Toyota billions of dollars and was the initial key to their success.

Do what Ohno did and go out there and ask people to change and watch the magic happen. Look around the work area of your subordinates and develop your problem identification consciousness.

If someone is just waiting, see if you can help find work for him or her to do. Ask them to tell you the problem.

> I once saw at a Toyota subsidiary a 7-ton press stamping out the tops of automobiles. The changeover took just seven minutes while I understand General Motors did the same thing in 40 hours. Since accountants at General Motors thought that inventory was an asset, General Motors felt that they did not need to reduce the changeovers. They just produced tons of inventory and thought that the excess inventory was producing a very nice profit for them. I think both General Motors and the accountants should reconsider the whole idea of inventory being a valuable asset.

---

[16] SMED is single minute exchange of die – all change-overs to be done in less than ten minutes.

It is in the very nature of Kaizen that it has to be done with nothing – no time, no money, and no-one to help out – but people without Kaizen ability say things like, "We could do it if we only had the time," or, "We could do it if only we had some money." However, if we had all the time and money we wanted, we could do whatever we liked, and we wouldn't need Kaizen in the first place. But life is not like that, and the very fact that we have no time or money means that we need to use Kaizen to change the way we do things. You seem to have the time to do what you always had done before but don't have the time for new things.

Another word for constraints is resistance. Whenever we want to change we meet some form of resistance. It is just the way our minds work. No matter how small the change, the thought rests with us that it might not work. If we really want continuous improvement, we have to overcome this "fear" of failure, fear of making a mistake.

In other words, the ability to do Kaizen is nothing more than the ability to cope with reality, or the ability to deal with constraints. This ability is to get the job done – an ability that cannot be acquired through multiple-choice-test education. When you do Kaizen, you will ask yourself why haven't we done this before?

Why Is Kaizen OJT (On-the-Job Training) Needed?

Improving one's way of working while actually doing the job develops Kaizen ability. This is where the significance of, and the need for, Kaizen OJT lie, because only practical training can develop the ability to deal with change. This is because in real life there is an infinite variety of practical constraints that differ from industry to industry and workplace to workplace and are changing all the time. It is impossible to teach people how to deal with these by rote learning in a classroom, which is why Kaizen OJT must be the mainstay of Kaizen training, with the trainees:

Developing Kaizen Ability While Doing Kaizen

Doing Kaizen While Developing Kaizen Ability.

Of course, the first two parts of the three-part definition of Kaizen (changing the method and small changes) can be taught in a classroom style, using lectures and textbooks, and trainees can acquire some knowledge of Kaizen in this way. They can at least learn what it is all about. However the third part of the definition (the ability to deal with constraints) cannot be taught in this way and has to be acquired through practical training (OJT) by actually doing Kaizen.

So, what exactly is this 'ability to deal with constraints'? The following three items can sum it up:

① **Avoiding or Dealing with Constraints**

② **Surmounting Constraints**

③ **Breaking Through Constraints**

A constraint is any kind of barrier. What would you do if you found your way obstructed by a barrier? If it were as flimsy as paper, the quickest way of getting past it would be to use force to break through it, but this would be impossible if it were a wall of reinforced concrete. In that case, rather than trying to break through it, you would have to try to climb over it or find a gap in it.

Real-Life Case Studies

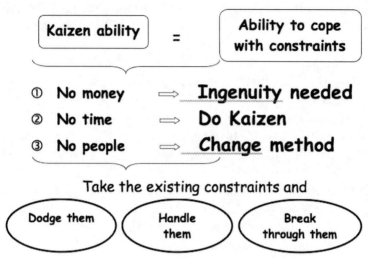

Fig. 32 <Kaizen ability – ability to cope with constraints.>

In other words, we need to adjust our response depending on our own capability and the size of the constraint. That is to say, we need to choose our method or vary it in accordance with the situation. This is exactly what is referred to as 'The ability to cope with reality' or 'The ability to deal with constraints.' People without this ability, like flies buzzing against a windowpane or a person repeating the only thing they know, persist in trying the same unsuccessful method.

If it is a weak barrier, break through it. In such a case, no ingenuity or Kaizen is needed. People who can choose their means and vary their methods according to the situation can make use of all sorts of strategies and tactics.

I always wondered about, children going through such difficulties getting through all those years of school. They face the intensity of learning, the aspirations to achieve, the criticism from teachers and parents, the enormous hours of homework, the preparation for tests, the tests themselves, over so many years supposedly to prepare you for life, to give the knowledge, the tools, the skills, the techniques to succeed in life, only to be followed by such tedious,

repetitive boring work to do. Somehow our educational system got out of kilter. How to get back to where it should be as an ongoing creative process of discovery and joy? It surely has not come from our politicians, the educators, nor our executives and managers. All of those with their advantages seem to want to keep things "Just the way they are." It should not have to be that way. There is a way to change our destiny; change is vital. I like the phrase, "If not me, then who?" If not given to me then I must rise and take the responsibility to change my life.

With Quick and Easy Kaizen, this very simple process of asking people to identify problems and find solutions that they can implement on their own, people can find slowly a new way to bring back dignity to their work life.

Instead of people waiting for managers to do things for them with Quick and Easy Kaizen, we are empowering people to become more responsible for improving the work area around them. If they see a defect or a potential defect, we want them to solve the problem right at the moment of discovery for if the defect moves forward it adds substantial cost.

I remember when I first started Productivity Inc.; I visited a cable company in Connecticut. I asked one lady who I saw very adeptly spinning two rolls of cable at the same time, and asked her what she did when she found a defect. She told me nine years ago when she first started working in the company she discovered a defect on a cable and put a tag on it. Her supervisor came over and saw the tag and ripped it off saying, "What you're trying to do, take away the job of the quality inspector?" Unfortunately, she learned what to do from then on.

Real-Life Case Studies

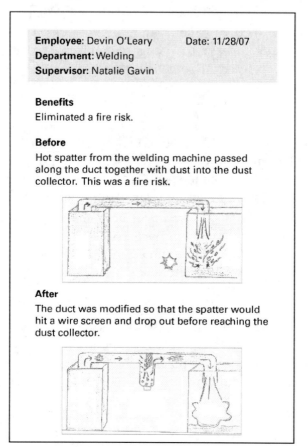

Fig. 33 <Eliminated a fire risk.>

It really doesn't matter what you do as long as you are given the opportunity to grow, to learn, to change and be creative. I could start by washing dishes but I don't want to wash dishes only for the rest of my life. I could start off by washing dishes then learn how to cook and be given the opportunity to work towards being the best cook in the world.

General Motors (GM) built cars and we bought them. I remember the last American car I bought was a 1980 Buick station wagon. Since, I expected to have a number of problems with the new automobile, I placed a yellow pad of paper and a pen on the seat

next to me. Whenever, I detected a quality problem, I would write it down on the sheet of paper. After a few weeks, I would take the car to the dealer to have the items repaired. I accepted this was normal. I never heard of someone getting a new car from Detroit without problems.

One day, I was visiting a GM plant in Detroit and noticed a quality inspector checking the tolerances on doors. I went over to him and asked, "What are you doing?" "Inspecting the car doors, insuring that they are in tolerance to specifications," he said. "What do you do when you find a defect, the door being out of tolerance?" He said, "I notify the punch press people to adjust the press." I then asked, "How many doors have been stamped after the one you are checking?" He said, "Oh, around 5000." What happens to all of those cars? "No worry," he said, "We have very good rubber mallets," and we both laughed.

My wish was that all of the problems would occur before the warranty period was over. It was just normal when you bought a new car to have many problems. It was acceptable. But, the Japanese changed the "ball game." With a new Toyota, you did not expect to have any problems, at all.

I bought a Lexus 13-years ago, and the only problems I have had in all these years were to replace the windshield wipers and get a new structure to hold up the hood. I would love to get a new car but there is nothing wrong with the old one.

Chapter VII

Practical Constraints

Doing Kaizen without Resources

Kaizen is a battle against practical constraints and overcoming resistance to change. To do it, we have to overcome those constraints and learn how to break through the resistance to change. In any case, whether we are doing Kaizen or not, our jobs are subject to a wide variety of constraints, such as:

- **Lack of time**
- **Lack of money**
- **Lack of people**
- **Lack of expertise**
- **Lack of connections**
- **Lack of equipment**
- **Walls imaginary or real to climb over or move around**

The biggest constraint is our fear of failure, fear of making a mistake, fear of lack of approval; many of these fears go back to our childhood. I am not being light about our fears but if we really want continuous improvement then we have to overcome our fears. We have to give people assurances that they will not be punished for making mistakes. That is why the Hino Mistake Board is such a great idea to encourage people to display their mistakes to everyone else.

"Drive out fear, so that everyone may work effectively for the company." - W. Edwards Deming

In 1951, Dr. Deming was invited by the Japanese Union of Scientists and Engineers (JUSE) and Gen. Douglas MacArthur to

speak and teach around 300 top executives from leading corporations in Japan. Dr. Deming was the spark, the inspiration that led Japan from a nation noted for making cheap products to one that produced some of the world's finest products. At the end of his speech, JUSE offered Dr. Deming an honorarium. Dr. Deming refused. He told them to take the money and to start a quality prize. JUSE started the Deming prize and virtually every large corporation in Japan competed and used the desire for that prize to lead their quality efforts. In 1965, Toyota won the Deming prize.

Of course, Dr. Deming was right; we must learn how to root out fear from the workplace.

Don't Just Write People off as 'Unmotivated'

The constraints are the same, but people's reactions to them are diametrically opposite. So where on earth does this disparity come from? Those who have not thought much about the issue may simply dismiss the naysayers (people that are always negative,) saying that they lack motivation. However, once it is said that people just lack motivation, it is the end of the matter, and things can go no further.

On the other hand, if an organization is something that can get ordinary people to do extraordinary things, then surely operating an organization or managing a business is all about getting as much motivation as possible out of ur motivated people. To do this, we have to find out why they are unmotivated, as this might give us a clue as to how to motivate them.

A person is never either totally motivated or totally unmotivated. Just because someone is not motivated to do a particular thing doesn't mean that he or she is not motivated to do anything at all. For example, some people appear completely uninterested in their

jobs but suddenly become very animated when talking about a party or their favorite pastime.

What this tells us is that the difference between being motivated or unmotivated toward Kaizen is merely a difference in the person's attitude toward constraints, arising from nothing more than knowing or not knowing how to handle them. Let's examine this by using a specific example.

One of the rules of Kaizen is, 'Attack the problem from many different angles,' which is the same as saying, "If this doesn't work, let's try that; and if that doesn't work, let's try this." Put another way, it means, "Don't get fixated on or hung up on one way of doing things; think of another way of doing it, or a different means to achieve the goal."

Kaizen Power Equals Multiple Ideas

This means that Kaizen power consists of the ability to come up with as many different choices as possible. This is because in real life we are limited in what we can do by many different restrictions. If we can only think of one idea for improving something, but that idea is impractical because of cost or technical problems, then we are stuck. However, what happens if we can think up many different possible solutions?

If our first idea won't work, we can try another; and if that doesn't work, we can try yet another. In this way, we can go on trying one idea after another until we find one that does work. If the barrier we are faced with is weak, the quickest way of getting past it is to break through it by force; but if that is too difficult, we can use another approach and try to dodge around it or handle it.

> When faced with a problem, don't we often get stuck on trying to solve it by the same approach,

Practical Constraints

banging our heads against it like the fly banging against the windowpane? When this happens, we should try uttering the words 'dodge it' and 'handle it' to ourselves.

This might help us to notice that there are many other possible approaches to solving the problem. At the very least, it might help us to stop stupidly banging our heads over and over against the same brick wall.

At any rate, 'Don't get hung up on one particular method or means' is one of Kaizen's most important rules. Devising many different possible ways of solving a problem helps us to dodge it or handle it.

Incidentally, 'dodging' a problem means 'getting round it,' 'avoiding it' or 'evading it,' while 'handling' a problem means 'skillfully dealing with it.' In martial arts and fighting sports, 'dodging' an opponent's attack means avoiding it, while 'handling' it means turning the tables on the opponent and attacking him or her. When addressing problems, 'dodging' them means avoiding a head-on assault for the time being, and minimizing the damage, while 'handling' them means solving them by turning defense into attack.

When faced with a problem, don't we often get stuck on trying to solve it by the same approach, banging our heads against it like the fly banging against the windowpane? When this happens, we should try muttering the words 'dodge it' and 'handle it' to ourselves.

Fig. 34 <Doing Kaizen – Battling with constraints.>

Practical Constraints

Employee: Lauren James   Date: 09/21/07
Department: Cutting
Supervisor: Manny Figueroa

Benefits
The knobs now go on to the next process free of debris (saving around $75 per month).

Before
Cutting debris came down the chute with the knobs into the box. This could create problems in the next process.

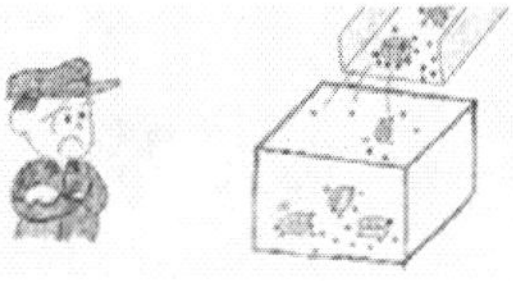

After
Holes were drilled in the bed of the chute, and a tray placed underneath, so that the debris would fall through into the tray.

Fig. 35 <Knobs now go on to the next process."

Chapter VIII

Solution–Compromise–Kaizen

The Three Approaches to Solving Problems

When faced with a problem, what behavioral pattern do we usually follow? How do we respond, particularly when the problem is with another person, and there is a conflict of interests?

Kaizen focused on doing things better can produce some conflicts as my improvement might make your work more difficult. So we need to find ways to compromise for the highest good.

Aren't the following two approaches the ones most commonly seen?

① **Confrontation – Threats – Conflict (the Coercive Approach)**

② **Negotiation – Concession – Compromise (the Conciliatory Approach)**

The Coercive Approach: Using Force

Let's use the simplest possible example to think about this. Imagine that a very tall person and a very short person are working at the same bench. The tall person might say, "This bench is too low, and it's hard for me to work at it. Let's make it higher." On hearing this, the short person would probably reply, "You've got to be joking; it's too high as it is. We can't possibly make it any higher. In fact, it ought to be lower."

Solution–Compromise–Kaizen

In this case, the two persons' interests are diametrically opposed. If the bench were made higher, the short person would have a problem. If it were made lower, the tall person wouldn't like it. Any change to the height of the bench would make it easier for one person but more difficult for the other.

This means that neither of the two can simply accept the other's request, because it would result in a disadvantage to the person who did so. Often, one person's advantage is the other's disadvantage.

When a problem like this occurs, some people might try to solve it is by force. This method of solving the problem consists of one party unilaterally attaining their demands through the use of threats or actual force. The winner is the one who is physically stronger.

Sometimes, instead of physical force, a person uses their higher social standing to get their own way, saying things like, "I've been working here longer than you, so you'll do as I say," or "I'm senior to you, so you'll just have to put up with it."

In any case, whether the force employed is physical or social, this approach, in which the stronger person wins and the weaker person has to grin and bear it, is the most primitive method of solving problems.

The disadvantage of the 'law-of-the-jungle' type of approach described above is that it incurs the resentment of the loser. This kind of resentment can build up in a society and create insecurity and instability, because of the possibility that at some stage the loser will retaliate and try to get his or her revenge.

Although this might have been the way they did things in civil wars or the Wild West, it is completely unacceptable in normal modern society. We need to find another way. If one party is overwhelmingly stronger, he can refrain from imposing his

demands in their entirety. He can demonstrate a certain amount of 'consideration' to the other party as the price of social stability and freedom from the concern that the loser might be plotting his revenge. He might then say to the weaker party, "I really want the bench to be 10 cm. higher, but since I emphasize with you, I'm prepared to stop at 7 cm."

Fig. 36 <Conflict of interests.>

The Conciliatory Approach, Using Kind-Heartedness and Consideration

Will the downtrodden weaker party really feel grateful to the oppressor for his magnanimousness? He might do so initially, but he cannot be relied on to go on doing so. At some stage, he will

• THE COERCIVE APPROACH •

Fig. 37 <The coercive approach.>

begin to wonder why he has to keep on submitting to the stronger party even though he is being treated unfairly. Rather than feeling grateful for the bench having been made only 7 cm. higher, he will feel resentful that it wasn't made 10 cm. lower.

Since he is weaker, he can't achieve what he wants by the use of force. This is when he starts 'negotiating' and says, for example, "Make the bench 7 cm higher? I can't believe you'd even suggest that. It's too cruel. It should be 5 cm at the most." In response to this, the stronger party will probably suggest a compromise, saying something along the lines of, "Well how about splitting the difference at 6 cm? Let's make a deal on that."

By repeatedly negotiating in this way, the two parties eventually reach a compromise determined by factors such as their relative strength, negotiating skill and readiness to show consideration to each other.

Whether the dispute be between individuals or nations, these are the two typical patterns that are followed, aren't they? Of course, real-life situations are more complex, and the two patterns sometimes get mixed up, or double back on themselves. Sometimes the negotiations break down just as the two parties are about to reach a settlement, and war breaks out again.

Sometimes the two parties find a compromise because they are tired of fighting each other. Sometimes they pretend to be negotiating in order to buy time.

• THE CONCILIATORY APPROACH •

Fig. 38 <The conciliatory approach.>

What would happen then? The use of a step by the short person would not cause any problems for the tall person, and the use of a work stand by the tall person would not inconvenience the short person.

Solution–Compromise–Kaizen 147

If we address the problem by changing the method in this way, we can avoid the situation where one party's advantage becomes the other party's disadvantage. In other words, a Kaizen-type approach to solving problems can increase the sum of the two parties' benefits.

Sometimes the two parties find a compromise because they are tired of fighting each other. Sometimes they pretend to be negotiating in order to buy time.

☆

At any rate, the second approach, where the two parties negotiate, make concessions and reach a compromise, is a little more civilized than the first, where one party forces a solution on the other. For this reason, whether with individuals or societies, the second approach to solving problems becomes more prevalent as the parties mature. It is certainly more peaceful.

③ The Kaizen-Type Approach, Where the Method is Changed

However, neither of these approaches to solving problems is Kaizen, because they do not change the way things are done. They do not introduce a new method; they merely change values and proportions while keeping the existing method.

Because of that, one party's gain is the other's loss, and there is no change to the sum of the two parties' benefit and satisfaction. In other words, the 'pie' stays the same and the only the difference is the proportion in which it is shared.

☆

In contrast to this, in Kaizen, we start by thinking about how to change the method. For example, we might say, "If the bench is

too high for you, why not try standing on a step?" or, "If the bench is too low for you, why not try using a work stand to raise the working height of your side of the bench?"

Fig. 39 <Splitting the difference.>

Whether there is conflict, or concession and compromise, any solution that does not change the method merely consists of each party's trying to gain an advantage over the other, with no increase in their overall level of satisfaction. If the total satisfaction of both parties were 10 units, it would simply be a question of whether those 10 units were shared in the proportion of 7 to 3, 5 to 5 or some other ratio, depending on how strong the two parties were in relation to one another at the time. The only difference would be whether the ratio were decided using force or peacefully. There would be no change to the overall structure. What satisfies one party dissatisfies the other. What makes one party happy makes the other unhappy

Solution–Compromise–Kaizen

Or, the two parties could put up with things for each other's sake and share the disadvantages and discomfort. In any case, there would be no change to the total level of satisfaction.

What would happen if even one of the parties changed their method? The total satisfaction of the two parties would increase by that amount at any rate. Also, if both parties improved things for themselves (without affecting the other), then their total level of satisfaction would become even higher.

Fig. 40 <Mutual satisfaction and sacrifice.>

Satisfying Both Parties through a Kaizen-Type Approach

Sometimes we hear people involved in Kaizen saying things like, "This improvement was good for me, but it inconvenienced some other people," or "Their improvement was OK for them, but it made things worse for me and gave me more trouble." However these were probably not real Kaizens that changed the method, the

way the work is done. We should discover how to change the method through repeated Kaizens, trying one after another until one is found that works.

Of course, not all problems can be solved in Kaizen style. Because of all the constraints that exist, it is sometimes impossible to change the method at that time. Let it rest and you can get back to it later.

As the next best method, one has to take the route of concessions and compromises, making the best possible use of strategies to resolve the conflict through compromise. When negotiations break down, then one probably has to resort to force, with the beaten party compelled to comply with whatever solution he is subjected to. However, these are always the measures of last resort.

Start by Thinking How to Change the Method (the way you do things)

People who are no good at Kaizen start off by squaring up for a fight or looking for a compromise. The idea of 'changing the method' is absent.

Everything has its proper order. When faced with a problem, the first things we should think of are:

- Is there another method?
- Is there any room to change the method?

Only if this is impossible should we think about conflict or compromise. The problem is if we get the order back to front, we never even reach the stage of thinking about Kaizen.

Fig. 41 <This makes is much easier.>

Incidentally, in the example we have been discussing, there are of course other possible ways of changing the method than using a step and a work stand. We could, for example, make a two-level bench, or buy separate benches of the right height for each worker. After all, the problem arose in the first place because two people of very different stature were being made to work at the same bench.

Therefore, the problem would disappear if we eliminated this precondition. If it were possible for each person to work at a separate bench, the problem would be solved. It is only if this were made impossible by cost or space limitations that it would be necessary to think up a different method, and this is when the idea of using a step and a work stand would emerge.

Fig. 42 <Satisfying one party does not increase the other's dissatisfaction.>

In other words, if we had limitless money and space, we wouldn't need to bother with Kaizen; but life is not like that. In reality, available money and space are limited, and this is why we need to do Kaizen, looking for ingenious ways of changing the way we do things.

The Method Decides whether You Stay in Hell or Go to Heaven

What is more, since human beings possess those troublesome qualities known as pride and emotion, the longer the struggle goes on, the further away they get from the Kaizen-type approach to solving their problem.

☆

Solution–Compromise–Kaizen

A Buddhist parable tells the story of some people who had died and gone to Hell, and whose fingers grew very long; longer than their arms, in fact, so that they were unable to put food in their mouths and starved to death. However, there was another group of people who had died and gone to Heaven, whose fingers also grew longer than their arms; but these people were able to enjoy eating all of the delicacies offered and did not starve to death, because they put food in each others' mouths whenever they were hungry.

This fable could be dismissed as smacking of pious preaching; but someone with the Kaizen mindset would be more likely to say, "Wow! That's a great example of using the Kaizen-type problem-solving approach to change the method!" It's certainly true that what happened was the same for both groups of people – their fingers had grown longer than their arms – but their experience was heavenly or hellish depending on how they approached the same problem, and the same can probably be said of our own experiences at work.

THE RIGHT ORDER OF THINKING

- How about striking a deal there?
- Start by thinking about how to change the method
- I wonder if there's a better way?

↓

Negotiate – concede – compromise

- If that's the way it is, I'll have to fight!

↓

Do not allow conflict!

Fig. 43 <The right order of thinking.>

Chapter IX

Principles – Rules – Formulas

A Simple Kaizen Reveals the Standard Formula

Let's take a certain university student's part-time job as an example of how simple Kaizens are, and how they are something that anyone can do.

A Kaizen for Reducing Inefficiency in a University Student's Part-Time Job

One of the features of Kaizen is that it cannot be properly studied without examining practical case studies, so its study and research are based not just on theory and logic but also on people's own real-life examples. Of course, university students do not yet have full-time jobs, so the only examples they can produce are those from their part-time jobs or from helping out around their homes. One student at the Sanno Institute of Management in Tokyo said that she had a part-time job at a food company, and that one of the jobs she had to do was to scoop out sugar from a container with a measuring spoon and use a small scraping stick to level off the sugar in the spoon so as to get exactly the right amount. The problem was that the scraper sometimes went missing and she had to waste a lot of time looking for it.

In workplaces without Kaizen, they would probably just issue a warning, telling everyone to put the scraper back in its proper place when they'd finished using it. But merely doing that would not fix the problem permanently, and the problem would be bound to keep cropping up. However, this particular student had been taught at college that Kaizen is all about changing the method, so she immediately started thinking of how to do so. She thought to herself, "It's a nuisance having to look for the scraper every time I

Principles – Rules – Formulas 157

measure out the sugar. I wonder whether there's some way of doing the job without using one."

She tried putting a large rubber band on the sugar container and scraping the sugar off on that while pulling the spoon out of the container, and the idea worked! She no longer had to look for the scraper each time. (But Bunji, we might now have to look for a rubber band – I guess not every idea is perfect. But, read on for Bunji is more clever then I thought.)

Anybody could do a simple Kaizen like this, whether they were a temporary worker, a part-time worker or any other kind of employee. However, we can use this kind of simple Kaizen example to learn about the generic principles and rules of Kaizen and then use these to improve our own Kaizen thinking.

Basing Kaizens Based on Fixing Locations and Making Things Visual

The first principle usually pointed out to those who are always rushing around in a panic trying to find things is that of keeping things in fixed locations, or having 'a place for everything, and everything in its place'. This is based on the fact that the reason such people can never find what they need is that they never put things back in the same place.

To improve this situation, they are told to decide where they are going to put things, and to always put them back there when they have finished using them. Then things will always be at hand when they need them. This is why many factories have shadow boards with the outlines of tools drawn on them, and tell their workers to put the tools back on the board on the right hook when they have finished with them. There are also lines painted on the floor or marked out with tapes, to show where trolleys and other articles should be located.

Fig. 44 <Scoop the sugar out.>

Of course, the student in this example knew about the Kaizen principles of fixing locations and making things visual, because she had studied them in her lectures at college. She therefore tried using a pencil tray to put the spoon and scraper in, standing them up in an empty can to save space, and even hanging them from the ceiling. In other words, she tried locating them horizontally, vertically and in various other ways, trying out numerous variations on the theme of 'fixing locations'.

However, these ideas did not satisfy her, so she went a step further.

Kaizens Based on Integration

The next thing that occurred to her was that; since the spoon and the scraper were always used together, why not combine them into a single unit? She therefore tried tying the spoon and the scraper together with string. The spoon and the scraper were now one, so when the spoon was picked up, the scraper came along with it, and there was no need to go looking for it. This is an example of a Kaizen based on integration; that is, combining things into a single unit. The principle of integration can also be seen in things like children's gloves. Children often lose one of their gloves, so the left-hand one is sometimes tied to the right-hand one with string, preventing just one from getting lost.

I was one of those children. When young I loved football. I still do, and I would always lose my gloves and my lunch whenever I would go to see the New York Giants play at the Polo grounds. I would get on the train and before I got to the stadium my lunch and gloves somehow disappeared. My mother would sew the gloves onto my jacket and also tie the lunch around my waist.

Now, I often keynote conferences and it is very easy for me to wander, tell a story, and forget where I started off. I need some kind of a Kaizen that will help me remember. If you have any ideas please e-mail me Bodek@pcspress.com.

Things used in sets can often be joined together like in the above example, in a type of Kaizen called 'integration' or 'packaging'. It takes a lot of time and effort to decide on and maintain fixed locations for many separate objects, but it needs to be done only once. Integration is therefore a type of Kaizen that saves time and trouble and improves efficiency.

Fig. 45 <Kaizen makes it easy to find things.>

Kaizens Based on Simultaneity and Single-Touch Operation

However, this student didn't even stop there, but went on to try yet another Kaizen, which could be called a 'simultaneous' or 'single-touch' Kaizen. Tying the spoon and the scraper together with string helped to prevent them from getting lost, but she noticed that using the spoon in conjunction with the scraper meant that she had to use both hands. She thought that, while she was at it, she might as well try integrating the scraper and the container. What happened when she made the scraper and the container into a single unit? She now found that she could scrape off the excess sugar in the spoon using one hand only.

In other words, scraping the sugar to make it level was made simultaneous with scooping the sugar out of the container. She used a rubber band to begin with because this was the easiest way

of testing her idea. Then, because this worked well, the next thing she did was to fix the actual scraper to the container.

The following is a good example of the way in which, even with the same integration-type Kaizen, the method of doing the job and the efficiency with which it can be done can change greatly, depending on what is fixed to what. In this case, why did mounting the scraper on the container make the job easier and more efficient than tying it to the spoon? It was because it fixed one of the elements, reducing the number of elements that needed to be adjusted. When the scraper was tied to the spoon, both the spoon and the scraper were still movable relative to each other and therefore fine adjustments were required with both hands, not just one. Even though the operation was simple, it required that much more care and was that much slower; and even though it only took a short time to do, it was considerably more tiring when done for extended periods of time.

However, when the scraper was mounted on the container, the only fine adjustments needed were where to position the spoon, and so the job could be done with one hand.

This is a good example of a Kaizen that obeys the following two Kaizen rules:

- Reduce the number of variables
- Reduce the number of adjustments

When people develop a Kaizen mindset, work becomes so much more interesting. If we come to work doing the same job over and over again every day it can become very boring. But when we are given the ability to continuously improve it, our work becomes more interesting and a lot more fun. The challenge, of course, is for managers to experiment and allow people to look for problems

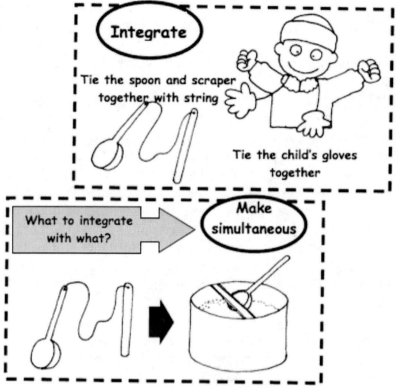

Fig. 46 <Integrate.>

and to come up with solutions and if at all possible to implement those solutions on their own. I hope those managers that are reading this book will be brave and start this simple but marvelous process.

Fix One of the Elements

Imagine that you have arranged to meet a friend at the exit of a particular train station at a particular time, but that you've been waiting for a while and he hasn't showed up. You begin to worry, and start doubting your memory, thinking, "I'm sure we arranged to meet at the West exit, but perhaps one of us misheard or got it

wrong. I wonder whether he's waiting at the East exit." Then you think you'll take a quick look to see if he's there, and start moving in that direction. Unfortunately, your friend, who is waiting at the East exit, thinks exactly the same thing and starts moving toward the West exit. The typical scenario of two people missing each other and failing to meet up has started. If it's a small regional station, there's no problem, but if it's a large metropolitan terminus, often the two of you miss each other and end up wondering whether you were fated not to meet.

This is a typical example of how the situation becomes complicated when both actors in the drama move. If you had agreed beforehand that one of you would remain in the same place no matter what, even if you felt uneasy, then the chance of missing each other would have been considerably reduced. Of course, if neither of you moved, then you would never meet. The best combination is thus to have one party move and the other stay put.

Don't Adjust; Set

Translating these examples to the workplace leads us to the following two rules of changeover Kaizen:

- Don't adjust; set. Set; don't just adjust.
- Don't measure; gauge. Gauge; don't just measure.

When positioning something in order to cut it or fix it, having to make fine positional adjustments takes time and creates variation. The result of these adjustments is waste. Therefore it is recommended to use devices such as blocks and surface tables to enable the work piece to be located by butting it up against something and positioning it with a single action, without the need for adjustment. This is another example of a Kaizen for reducing the number of variables, variable dimensions and so forth.

Fig. 47 <Reduce variable elements and adjustments.>

Measuring, which usually entails taking detailed readings, is also a source of inefficiency and error. When we take readings, what we often want to know is not what the readings themselves are but what range they are in; i.e. whether they are inside or outside the acceptable limits. In other words, we are using them not so much for measurement but for making a decision. Taking readings and then comparing them with a chart to decide whether something is all right or not is a waste of time.

For example, when calculating the cost of mailing an item, weighing it and then looking the weight up in a postage table to find the price of the stamps is not only unnecessarily time-consuming but also error-prone. Offices that send a lot of mail should therefore mark the cost directly on the scales they use to weigh the mail, or buy a special weighing machine that indicates the price of the postage. This would be a Kaizen that made the weighing of the mail simultaneous with the calculation of the postage.

Chapter X

Three Rules for Doing Kaizen

The Standard Formula for Quick and Easy Kaizen

A Kaizen is useless unless it is implemented. No matter how marvelous an idea might be, if it is not acted on, it is no more than pie in the sky – and, as everybody knows, pies in the sky do not make a satisfying meal. What is more, a pie that cannot be eaten has no value as a pie. In other words, in Kaizen, an idea that cannot be implemented is not a good idea. Only ideas that can be implemented are good ones.

But, when faced with a problem you might have many different ideas on how to solve it and you might have to test a number of different solutions. You also have to think about the question, "Are you solving the right problem?"

Thomas Edison and many great innovators tested thousands of different scenarios before they came up with the right solutions. The main idea is to get your mind thinking about the problem and allowing the flow of many ideas to come to you.

To carry out a Kaizen, we have to surmount whatever practical constraints stand in our way – and we can be certain that, whatever work we are engaged in, there will be constraints. People often talk about their constraints:

"We could do Kaizen if only we had enough money."
"We could do Kaizen if only we had enough time."
"We could do Kaizen if only we had enough people."

Three Rules for Doing Kaizen

However, these are ridiculous things to say, because if we had enough money, time and people, we wouldn't need to do Kaizen in the first place. If we had unlimited time and an unlimited budget, we could do anything we liked. It would be entirely up to us. Improvement ideas might not be necessary.

But in practice we have to get our jobs done within the constraints of limited management resources – a limited amount of time, a limited amount of money, and a limited number of people. We always work in conditions of scarcity, with insufficient money, not enough time, too few people, and too little equipment. That's life – and that is exactly why we have to look for ways of changing our methods and improving the way we do the job.

Fig. 48 <The 3 rules.>

With the old type of employee suggestion scheme, there was hardly any need for the people putting forward the ideas to take these constraints into account, because they were only responsible for making the suggestions, not for implementing them. After all,

these schemes were of the 'I propose, you implement' type, so all the proponents of the ideas had to do was blithely suggest doing this and that without having to bother about troublesome things like constraints.

With a practical Kaizen system, however, everyone is responsible for either carrying their ideas through to completion, or working closely with support staff to insure the ideas will be implemented. You have to think about how to get around or overcome the constraints, and this sharpens your ability to deal with reality. It is why the 'I propose, I implement' type of Kaizen system helps with people development.

At some companies I work with the person who comes up with the idea implements almost 80% of the ideas without the assistance of co-workers, but at Autoliv it is around 10%. Autoliv has 13 people, coordinators, and specialists, each assigned to a 60-person team. These coordinators support the workers and help them implement their creative ideas. It has been a very powerful process for Autoliv where 63 ideas per employee were implemented last year and with 96 as the new goal, but it does have a drawback and is different from what I teach.

I want the workers to build their skills and capabilities from their own ideas by implementing their own ideas. The specialist grows, has an amazing job in implementing numerous ideas from the workers who generate lots of ideas but the worker does not have the same opportunity to learn new skills to grow from her own ideas. Autoliv has a great system but it could be much better if it gave the worker time away from his line to implement his own idea.

Toyota has one team leader for each group of four to eight people. The team leader spends 50% of the time working and 50% of the time training, coaching and supporting the worker. Autoliv differs from Toyota for their team leaders spend about 90% of the time

working, and producing products, and only 10% of the time coaching and helping workers implement their own ideas.

In February 1981, I led 19 senior executives on a study mission to Japan. At first I was extremely nervous for I had no idea what to expect. But it was magical being introduced to the Toyota production system, quick changeover, visual factory, 5S, and the Japanese suggestion system.

For me it was a gamble to take over 19 top managers to Japan on a study mission when I did not know at all what to expect. I knew the Japanese were the world's leaders at the time in quality and productivity improvement but I did not know why; I didn't even know if I could discover why. I knew Japan was doing something valuable but I had no idea what it was and I didn't know if we would find it. But, I do believe in miracles and that first trip was absolutely great and introduced us to the Toyota Production System, the Canon Production System and many other powerful tools and techniques that were helping Japan to move forward.

At first, Toyota and other Japanese companies copied the American Suggestion System but, around 1970, they looked carefully at the suggestion system and expanded it. They now wanted all employees to participate in problem solving activities. And, slowly during the 1970s, suggestions started to climb whereby instead of getting one idea every seven years from the average worker (like in the American system), the average in Japan rose to close to 24 ideas per employee per year and at Toyota it rose to 47 ideas per worker per year.

The significant difference was that the worker that came up with the idea was the one to implement the idea. For the past 10 years I have been following Bunji's advice and teaching companies in America to focus on having the worker who came up with the idea become responsible for the implementation of the idea.

But, Autoliv is introducing us to a new approach to Quick and Easy Kaizen.[17] It gives us a new, vital and powerful addition to the suggestion system. It redefines the responsibility of management and says that a managers job is to support and assist the implementation of the worker's suggestion.

Think about it: of all the people in an organization – the managers and supervisors, the accountants, the customer service and HR representatives, the people in maintenance – it is the worker who builds the product that the customer buys. And, the worker often knows what should be done to make his or her work easier and more productive. As management educates the workers and teaches them how to express their needs, the workers become more capable in submitting improvement ideas. When managers see the improvement that results from the worker' contributions, they begin to recognize that a vital part of their responsibility is to assist the worker to be more productive.

Remember:

1. To get started with a new suggestion system we want the worker to focus on small improvement ideas and to become responsible for the implementation of those ideas.

2. But as the system matures and supervisors and managers recognize the intelligence, ingenuity, and creativeness of their workers, they begin to understand that their new role is to support their workers and to help them implement their ideas.

And as we said earlier "resistance to change" is probably the hardest constraint to overcome. Please do recognize that whenever you want to change "resistance" is always there. What I do to overcome resistance is to take a deep breath, hold it for the count of 10, and attempt to be more detached from the situation. This allows me to overcome the "resistance" standing in front of

---

[17] See the Tom Hartman interview in the back of the book.

me and to make the change. Try it and see how it works.

Change

In our mind, we think to change is easy, but in reality for most people change is very difficult. We fall into patterns. Try to lose weight, to stop smoking, and to stop drinking too much. It is not easy to overcome our patterns. It is difficult to change our reaction to the situations with which we are confronted in life. Most of us aspire to do something different and yet we seem to continually fall back into the same patterns over and over again.

But, at work with proper supervision, and proper leadership people can change their way of working. When your own mind tells you not to do something different you can just ignore it. But, when the boss tells you to do something different you don't have much choice because the boss pays you, and the boss has a role, a greater responsibility for the well being of the organization not just for the individual.
"Failure to Change is a Vice!"

> *I want everyone at Toyota to change and at least do not be an obstacle for someone else who wants to change.*
> **Hiroshi Okuda, former Chairman Toyota**
> *Fig. 49* <Failure to change is a vice!>

To me Okuda has a marvelous statement. I use it in all of my workshops. Imagine, the chairman of the largest and most successful automotive company in the world telling his or her employees they must change. Toyota, until this recent recession, had something like $50 billion in the bank and yet the chairman wanted everyone to grow and to change so that Toyota could be better. I've always liked his statement but the question is how can you get people to change?

Please recognize that all people resist change and see constraints in front of them. The manager's job is to help people overcome those practical constraints and do a Kaizen. In fact, I feel that the prime job of a manager is to lead change. Managers should apply the following three rules:

① **Attack on Different Levels**

② **Attack from Various Angles**

③ **Attack One Part at a Time**

Let's examine each of these in order.

① Attack on Different Levels

To find opportunities to make improvements, you have to be able to see things differently, if not you just see things today as you saw them yesterday. It is like the story of the fish not knowing it is swimming in water. Without seeing things clearly we often overlook opportunities for improvement. Taiichi Ohno once said that his greatest gift was in his ability to see waste. From his unique ability to see, new things could be done; he was able to lead Toyota from a company that was noted for making "junk" to producing the Lexus -- one of the finest automobiles in the world. Jokingly, he would say I am not going to share my gift of seeing with you. You will have to find it on your own.

Ohno saw non-value adding wastes and once he saw them and understood them he would ask others to eliminate them. He defined waste as: inventory, defects, waiting, excess motion, transportation, overproduction, and using the wrong process. Once

Three Rules for Doing Kaizen

he discovered these wastes, he would challenge others to eliminate them. In fact, virtually every day, Ohno would challenge people to identify and eliminate waste.

Most of us in America and elsewhere outside of Toyota just didn't recognize that things like inventory, and motion were really wastes to be bothered about. Let's look at waiting as a waste. When I first started to visit manufacturing plants in the early 1980s, I was amazed to see the wastes of human talent. For some strange reason, managers and accountants were more concerned that the machines were producing the products, and less concerned with the people who just stood there and watched the machines. To me it was so deadly, so inhumane, to see a human being coming to work and paid to just stand and watch a machine.

I remember watching in the early 1980s a man at a factory sitting and watching glass being extruded to become optical fiber. I knew it was important to insure the quality of the glass fiber, but I could not imagine how a human being could work all day just looking at the glass being extruded.

It reminds me of 9/10, the day before 9/11 – the attack on the World Trade Center, when I passed through security at the Portland, Oregon airport. I looked at the person staring at the TV screen trying to detect things that people were taking onto the airplane. I knew that this was an impossible job to do well. How can a person look at a screen for seven hours and see clearly? Impossible! I turned and looked at these people and told them that they would never be able to detect anything. The next day, in Austin Texas, like millions probably billions of people throughout the world I was shocked when the planes struck the World Trade Center in New York City.

Ohno focused on human beings and said it was all right for the machines to wait not for the human being.

As everyone knows, the best solution to a problem is a radical one that uproots it and fixes it for good. But just going around shouting something as obvious as that isn't going to get us anywhere. Of course, there would be nothing better than being able to implement a radical solution right away. If that were possible, then we should do it without delay. There would be no need to hesitate, and no need to put off solving the problem.

But what happens in practice? Real life is not usually as kind to us as that. When we try to implement a radical solution, it often turns into a major project; in other words, it entails big changes (which are tough), not the small changes we pursue in Kaizen. It also costs a lot of money, takes a lot of time, raises a lot of technical issues, necessitates many complicated administrative procedures, and engenders much resistance and opposition both inside and outside the business. A radical solution cannot be implemented without breaking through such barriers.

The problem with the old suggestion system, which originally started out as an employee participation system, ended up as a cost-saving system and very few of the employees would participate. The average employee would submit on the average one idea every seven years while at Autoliv they are receiving 63 ideas per employee per year.

If we insist on nothing less than a radical solution, we may never be able to get anything done – and while we are trying, all sorts of other problems are popping up all around us. If we leave these unchecked, accidents and quality defects will increase, losses will mount, and if we still do nothing about them, we will forfeit our credibility, our customers will desert us, and we will end up bankrupt.

In view of this, it is clear that it is not wise always to insist on the perfect solution; rather, we should give priority to the less-than-perfect solution, which curbs the problem and reduces the damage, even a little.

Use the 'At Least' Concept to Start Where You Can

People who are good at Kaizen, those able to choose their means and methods flexibly in response to the circumstances, do not always insist on a radical solution. They assess the situation, and if they see that it would be difficult to implement a big solution immediately, they apply the 'at least' concept, and begin implementing a Kaizen right away, contenting themselves with a not-so-radical interim solution.

For example, when faced with a quality defect, they know that the best solution would be one that eliminated it. However, if it is difficult with the present level of technology to reduce the defects below a certain level, then they try at least to think of a faster and more reliable way of detecting them. If they see that a certain percentage of quality defects is inevitable at present, they think, "Well if that's the case, we can at least try to make sure we prevent them from leaving the factory gate."

If 'Best' is Impossible, Start with 'Better'

Quality Control (QC) textbooks admonish, "You can make your inspection procedures as rigorous as you like, but this will do nothing to improve quality. Rather then making defects and then trying to detect them, you should set things up so that you do not make them in the first place. This is what is meant by building quality into the product by means of the process."

If you ask, you can get. Gulfstream Corporation was serious If about eliminating defects and I taught a group of managers to teach 1000 people in one of their plants Dr. Shingo's Poka-yoke system. Last year, just one year after the training, 1000 people

implemented 4000 Poka-yoke[18] devices. A Poka-yoke device is used to prevent a defect from occurring.

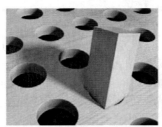

Fig. 50 <You can't put a square into a round hole. Picture from John Grout http://csob.berry.edu/faculty/jgrout/pokayoke.shtml>

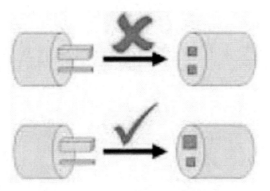

Fig. 51 < The plug only goes in one way.
http://csob.berry.edu/faculty/jgrout/pokayoke.shtml>

---

[18] Poka-yoke is a Japanese word meaning mis-proofing, having workers create simple devises that do not allow a defect to occur. The key to your house is a Poka-yoke – you can only put in the lock one way.

Three Rules for Doing Kaizen   177

Fig. 52 <Laser Poka-yoke device - *http://csob.berry.edu/faculty/jgrout/pokayoke.shtml*>

In the above figure, when you remove a part, you break a light circuit and the computer knows you have removed the correct part in the right sequence. When I visited a Prius plant in Japan, I saw one worker collecting all the small parts needed to assemble one car into a large bin. A lit green light told him where to go to get the next part, and every time he removed the part from the bin his hand broke a light circuit. The computer knew when his hand broke a laser beam and then directed him to the next bin.

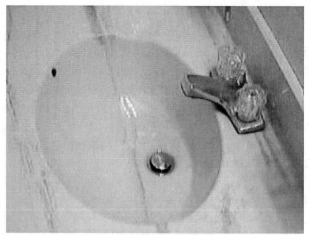

Fig. 53 <Even your sink has a Poka-yoke device. The small hole is used so that water will not overflow.
http://csob.berry.edu/faculty/jgrout/pokayoke.shtml>

Fig. 54 *<Aim for the best but start with 'better.'>*

Our textbooks can guide us and be absolutely right, but what actually happens in practice? We can't suspend our operation or turn off all the equipment and stop production just because we haven't yet been able to find a way of eliminating our quality problems. Even though the situation is imperfect, we still have to go on making the product. We have to produce our quota every day. That is the reality we are faced with.

That being so, the first thing we need to do is strengthen our quality inspection procedures to ensure that <u>at least</u> we are not letting any defectives slip through. We have to start by finding some way or other to address the immediate problem. Yes, we can learn and put Poka-yoke into practice.

Three Rules for Doing Kaizen

Of course, when all is said and done, the <u>at least</u> strategy is no more than dealing with the symptoms of the problem. We will never be able to prevent the defective items from being produced until we implement a solution that solves the problem's basic causes. We would just have to go on making our inspection system stronger and stronger.

With the <u>at least</u> approach, though, we take the causes of the problem one at a time and eliminate them if we can, starting with the easiest. The fewer causes we eliminate each time, the smaller the scope of the action we need to take.

Of course, this will not permanently solve the problem; because many of its causes remain unsolved; it will continue to rear its head. But it will definitely get smaller and smaller as we chip away at its causes one by one. The more solutions we implement, the better the situation becomes.

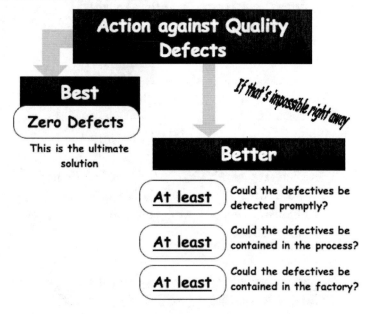

Fig. 55 <Action against quality defects.>

② Attack from Various Angles

Try to step back and see things differently. Both Dr. Shingo and Mr. Ohno had the amazing ability to see things from a different perspective, beyond the obvious. Ohno knew that the biggest obstacle in manufacturing was excess inventory. Prior to Ohno and Shingo most people, virtually all accountants, thought that inventory was a valuable asset. But Ohno knew that inventory was a terrible waste. It took up valuable factory floor space, it hid defects, and it was a major block to get just-in-time working properly. The main focus for Ohno and Shingo was to reduce lead

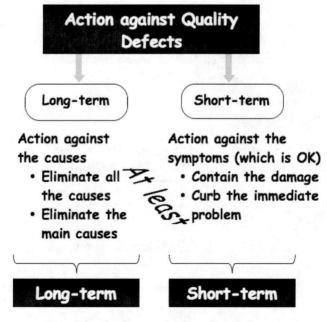

Fig. 56 <Action against quality defects.>

Three Rules for Doing Kaizen

Time. Having mountains of inventory in the plant was the prime obstacle.

I remember my first visit to Toyota in 1981. I saw 18 engines being delivered to the line while at the Oldsmobile plant I had visited just a few months earlier 1000 engines in the plant were waiting to be assembled.

Yes, when you learn to see things from various angles, enormous new opportunities exist for you. A cleaning lady came through our house, did her job quickly and left. Afterwards, my wife later looked carefully around the house and saw spider webs up on the ceiling. The cleaning lady was following her routine and just did not see the spider webs. Without being critical it is our job to help her learn to see from different angles.

Break through the Limits with a Combination Play

The relationship between 'cost' and benefit in Kaizen is similar. For example, when we address a quality problem, our first actions often produce gratifying results in terms of reducing the defect rate. But, as we proceed, the marginal results we achieve get less and less, and we eventually go up against a brick wall, where, no matter what we try, the defect rate stays the same. Either that, or we reach a point where it would cost more to produce a further decrease in the defect rate than the money we would save by doing so. This is what happens if we get hung up on one approach and keep going down the same route; eventually we reach the position when what we are doing is just costing us time and money and giving us no benefit at all. Rather than Kaizen (changing for the good), it has become Kaiaku (changing for the worst).

When we get stuck on one approach, a Kaizen master remembers the Kaizen rule of 'Attack from Various Angles,' and tries changing the way he is viewing the problem, looking at it from a different perspective, or trying a different method.

A 'Combination Play' Kaizen for a PC

Sometimes a clock or an hourglass icon appears on your computer screen when you have clicked the mouse and are waiting for the display to change.

This is a good example of a Kaizen in the world of high technology – a 'combination play' Kaizen, in fact. Really, it would be best if the waiting time were zero. We would all like the required data to be retrieved, and the display to change immediately when we click the mouse. But this is not always possible. So, what should we do about it? Should we just give up and do nothing, saying that the operation cannot be speeded up with today's technology?

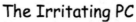

This stupid PC! Is it working, or what?

Fig. 57 >The irritating PC.>

This is in fact the way people who are no good at Kaizen think. But skilled Kaizen practitioners make good use of the 'combination play' rule. They accept that it is impossible to make the operation any faster because of technical and cost constraints, but they try to look at the problem from a different angle and do another sort of Kaizen. For example, they might think, "I wonder

if we could do a Kaizen that addresses the psychological aspect of waiting."

He/she comes up with the idea of showing a clock or hourglass icon on the screen whenever the user is forced to wait; and in fact, that alone considerably reduces the user's stress level.

A Small Difference Can Make a Big Difference

Of course, we would make no progress if we were satisfied with having averted the user's dissatisfaction and simply left it at that. As well as somehow getting over the immediate problem with small changes, we also need to look for radical solutions and do research. The hourglass idea is no more than a stopgap measure. If a competitor revolutionized the PC world by developing a lightning-fast new machine whose screen changed instantaneously, the conventional machines would immediately become worthless. There is a world of difference between the effect of a Kaizen and the effect of an innovation.

Fig. 58 <When you see the hourglass, you don't get annoyed.>

But even so, what would happen if PC developers ignored Kaizen and focused exclusively on finding radical solutions? If two PCs cost about the same and had substantially the same functions, buyers would choose the one that was easier to use or caused less stress, wouldn't they?

In today's highly competitive society, a very small difference can make a very big difference. This is particularly true when two companies' technological capabilities are more or less equal, and it is why even high-tech industries cannot afford to neglect low-tech Kaizens.

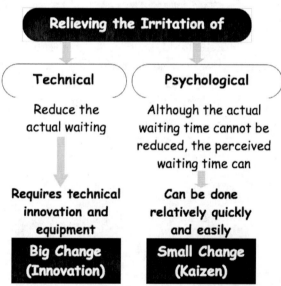

Fig. 59 <Relieving the irritation of>

If we look at how the world is today, we see that the strongest companies are those that carry out just the right combination of small changes and big changes. They maintain their advantage and keep themselves in the lead by skilful use of 'combination plays'.

A Kaizen Like That Can Soon Be Done

Three Rules for Doing Kaizen

A similar example of Kaizen by means of a 'combination play' can be seen at train stations and subway stations. Systems have recently been introduced that show passengers where the next train is at the moment. Lighted displays now show everyone information, such as whether the next train has arrived at the previous station or has already left it and is heading towards them. Just a simple thing like that can considerably alleviate passenger's stress and irritation at having to wait.

Fig. 60 <Problems.>

Waiting itself stresses us; our biggest source of irritation comes from not knowing what is happening, or how long we will have to wait. People feel irritated if there is no announcement or explanation of a delay. But just announcing the reason for the stoppage, together with an estimate of how long it will take for normal service to be restored, makes everyone feel far less stressed about it.

Unfortunately, at the average manufacturing company that I have visited in the last number of years, the average worker does not know what is fully expected of them. Sure they know how to make their product but they don't know how many products they should make each hour. They often don't know if they are ahead or behind schedule. Toyota and other companies implementing Lean have an Andon system, which tells the worker if they are ahead or behind schedule; they know if they have to work overtime that day. Question: Do you keep your workers informed?

Fig. 61 <Relieving the irritation of waiting for a train.>

Unskilled sales representatives apologize when a delivery date is delayed for some reason or other but do nothing else. But, even if they cannot do anything about the delay, Kaizen-minded sales managers at least provide their customers with information, continually contacting them to update them on the progress of the order. This allows the customer to adjust their plans, and also helps to reduce their irritation and feelings of distrust.

Earlier in my life, I managed a data processing company and serviced a large survey organization. One day, I was called into the office of the senior vice president, on a Monday, to talk with him and also to meet with a manager of one of their departments. I was

asked by the manager, "When will I get my job?" I said, "I don't know!" The manager looked at me and was very unhappy about my answer and stormed out of the room. The vice president looked at me and asked, "Could you deliver the job by Friday?" Since the work was new to me, I really didn't know if we could deliver the job by Friday; but there was a good chance we could do it. The vice president told me I should have told his manager that the job would be ready on Friday at noon. By telling him my best guess, he would be able to call his client and both of them would be able to live peacefully during the week. The vice president then asked me, "Would you know on Friday exactly when the job would be completed?" "Yes, I should be able to know exactly when the job could be done."

The vice president said, "On Friday morning you should call my manager and let him know if the job is going to be delivered on time or exactly when it should be delivered." If I delivered it at noon on Friday then the client would be very happy. If I called him later during the week with the exact delivery date, he might not be happy with us if we were going to be later then Friday, but he then could call his client to alert him or her about the delivery date. The lesson I learned was to be up front and truthful but at the same time to do whatever I could to take away the anxiety from others. It was a great lesson for me on how to serve other people.

③ Attack One Part at a Time

One of the key principles of Kaizen is to attack one part at a time. This is because most problems are due to multiple causes interacting in complex ways. If a problem only had one cause, then only one solution would suffice. Multiple causes require multiple solutions. The problem is not completely solved until all of its causes had been eliminated.

This means that we cannot usually do just one Kaizen and then say, "Great. Job done." Kaizen means continuous improvement – unending, one improvement idea after the other. There is an old saying that when you solve one problem you create at least one more. So when a person implements Kaizen, one of their ideas is to stop and think, "What is the next thing to look for? Is their another problem and another problem?" To me, it is one of the prime jobs of a manager is to educate, train, coach and help workers to identify problems and help them to solve them.

In 1980, when I started the Productivity newsletter one of the first things we discovered was Quality Control Circles, whereby workers in small groups would get together to solve quality problems in their work area. This was a very powerful discovery for me; I thought it was the significant reason the Japanese were able to produce such high-quality products. Quality Control Circles were very powerful in bringing out the best ideas from workers and giving them the opportunities to solve those problems on their own. Circle activities were tried in America but did not last long. They are still used by almost every large company in Japan. I would recommend that you relook at Quality Control Circles and consider the process for your organization.

What we are trying to do in this book is to inspire you and to help you create a new culture where people can work with dignity and be a real part of a productive and thriving company. People are filled with creative ideas. A fundamental part of human behavior is to be able to evolve and solve problems and advance society forward.

Kaizen requires a sustained series of attacks, like a boxer knocking down his opponent with a barrage of blows. We can eliminate a problem's many causes one by one if we attack them from various angles, on different levels, and by different methods, rather than trying to solve the problem all in one go.

Respond Flexibly 'For the Time Being'

The phrase 'for the time being' neatly expresses the idea of applying multiple solutions and mounting a series of attacks on the problem. Indeed, it is a key phrase that helps us to overcome practical constraints and put our Kaizen ideas into action. Doing what we can do 'for the time being' means chopping the problem up and not trying to solve it all at once. It means splitting off its many causes and addressing them one by one; in other words, attacking the problem one part at a time.

Standardized work is a very powerful Toyota developed tool. The goal of standardized work is to find the absolute best way of doing something and having everyone follow the best way. It is like observing LeBron James shooting in those three point shots and then being able to follow him and do the same. Of course, each person is different; each person is different physiologically. There is a best way to do something and we want everyone to follow as close as possible that best way. We want to get the exact results that we want. Managers should help workers find the best way. It doesn't mean that the best way is fixed forever, no; it can always be improved. Even LeBron continually practices and continually looks for new ways to be even better.

Some people try to solve the problem at one fell swoop. This gives them so much to think about that they never actually get around to doing anything.

It is certainly true that making big changes requires one to think carefully, investigate thoroughly, do all the necessary calculations and proceed systematically, but none of this is needed with a simple Kaizen. What is more, we live in a world where we don't actually know what is going to happen until we try something out. Doing a single Kaizen can reveal causes of the problem that had been hidden up until that point.

Fig. 62 <Big ideas but small.>

If, despite this, we insisted on working everything out in our heads before we took any action; we would end up doing nothing at all. Even if we did all the calculations and put together a perfect plan before starting any Kaizen; there would still be no guarantee that everything would go according to our plan. Problem causes we had not noticed at the planning stage have a habit of springing up unexpectedly in route. What is more, the environment surrounding us is constantly changing, so it is no wonder that we are continually faced with circumstances that we had not planned for.

If we adopted the stance of taking no action unless we had understood and accepted everything and worked it all out; we would be unable to respond appropriately to changes in our environment. On the other hand, those good at doing whatever they can 'for the time being' are also good at coping with change, because they are the type of people who can think while they are walking, walk while they are thinking, act while investigating, and investigate while acting. In fact, they have the advantage of being

able to fly by the seat of their pants, play it by ear, and deal with the unexpected.

Multiple Causes Have Multiple Solutions

People who can divide a problem up and act on a part of it 'for the time being' instinctively understand that, because multiple causal factors are operating in any situation, many solutions are possible. Of course, those who have studied QC techniques probably also understand this theoretically as well. The cause-and-effect diagram (also known as the Ishikawa diagram, or fishbone diagram), for example, depicts the idea that problems have multiple causes and that therefore multiple solutions are required.

After teaching a division of Boeing Quick and Easy Kaizen, one of my students submitted an idea to her supervisor. The worker left the supervisor's office and turned to a friend of hers, a fellow employee, and told her that her supervisor told her that her idea was not correct, "It was not what the company wants or expects from this Quick and Easy Kaizen." The employee then said, "I was so embarrassed that I will never submit an idea again."

They certainly won't want to expose themselves to a second dose of embarrassment by trying another Kaizen. They might even get a fit of the sulks and say something like, "OK, OK, I'll leave things alone and steer well clear of Kaizen and that sort of thing from now on. Just let me get on with doing the job the way I've always done it, and I won't cause any more trouble."

In workplaces that are good at Kaizen, though, you won't hear people saying anything like that. What you will hear is, "If the first Kaizen doesn't work, try another; and if that doesn't work, try yet another." They think it's fine to keep on trying different Kaizens until one eventually works, and that if one Kaizen fails, it's a good chance to try a different one. This is exactly what the three Kaizen

rules of attacking from various angles, attacking on different levels, and attacking one part at a time mean. They mean that it's fine to try out an idea at least for the time being, and if it doesn't work, to think of a different solution. When we take some action, it can result in a different problem coming to the surface. All we need to do then is solve that one and move on to the next. That's all it is, and it is how things get progressively better.

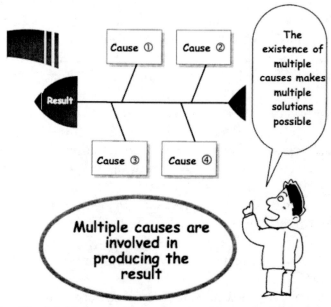

Fig. 63 <Multiple causes are involved in producing results.>

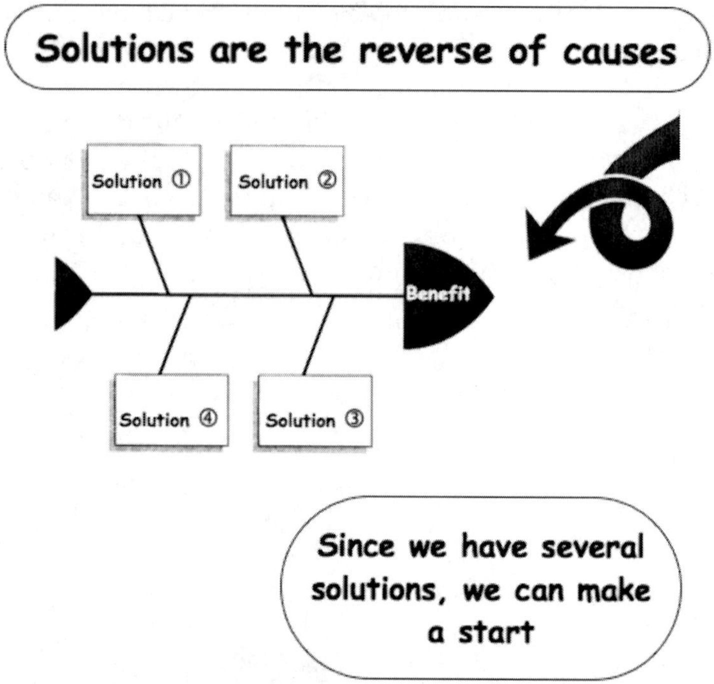

Three Rules for Doing Kaizen

Solutions are the reverse of causes

Solution ① Solution ②

Benefit

Solution ④ Solution ③

Since we have several solutions, we can make a start

Fig. 64 <Solutions are the reverse of causes.>

High-Tech Industry also Uses Successive 'For the Time Being' Solutions

Computer software is in fact developed by this method. Once a program is provisionally ready, it is distributed for beta testing (a process in which bugs are detected and the program is improved) before the final version is put on sale. And it doesn't even end there, even after it has been launched, improved versions, updates, are brought out in response to users' complaints and suggestions, and the program continues to evolve.

A software program is such a complex thing that it typifies the idea of not knowing whether something will work or not until it's been tried or only knowing how things will turn out once some action has been taken.

This is why software developers have adopted the approach of putting their programs on sale after developing them to a certain level ('for the time being'), then releasing successive new versions as they find and fix their flaws. It's interesting that even a high-tech industry such as computer software development employs the low-tech Kaizen principle of trying one Kaizen after another. I wish Microsoft would read this book for I still have a lot of problems with their "Word," program.

Fig. 65 <Computer software development is also a series of Kaizens.>

Three Rules for Doing Kaizen

Kaizen is like a game of chess with special rules. We can take our moves back as many times as we want. This is why in Kaizen it is recommended that we start small. If any change we make is within the bounds of our ability and authority, we can easily reverse it. Even if we botch it, we can fix it somehow or other. However, if we do something that is beyond our power to reverse and it goes wrong, we're in big trouble. We could get blamed for it, and do irreparable damage. That's why big changes should never be undertaken lightly. But there are no such problems with Kaizens that we are able to do ourselves. Even if they fail, we can still recover. In other words, the route the Kaizen master should take is to start doing whatever he can, and do as much as he can.

On my last trip to Japan, I visited a Toyota plant and saw what looked like a new worker being trained. Using a crane holding a large engine, he somehow allowed the engine to crash onto the floor where oil was pouring out from it. The trainer did not scold or blame the worker for the problem. He only used it as an opportunity to continue training. How would you handle the situation?

If at First You Do Succeed...

Of course, as well as remembering that, "If the first Kaizen doesn't work, try another; and if that doesn't work, try yet another," we should also remember that, "If the first Kaizen works, do another; and if that works, do yet another."

If we study Bunji carefully, and follow his principles, we can see how we would be able to bring out dozens and dozens of new creative ideas from every worker. It is the attention of the supervisor and the manager on the worker and being aware of the vast talent that lies within each worker that makes continuous improvement work.

Naturally, when people do a succession of Kaizens in this way, they can sometimes end up going round in a circle and finding themselves right back where they started. They can then be heard to complain, saying things like, "What! We might as well not have done anything in the first place," or, "What a pointless waste of effort that was!" But, actually, this is fine in its way. The mere fact that they now know that the particular method they tried doesn't work is progress. It presents them with the opportunity to think about the problem from another angle or attack it by a different method, and paves the way to a broader range of ideas and options. For example, if we have changed the length of something many times without any good results, that tells us that its length is probably not a cause of the problem, and the next idea that might occur to us is to try changing its width.

Fig. 66 <In Kaizen, you can take your move back.>

Then, if that doesn't work, it opens things up for us to be able to think of various other approaches and methods, such as changing the angle, the material, or the attachment position.

Three Rules for Doing Kaizen

Kaizen experts learn the principle of coming up with multiple ideas as they experience this process of going round in a circle and ending up back where they started.

Even the paragon of inventors, Thomas Edison, didn't regard an unsuccessful experiment as a failure. He thought of it as taking him one step closer to success, and ended up making some wonderful inventions.

The principle of Kaizen could also be regarded in this way as a technique for turning failure into success. It treats failure as an opportunity for broadening one's outlook and thinking more flexibly.

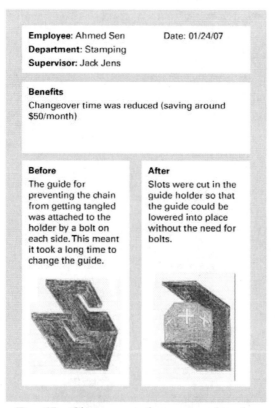

Fig. 67 <Changeover time was reduced.>

Chapter XI

Real-Life Examples

① **The Spirit and Technique of Kaizen**

② **Enforced Kaizen**

③ **Anyone Can Do It, Every Day**

④ **Established Formulae and Key Words**

The Spirit and Technique of Kaizen

When implementing a program of work improvement, we need the following two approaches:

① **The Psychological Approach**

② **The Technical Approach**

Simply put, this means addressing the spirit and the technique of Kaizen. If either of these is missing, the Kaizen program won't last. Of course, it will only get off the ground in the first place if the company's employees feel inclined to improve the way they work. But motivation alone is not enough to keep the Kaizen program going. Although Kaizen is simple, it requires more than just idealism and a gung-ho attitude; it also needs specific techniques.

Real-Life Examples

Let's set out the principles and rules relevant to the spirit and technique of Kaizen that we need in order to do it.

We Have to Think for Ourselves – No-one Can Do It for Us

Work Smarter *and* Work Harder

In the late 1970's, there was a very popular phrase used by American Unions. "Work smarter, not harder."

And I think they meant it. They wanted the worker to be treated decently at the workplace and they liked the concept "work smarter, not harder."

But unfortunately, after spending years studying the world's most important management techniques, rarely did I find that the unions understood the phrase: "Work smarter, not harder." What did the union do to help people work smarter?

If you went down to the factory floor, and you saw the way people work, it would be very hard for you to distinguish between a person and a machine. I'm being a little facetious, because you physically can tell the difference between a worker and a machine. But they were treated the same. The worker was working like a machine, doing the same thing over and over again.

At one small company, I was watching a woman working on a punch press. She bent down, picked up a piece of metal with the left hand, put the metal into the punch press, then put both her hands onto two separate buttons so send a signal to the machine to punch the piece. This safety mechanism was in place so that when the die came down to press against the metal, it wouldn't hurt the worker's hands. Then when the press went back up, the woman

reached in with the right hand, took out the formed piece of metal, put it down on a stack over to the right, and kept doing it over and over again.

When I turned to the manager, who was next to me, I said, "How many plates is she going to do in a day?" He said, "She's going to do 5,000." And what is she going to do tomorrow? I asked. "She's going to do another 5,000." It was a little bit of a shock to me to think about how the work was designed with such repetition without considering the needs for some creative input from the worker.

It was November 1980, when I visited an Oldsmobile plant in Tarrytown, New York. I went to the Oldsmobile plant because a few months later I was going to go to Japan on a study mission, my first study mission. I wanted to get a comparison, a visualization, of what American factories looked like compared to what I was going to see in Japan.

As I was walking around Oldsmobile's assembly line, I noticed one particular worker, whose job was to put brake fluid into every car on the line. I was amazed to see a human being working so slowly. To me, it was devastating to come to work every day and to do that kind of job. It was deadly. I turned to the guide who was walking with me and said, "How long is he going to do that?" He said, "I don't know how long he's going to do that, but he said, "Norman, we had a man in this cplant who for 43 years did nothing other than put a tire on a hook to send it to the assembly line."

Imagine getting up, going to work, and your job is to pick up a tire, put it on a hook. And that's all.

The irony in this story is that the guide turned to me and said, "You know, he only collected two retirement checks."

Imagine that what management does, to be expedient, is to take the workers that have gone through so many years in our school

system, to learn, to inquire, to grow, to want to really do a good job in life, and then to be given these boring jobs that industry has set up for them. I can't fault the worker for they need the job to feed their family. But, I do ask the manager to start to see if work can be made more challenging.

"Work smarter, not harder." What does work smarter mean? Surely it means to use your brains to work more efficiently. I think General Motor's bankruptcy reflected their inability to develop people properly. It is called Karma. The bible says, "As Ye Sow, So Shall Ye Reap." General Motors did not know how to use people and now suffers from that neglect. Unless they learn that lesson now, they are just prone to fail again. People are not like machines. People can be very creative on the job with the right understanding and leadership from management.

Look if Gulfstream can get 33-implemented ideas per year per employee so can you. Quick and Easy Kaizen is not the end-all to cure all problems for people going to work, but it is a very powerful beginning to empower people to become responsible for making their own work easier more interesting and to build their skills and capabilities. Instead of workers waiting for supervision to improve their work lives, the company is now saying to the worker, "You can now participate with us in making a better company for our customers and all of our employees."

I once saw a cartoon, and the cartoon showed a box, and above the box was a sign that said, "Leave your brains here." You'll get them back when you leave at the end of the day.

Yes, we wanted workers to come work and use their bodies not their brains. The other part of the union's motto is also misunderstood - "not harder." Even that is wrong. We want people to work as hard as they can physically, and mentally.

"Work smarter, not harder. So what could unionism do? Some unions have a tradition of educating their worker, like those of carpenters and electricians. There are certain unions where members spend many years apprenticing, learning your skills, and having to pass tests to show that they have achieved certain levels of skill - to be certified as a master.

These unions follow the model of working smarter. But most American unions, like the automobile unions, didn't care at all if the worker used their brains. They wanted the worker to be paid well and to have a good retirement plan, but they missed the most important element, which was to be fulfilled creatively at work.

Once, I was at a Ford Motor Company engine plant inside of Cleveland. A friend of mine, Gifford Brown, was the plant manager. Gifford spent $2 billion of Ford Motor Company's money to build the most advanced automotive engine plant in the world. This plant was designed to produce engines to what Ford called their World Car. Most of the machines used in the plant were made in Germany.

I came into the plant just when the machines were being installed. I watched the motors going along the line; the assembly work was done almost completely by automation. I looked at the workers, and what did I see? I saw workers sitting there having cups of coffee, smoking cigarettes, and reading newspapers. They were there only to attend the machines. If the machine did something wrong, they would respond. The workers made good money but the work was terribly boring.

This system was designed for machines, but not for people. And what is the result of applying that kind of technology? Just look at General Motors. Look at Chrysler, going bankrupt.

Recently, I saw on the Internet a new Volkswagen plant in Dresden, Germany, a new Lean Center, designed to be ergonomically correct. It gave the worker the best possible

working conditions and gave them the opportunity to continuously build their skills while they built a superior product for the customer.

We do want to continually educate the worker to have the knowledge necessary to fully participate in the improvement process. The worker knows the job. The worker knows his or her machines. The worker knows what quality is. Autoliv teaches the workers TPM, 5S, standardized work, etc. The more the worker knows, the more multi-skill they are and more improvement ideas that they can come up with.

When I keynote a conference, I often ask the question, "What is your most important asset?" And people will say, "People are our most important asset."

And then I'll say to them, "If they're the most important asset, why aren't they on your balance sheet?" Your balance sheet represents the financial worth of a company. If you look at it, you'll see cash, you'll see accounts receivable, you'll see investment in technology and machines. You rarely will ever see investment in people. It's ironical. People are just written off. They're just expenses. They're treated as necessary evils. But people are the real assets of the company. When management knows how to properly invest in its people the payback is enormous. I am sure that accountants can figure out a way to show their investment in people's training on the balance sheet. If cleverly done, this could both insure skill building and long-term loyalty from employees.

When we don't have people work smarter *and* harder, then they're expendable. Then we easily send the work overseas, because what are we losing? We didn't make any real investment in them.

How can you get rid of a LeBron James ? How can you get rid of any scientist, any genius in your company, anyone that has

developed your treasures? You should never get rid of innovative people.

So what do you do? I like the motto **work smarter *and* work harder**.

How do we challenge and get people to work smarter *and* harder?

In my studies I found a very simple process in Japan. They very cleverly looked at the American suggestion system and they copied it exactly. Initially, they got the same results that America did, like, one idea every seven years from the average worker.

But Toyota and the other Japanese company adapted the system and said, you know, it's a waste. People have real talent and we are getting very few ideas from them. How do we bring it out?

Then they slowly changed the system to a really participative management system. People know their job the best. We should be focusing on how to get people to manage their own work and solve the problems around their own work area.

That means, when a problem occurs, we want the person working on that job to be responsible for identifying where that problem came from and to find the solutions. We want to make that person responsible for detecting quality problems.

Another brilliant thing that Toyota did, in addition to extending the suggestion system, was to have the worker stop the line every time there was a problem. Toyota was serious about not allowing a defect to be passed to the customer. So they established the idea that the next person who gets your work is your customer, and you should not pass a defect or a problem to the next worker.

When I was in Georgetown with a group of people from the construction industry a few years back, someone in the audience

asked Gary Convis, president of Toyota in Georgetown, "Gary, what do you expect from your employees?"

Gary said, "You know, I expect only two things. One, I expect them to come to work. Two, I expect them to pull the cord.

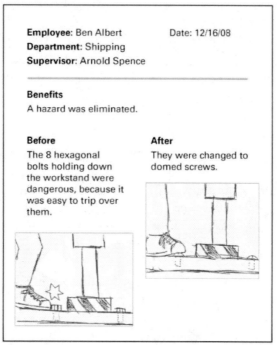

Fig. 68 <A hazard was eliminated.>

Imagine the second most important thing to Gary was people pulling the cord, because he wanted to empower workers to use their intelligence, to solve the problems that they were faced with at the time the problem occured. Look what Toyota did. In 1950, they were known for making junk. They almost went bankrupt, almost went out of business. And now they make the Lexus and they have close to $50 billion in the bank, enough money to get them through this recession.

I'm sure at this moment the whole automobile industry is in trouble. They're all losing money. But at least Toyota has enough

money to cushion them until the world turns around. And Toyota today is putting tremendous efforts on reducing their costs.

Work smarter, *and* harder. To work smarter is to challenge people to look around their work area and define ways to continuously improve. Because there are always problems, no matter what you do in life, there are always problems to solve.

Believe me, we want workers to work smarter. How to work smarter? Well, first, we have to educate them, don't we? If we want them to work smarter, then they have to know their jobs very well. So training is unending.

In the interview with Tom Hartman at Autoliv. (See appendix), we learn that his company is continually investing in people. Every month, they're training people, new things. Every month, they have scheduled training sessions with workers. And workers meet before and after every shift. They meet to discuss things that happened during the day - the problems that occurred to them and what they went through to solve them.

We really should want to have a learning organization. But what do we mean by a learning corporation?

The large corporations encourage a select group of people to innovate new products while all the other workers could be like machines. That was not a learning organization where innovation and new ideas can come from any worker. Of course, the ultimate, today, is what Canon has done.

When I visited Canon ten years ago, I saw around 72 people on a conveyor belt assembling copiers. A major problem with a conveyor belt is that it must move at the speed of the slowest worker. Since my last visit to Canon, the company went from a conveyor belt system where one worker would do very limited work, to cell technology where one worker builds the entire copier. Canon workers now work from 30 minutes to three hours building

an entire copier on their own. Think of the skill that's necessary to do that. Think about the education that is needed to have every worker totally multi-skilled, and to know everything about that copier in order to build it properly.

Canon calls this multi-skilled worker a "super meister." Meister is a German word meaning "master." Everyone is encouraged to grow on the job and to improve their skills to become a master at their jobs. With this new cell technology at Canon, they improved productivity from 30% to 50% over the conveyor belt system. They give each worker the opportunity to live with a new sense of dignity and self-respect. One woman said, "I build seven copiers a day with full responsibility for quality. I feel at the end of the day, I gave birth to seven new babies. I am very happy with my work."

Canon to me is the current state of the art of "Working Smarter *and* Harder."

Think about it, if you build skills, you lower costs not the reverse.

The psychological aspect is the first and most important thing to look at when thinking about making improvements, because Kaizen is something that can be done only by people who are motivated to do it. Our arms and legs can be moved by an outside force. We can be made to do physical work by the use of the carrot and the stick. Simple physical work can be controlled by threats of punishment and promises of reward but how about 'thinking' and 'coming up with good ideas'?

How did we ever create a system that asks people to come to work while leaving their brains at home? What a waste of human potential! The average person goes to school a minimum of 13 years from kindergarten through 12th grade, taught many different things; challenged from homework and tests to stretch their brains and then told at work not to use their brains. Crazy, isn't it?

No-One Can Be Forced to Do Kaizen If They Don't Want To

Even the smallest Kaizen requires some thought. To do a Kaizen, we have to think thoughts like, "This is odd," "I wonder why this doesn't work very well?" and "I wonder what would happen if we did this?" This is why no Kaizen can take place if the people involved don't *feel* like doing one.

Once someone begins to think that they would like to do something to make their job better, the next thing they think about is how they can improve it, and whether or not there is a better way of doing it. They themselves, on their own initiative, try to find that better method or special trick. People just need the encouragement from their supervisors to experiment to apply their ideas on improving the work area around them. They will probably be happy to be taught about implementing their own Kaizens, and they will probably absorb the teaching quickly, and promptly put it into action.

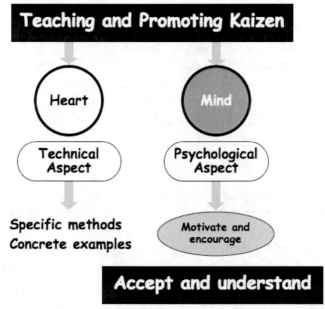

Fig. 69 <Teaching and promoting.>

So how can we motivate people to *want* to do Kaizen? The way to do this is to get them to realize that it is good for them to do Kaizen, and bad for them not to do it. And then to just ask them to look around their work are for things to make their work easier, more interesting and to build their skills and capabilities.

After all, people are very aware of what is to their advantage and to their disadvantage. Wanting to do what benefits us and not do what harms us is a sentiment we all share. In other words, to motivate people to do Kaizen, there is absolutely no need to use sophisticated reasoning or theory; all we have to do is to get them to see whether doing it would be to their advantage or not.

When I teach Quick and Easy Kaizen I always emphasize the reasons we are doing it are to make work easier, to make work more interesting, and to build skills and capabilities. I do not emphasize reducing costs or improving quality and productivity. Most companies, most managers continually emphasize the benefits for the company and not for the worker. We should reverse. Then the company will get happier employees and better results for its customers.

Use Concrete Examples to Convince People of Kaizen's Benefits

So, how should we go about getting people to see whether Kaizen is beneficial to them or not? We should use actual case studies to do so. If we explain Kaizen to people using specific, real-life examples from their own workplace, they will understand its benefits immediately.

Recently, one of my clients sent me a video of a worker working on a bending machine. At first, the worker looked at the specifications carefully for this particular job and then moved his body 90° to dial the specifications into the computer. Then he

moved another 90°, and took an additional four or five steps with the first piece of metal and placed it into the bending machine, putting his hands on two buttons and then bending the metal. He then took the formed metal and turned 180° back to the original table and carefully checked the bent metal with his quality tools to make sure the bend was calibrated correctly. He noticed a slight difference that required him to redial the computer and to turn and run another piece of metal to make sure the bend was correct. After doing these tests twice, he felt confident that the balance of the pieces would be bent correctly.

Later, I went to see the worker and told him that I had seen him on video and asked him what he could do to improve his process. He told me that if maintenance would move the computer in front next to the bending machine and if they put a table to the left in front near the bending machine, he would be able to do his work without turning repeatedly. Yes, he had all the answers but management never asked him.

But, after that last visit the worker did implement all of his ideas and he now no longer has to turn around. When I saw him on my last visit, he was very proud to show me what he had done.

Kaizen is about selecting the means and altering the methods of doing things within the bounds of what is possible, and, as long as the world continues to change, the bounds of what is possible will continue to expand.

When we examine an example of Kaizen and compare the way in which the job was done before with the way in which it is done now, we see that the work objectives can now be achieved more easily, efficiently, comfortably and safely. It is immediately obvious whether doing or not doing the Kaizen was beneficial. At least, if the example relates directly to the work the people are doing, they will have no problem in understanding it, because they themselves personally experience its benefits in terms of being able to do their jobs more easily and safely.

Real-Life Examples

There is nothing more convincing than actual experience. It is obvious at a glance from the cartoon below which of the two ways of moving the block of stone is better. The worker has to shift the block in order to get paid, and there is no room for discussion about which is better – stubbornly clinging to Method ① without even trying to change it, or changing to a method such as in Method ② within the bounds of what is possible and permissible so as to be able to shift the block more easily and safely.

Fig. 70 <Which Way of Doing the Job is Easier?.>

Even Pre-Schoolers Can Spot Differences

However, this kind of simplified example does not work with everyone, since some people are deficient in the ability to understand abstract concepts. They are likely to say something like, "Our work is not as simple as shifting blocks of stone. It's in a

totally different dimension." The only way to convince people like that is to use real-life examples of improvements to their actual workplaces or the tasks they are actually doing.

People know how to make their work easier and more interesting, if we just stop and ask them. Unfortunately, people are so filled with fear at work; afraid that they might make a mistake and lose their job that they do not come up with ideas to make their work easier and more interesting. They are willing to suffer and do the work tediously rather than to risk changing and the negative responses they might get for making a mistake. It is said that, generally just to keep the job, no matter how bad the job is, any job seems to be better than no job.

It is said that, generally speaking, the development of our intellectual faculties starts with the perception of differences and eventually proceeds to the point at which we become able to recognize commonalities. It is easy to understand this if we look at textbooks written for preschool children; those for younger children contain material that encourages them to look for differences in color, shape and so forth, while those for older children pose questions that get them to find things in common and put things in groups.

This shows that even pre-schoolers can spot differences, but recognizing commonalities requires a slightly higher level of intellectual capability. So people with a higher intellectual level are able to think, "Our Company is bigger (or smaller)…" "We have a different history from that company…" "Our business objectives are very different from theirs…" and "Our culture is different…" and go on to think, "But we work in similar ways," "But the nature of our work is very similar," and "But we use the same movements in our work." In other words, they are able to identify differences and commonalities and think about them separately. People with a certain level of ability to think abstractly like this can understand the advantages of various Kaizens, even if they come from

different trades and industries, and think about how they could apply them to their own work.

Nevertheless, overcoming this psychological resistance is hard, because it results from the arbitrary assumption that Kaizen is troublesome and difficult. People acquire this misconception when they confuse Kaizen (continual small improvements) with Kaikaku (major reforms). They wrongly assume that Kaizen means making wholesale changes to the way they do their jobs, and is therefore very difficult, so they tend to shy away from it. Either that, or they think they have to achieve the same results from it as a major reform, and so they cannot approach it in a relaxed way.

Psychological Regression When Faced with Kaizen

The failure to understand Kaizen, or the failure to even try to do so, is not merely a question of intellectual capacity; rather, it is a psychological, and emotional issue.

We should keep repeating that Kaizen is not difficult, and that it is all about changing how we work little by little over time. And we must not only explain this in words; we must also demonstrate it by showing them lots of actual examples. This is because the same words convey different things to different people. If we just say that Kaizen consists of 'small' changes and use no examples to show what small looks like, they might end up picturing Kaizen as consisting of much bigger changes than those we are looking for. But if we use real examples from their own workplaces, people will often be surprised and say, "What? Is that all you're talking about?" or "Is it OK just to do small changes like that?" and their view of Kaizen is transformed.

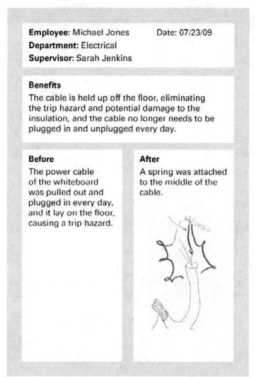

Fig. 71 <The cable is held off the floor.>

Once people have understood that Kaizen is all about small changes, things become much easier. When they see that minor changes are all that is required, they relax and become able to approach Kaizen with optimism, and they can escape from their regressive, fearful state of mind.

Real-Life Examples

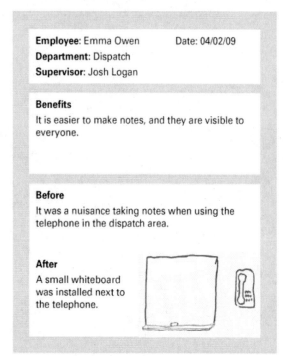

Employee: Emma Owen   **Date:** 04/02/09
Department: Dispatch
Supervisor: Josh Logan

Benefits
It is easier to make notes, and they are visible to everyone.

Before
It was a nuisance taking notes when using the telephone in the dispatch area.

After
A small whiteboard was installed next to the telephone.

Fig. 72 <It is easier to make notes.>

Chapter XII

Enforced Kaizen

Kaizen Only Lasts if Self-Directed

Kaizen is by nature a self-directed, autonomous activity, but enforced Kaizen also exists. This is the kind of Kaizen which people are directed to do by a boss or consultant saying something like, "Surely it would be better if you did this?" or "Wouldn't it be more efficient to do it this way?" Employees on a company's payroll cannot just flatly refuse to do what their bosses tell them to. Neither can they ignore the advice of a consultant that their boss or their factory's general manager has engaged. So they grudgingly do what they have been told, while muttering to themselves things like "That won't work; it'll make things less efficient, not more." and, "That will certainly increase the work pace, but how would you like to be doing it?"

But what happens afterward? Will employees who have been forced to do one Kaizen go on doing more by themselves? Definitely not! All they will do is wait passively for the next instruction to do one. They will end up never attempting to do a Kaizen themselves but just waiting for orders.

If this happens, then what? The situation and the conditions will go on changing, but the working methods will remain the same. There is no way bosses and consultants can keep on following up everything the employees are doing, so everywhere in the company things will be happening that do not suit the conditions.

Look, in a sense when people come to work they must follow instructions, they have no choice. I think what we really want to do is to have people recognize that Kaizen is part of their job; using their brains in addition to their physical body is not something extra. But, since people have not been asked in most cases not to be problem solvers they look at Kaizen as something additional to

their work. We really want to change this. We want people to recognize that they know their job best and we need their help in order to stay competitive to improve everything, literally everything, at work.

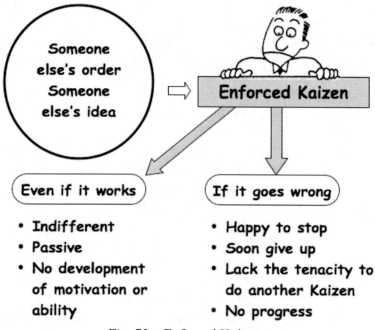

Fig. 73 <Enforced Kaizen.>

Enforced Kaizens Do Not Last

But as Bunji is trying to explain, when people feel that they are forced to do things, surely they have to do it, but the spirit we want of full cooperation is not there and you will not get the kind of results that you want. Certainly, a Kaizen ordered by a boss or consultant can deliver excellent results, but those results can be very short-lived. But, when people feel empowered and it is their own ideas the results will last much longer. People are proud of their Kaizens. Without further improvements, the original Kaizen

will end up, before anyone notices it, producing the opposite of the intended effect and lowering productivity instead of raising it.

Work is clearly defined for people. They know what to do from the instructions, but Kaizen is something different. We are asking people to be creative, to follow standardized work but also to look for improvements. So even though we want Kaizen to be part of everyone's job; it is different and we must take a different approach in order that people feel comfortable. Since Kaizen is creative and new to the worker, fear of making a mistake and being punished for making a mistake is one of the main causes for people to resist being involved in improvement activities.

Kaizen means continually improving the way the job is done in response to changing conditions and circumstances. Thus, if the people actually doing the job do not try to improve it themselves, the results of any Kaizen enforced on them by someone else will not be sustained.

It is certainly true that major, sweeping reforms cannot be accomplished without decisive action from bosses and consultants, of the type that does not take no for an answer, because massive reforms and large-scale innovations cannot be achieved through the kinds of watered-down changes that everyone in an organization is likely to agree with.

Kaizens should be done by the people who know the job best, i.e. by the people who actually do the job themselves. Of course, these kinds of Kaizens are on a completely different level than those ordered by experts; but they can deliver far better results in the long term. Kaizens directed by experts may produce excellent results at the time they are done, but they often do not last. And of course, there is no way we could ask experts to come in and do the same job for us day after day. We must not forget that a Kaizen that is not sustained will end up doing the opposite of what was originally intended.

Enforced Kaizen

One of the other harmful effects of enforced Kaizens becomes immediately obvious when one goes wrong; the lack of the tenacity required for keeping the Kaizen going. Kaizens do not always work the first time; sometimes a Kaizen done in good faith actually makes things worse, or creates other problems. How will employees who have been compelled to do Kaizens react when this kind of thing happens? They will probably be beside themselves with glee and as happy as sand larks, saying, "There, what did we tell you? We said it wouldn't work, didn't we? It was just as we thought, wasn't it?" If they go on to say things like, "Just as we expected, the way we've always done it is best, isn't it?" and "If it ain't broke, don't fix it," then the Kaizen has had it and all the resources spent on it will have been wasted. Enforced Kaizens easily come to naught over the smallest stumbling block.

Remember, people naturally resist change. It is the manager's job; probably the most important part of the manager's job is to help people overcome the resistance to change. But, forcing people to change is not sustainable.

With patience you will see those people initially reluctant to offering ideas slowly begin to feel less threatened as they see their fellow workers participating.

Self-directed Kaizens

On the other hand, what happens when a Kaizen that the person actually doing the job has thought of by himself/herself, and is trying to do on their own initiative, doesn't work? In this case, that person would not clap hands for joy. Rather, they would probably ask them themselves why it didn't work, and what was wrong with it, do some investigating, and ask for some advice. Then they would probably soon come up with the next idea for improvement, saying something like, "It'll probably work if I try this," "OK, I'll try changing this element, then," or "I'm going to try adjusting this

part," and actually try it out as soon as possible, moving the Kaizen nearer and nearer to success.

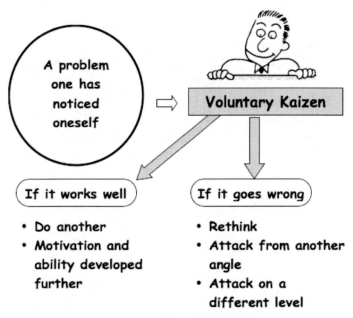

Fig. 74 <Voluntary Kaizen.>

Kaizens should not be expected to work well the first time they are tried; they usually only deliver results after repeated attempts. You try something, and it doesn't work, so you try something else. If that doesn't work, you try something else again, mounting a series of attacks by changing the method, the material, the angle, and so on. 'Enforced Kaizens' directed by others will never generate the tenacity and perseverance required to do this. These qualities only emerge with Kaizens thought up by, and implemented by, ourselves. They do so because we will fight to the finish to make our own ideas succeed.

Because Kaizens are by definition small changes, they do not require any special talent or ability. We just say "The person doing the job each day surely knows their job well and is aware of

the problems. With respect, patience and listening to workers they will allow Kaizen to work.

Bunji, from his 30 years of experience teaching Kaizen in Japan and in many other countries knows that focusing on small changes sustains Kaizen over the long term, but if we look differently at the infinite potential of workers and are willing to invest in them for the long-term then we can expect and will achieve results that are much more thoughtful and deeper Kaizens. If you are willing to train people, to educate them, to develop them all as if they were future engineers not just doing mechanical work but helping you to reinvent the workplace over and over again then you can expect them to do both small changes and be part of big changes.

Yes, you want to focus on small ideas but don't limit the scope of people. Yes, you do want to confine their Kaizen's to their own work area. If you can develop the kind of support staff that Autoliv did then the scope of the Kaizens can be vaster. But, give yourself time to become like Autoliv and just start off by asking all workers to come up with one or two small improvement ideas per month to make their work easier, more interesting and to build their skills and capabilities.

If there is one thing that people do require, it is the persistence to hang in there and doggedly and tenaciously see them through to the end. And the source of this tenaciousness (the most important thing in Kaizen) is their self-directedness.

Chapter XIII

Anyone Can Do It, Every Day

Simple Examples Are Truly the Stars of the Kaizen Program

What are the stars in Kaizen? They are small, everyday Kaizens that are accessible to everyone. At the very least, as long as we are asking all employees to do Kaizen continually, on a daily basis, they have to be of the kind that anyone can do every day. As long as we are calling our program or system 'Kaizen,' the concept behind it has to be that of making simple, minor changes to the way we do our jobs. If we were asking everyone to effect big, tough changes, then we would have to call it a 'reform program' or a 'major change activity.' Anyway, as long as we are calling it 'Kaizen,' it has to be about small, easy changes. This is the commonly accepted, universally-recognized definition in business.

Do all managers, those running Kaizen programs really understand that the aim is small ideas, I wonder? Are they really acting in a way that is consistent with this definition? For example, on what concepts do they base their choices when making compilations of Kaizen case studies or holding Kaizen events, and when selecting and presenting examples for these? Don't they tend to present only the best examples, or showcase just the best Kaizen practitioners? This is a shame, because it is counterproductive and harms what could be a healthy Kaizen program. We want everyone to be involved in continuous improvement. It is difficult for workers to come up with big Kaizens but everyone can find something small that will improve the quality of their work. It is the collection of all of these small Kaizens that gets everyone involved that adds great value to the organization.

Anyone Can Do It, Every Day   229

Innovation is not just the big ideas from a select few people. Innovation and long term sustained success will come from both the big ideas and from the massive effort from all of the people to make meaningful improvements.

I am guilty of showing managers wonderful examples of Kaizen for I want them to get excited about the process. If they only see small improvement ideas, they might not understand the power of Kaizens for their organization. However, it is in accumulation of small ideas from everyone that really allows the Kaizen process to succeed.

What and Who Are Case-Study Collections for?

Why do we make collections of Kaizen case studies in the first place? The purpose of a collection of case studies is to share Kaizens, thereby encouraging people to join in the Kaizen activities, and stimulate the Kaizen program. It is to let people know the good things that have been achieved through Kaizen so far and motivate them to do more. And since we are looking for improvement, we want people to look at other people's Kaizens and copy them. We don't care where the idea came from. Even though we are interested in creativity, we are more interested in making sure that defects are being eliminated and problems are being solved.

That being so, case-study collections should contain examples of the type that as many employees as possible can understand and learn from. If they didn't, there would be no point in going to the trouble of compiling them. They would just be a waste of time, paper and money. And promptly doing away with that kind of waste is exactly what Kaizen is about, isn't it? But, although this is true, isn't it also true that most examples show only examples that have resulted in big savings, are highly specialized, and make no sense at all to people from other departments? Not only that, but aren't they usually also described in great detail and in complex

terms, so that most employees are completely put off by them and aren't even faintly interested in or impressed by them? It would be all very well if the intention in compiling that kind of case study was to document and preserve them as historical records, but they are useless as a means of invigorating a Kaizen program.

Fig. 75 <Easy Kaizen examples.>

Far from doing that, they are more likely to elicit a negative reaction from employees and provoke comments like, "That's way above my head. I couldn't do anything as difficult as that." "There's no way we could do that sort of thing" and "Those Kaizens are irrelevant to us, anyway." Rather than invigorating the Kaizen program, they will probably decrease the participation rate and deactivate it. There's nothing more senseless than spending lots of time and money only to produce the opposite of the intended effect. It's completely crazy, isn't it? The more effort the people in charge put into compiling such collections, the more the Kaizen program is dragged down.

It is a challenge to select good examples of small ideas that show workers how simple the process is for them and to encourage them to participate.

Start by Putting Together a Collection of 'Easy Examples'

Of course, we also need to document and keep records of Kaizens that have produced major results. That would be absolutely fine, since such records would certainly be informative and useful for certain departments and particular employees. The desire to compile collections of those kinds of high-level Kaizen case studies is also understandable from the viewpoint of Kaizen promotion staff, since they want to demonstrate the results achieved through Kaizen to the company's senior management and persuade them of its benefits. So of course, they need to make that kind of report. But it is terribly wasteful to invest excessive amounts of time and money on just doing that, because senior executives do not have time to study such detailed compilations and reports anyway. All they will do is quickly skim over them and say, "Thank you. Well done." It's all well and good if their purpose is to show senior management how hard the Kaizen promotion staff have been working and what a good job they've been doing. But if their mission is to get the Kaizen program going, there is something else that needs to be done first.

The case-study collection we should give highest priority to compiling should be made up principally of easy examples that anyone can understand. Preparing such collections and distributing them promptly at regular intervals is the best way of sharing Kaizens and keeping the Kaizen activities on the boil. Wasting time and money on things of low priority and less importance, and not even addressing the top priority, while producing the opposite of the intended effect, is nothing less than a dereliction of duty.

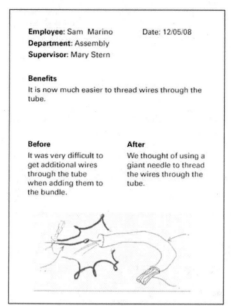

Fig. 76 <It is much easier to thread wires through the tube.>

Compile These Collections Speedily

Having said this, there is no need to spend too much time on compiling these collections of easy examples. In Kaizen, speediness is of the essence, so case-study compilations should also be produced promptly. People get anxious if they feel they have to produce a thick, impressive-looking document, and tend to keep putting off getting started on it.

Doing something 'for the time being' is one of the secrets of Kaizen, and the same thing applies to case-study compilations; it is important to at least make a start 'for the time being' and produce them as promptly as possible. All we have to do is look at a few Kaizens, choose one or two that seem interesting, easy to understand and relevant, make copies, cut out the interesting bits and stick these on a sheet of paper, and Bingo! we have our Kaizen News.

All we need is a pair of scissors and some glue. Even if we dress it up a little, all we need to do is underline a few things with a felt-tip pen, rewrite anything illegible, and add a few Kaizen keywords and simple comments. Even if the original Kaizen contains some mistakes, we mustn't do anything as foolish as retyping it on a word processor.

The cold and impersonal feeling of the printed word is inappropriate for Kaizen, which gives the highest priority to feeling relaxed and at ease. That's why the best way to document a Kaizen is in large handwriting, because this is the easiest to read, most personal form of writing. Going to all the trouble of re-entering the information onto a and word processor and printing it out is once again the height of folly.

I do know of many companies that have entered their Kaizens into a computer with the thought of establishing this data base of ideas for others to search. I agree with Bunji; it is a way of complicating something that we should keep very simple.

Since Kaizen means selecting the means and changing the methods in order to better achieve our work objectives better, we need to select the most appropriate means and methods to achieve our objectives efficiently and effectively when promoting Kaizen as well.

The Secret of Keeping Kaizen Going is Speed

Anyway, it is easy to produce a simple kind of Kaizen bulletin like this. It can be done quickly and easily, right there and then. Then all that needs to be done is to select the best method of sharing it for that particular workplace – whether that be pinning it to a board or sending it round like a circular. If we keep it simple enough, we could produce one every month, week, or each day without it being

too much work. A year soon goes by, so we could make a collection of case studies by collecting them all up after twelve months and stitching them together.

While people who find it difficult to get started on things say, "I'll get round to it any day now..." the situation moves on. This is indeed one of the key principles of doing Kaizen – that of splitting things up. What's more, bulky collections of case studies are not read very much anyway. The people who receive them just stuff them into their desk drawers, saying, "I'll get around to reading them as soon as I have time." They then suffer the fate of being discovered and thrown out several years later when the office gets a Spring-cleaning.

Fig. 77 <Our own Kaizen examples.>

Anyway, the point is that if the people producing the case-study collections and those receiving them keep on saying, "I'll get round to it any day now…" there is no way that the precious case studies are going to get shared. Information is pointless unless it is

communicated, at the time and in the place where it is needed, and information that is merely hoarded and not shared is worthless.

Producing and distributing the data promptly is the only way of keeping the job of doing so from becoming a burden, and is therefore also the only way of ensuring that this activity is sustained. Speed is the secret of keeping things going and should be the highest priority of those responsible for directing and promoting the Kaizen program.

I suggest that you hang up on a wall, not far from the workers, all of Kaizen examples, where everybody can see them, and continually replace and hang up new ones. People will go and look to see if you posted their example. It is human nature. I also like to ask people to vote each week, each month on the best example: the simplest, the most creative, the most beneficial for fellow workers, etc. I recommend you give out simple awards to those with the highest number of votes and also to the team that comes up with the most suggestions during that period.

In Oregon, DCI with around 100 people received on the average three ideas per week per employee. Each idea was hung up on a wall to allow all of the operators to view their own ideas and the ideas of their fellow workers. For most of the Kaizens, a picture was taken when the problem was identified and again after the Kaizen was implemented. The ideas were rotated each week. The workers would be able to look up with pride and see their ideas up on the wall. Also, they would encourage copying other people's ideas if they were faced with a similar problem.

Easy examples, not impressive, complex ones, should be the stars not only of case-study collections but also of Kaizen presentation events – but we tend to get this back to front, don't we? Company Kaizen events tend to focus exclusively on the superior case studies, or the ones that have produced the biggest results, don't they?

> # Easy Examples Should be the Stars of Kaizen Events Too

Recognize Simple Kaizens Appropriately

A certain company used to stage a massive event every year on the anniversary of its foundation, at which its employees assembled from all over the country to present Kaizens and receive prizes. But the more events were held, the lower the rate of participation in the Kaizen program became, and eventually only certain limited groups of employees were involved. The company therefore decided to change the event's format. Instead of it being all about large, complex, sophisticated Kaizens, they stipulated that eighty percent of the presentations should consist of simple, everyday Kaizens that anyone could easily understand.

This completely changed the atmosphere of the event. Previously, the presenters had proudly described their wonderful achievements at great length; now, all they had to do was put up a few slides that clearly showed what they had done. They didn't even have to talk much; all they did was say, "What we did was very simple – it was just as you can see here – it wasn't much, really. Thanks," and hop down off the stage.

However the company's president made some simple but appropriate comments on every presentation, saying things like, "You said it wasn't much, but what you've done is very important, you know. Before you made that improvement, we were causing problems for our customers, weren't we? But thanks to this Kaizen, our customers are delighted with us now, and we are also much more efficient. This is an excellent Kaizen. It's exactly the

kind of Kaizen I'd like everyone to do. Please go on doing Kaizens like this."

In retrospect, you will see that the success of Japanese industry has come from continuous improvement by everyone, all employees involved, and focusing primarily on producing high-quality products.

When the president made those remarks, the expressions of those in the audience changed. While they had been listening, they had been looking at the slides and thinking, "What, is that all? It's obvious, isn't it?" but now that the company's president was saying, "This is an example of an excellent Kaizen," it made them think, "If that's the kind of Kaizen they want, well I'm already doing it myself. I want to be up there presenting, too." As a result, the event became more and more popular every year.

Individual workplaces can also hold presentation events if they are kept simple. This particular company also holds monthly mini-events in individual workplaces every month, enabling the Kaizens to be shared even more extensively. Complexity and difficulty do not suit Kaizens, which are meant to be simple and easy. People should be able to think, "Oh, they're just Kaizens," and do them quickly and easily without feeling any pressure. Kaizen presentation events should therefore also be simple, easy to participate in, and held frequently.

Combine Case Studies with Keywords

How should we use our own Kaizen case studies as authentic training materials for teaching people about Kaizen? The best way is to use 'Kaizen keywords' in conjunction with the case studies.

Of course, using case studies by themselves is also effective, but they become much easier to use when combined with Kaizen keywords.

Kaizen keywords consist of the principles, rules and established formula of Kaizen, expressed simply and concisely, and they can be categorized as follows, in accordance with each of the Kaizen steps:

① **Observation keywords** (key words for helping people notice problems)

② **Ideation keywords** (keywords for helping people come up with ideas for solutions)

③ **Implementation keywords** (keywords for carrying out improvements)

Fig. 78 <Presenting high level Kaizens.>

The following tables show some typical examples of keywords, but it would be pointless trying to memorize this table. The keywords have to be understood in terms of specific examples and used in

conjunction with them. Even if the words do not mean much to people on their own, they will understand them and accept them if illustrated by concrete examples of easy, everyday Kaizens relating to work they are familiar with.

The same thing can be said about Kaizen coaching. If bosses couch their explanations in difficult, technical language, their people will have no idea what they're talking about. The bosses will just rattle on, mightily pleased with themselves, but what they are saying will be completely useless, and their people will end up feeling uncomfortable and trying to avoid them.

Kaizen is something that everyone should do every day as part of their job, so everyday words should be used to explain and advise on Kaizen, not hard-to-understand ones. It is recommended that they be used together with simple, close-to-home Kaizen examples for maximum impact. It is not appropriate to use difficult words to explain easy examples. Easy examples should be explained in easy words.

Examples and Keywords are the Weapons of Choice for Kaizen Coaching

A combination of case studies and keywords is the best ammunition for directing and coaching Kaizen. Just as an army cannot win a battle without bullets, so it is impossible to direct and promote Kaizen effectively without examples and keywords. When their people are facing problems, bosses who have plenty of these combinations up their sleeve can tell them things like, "Here's an example that might help," or "This is what we did in my last workplace," or give them specific advice, like "How about thinking of it in this way," or "How about addressing it from this angle?" But bosses who do not have these combinations to offer cannot give any specific advice, so anything they say is inevitably abstract. All they can do is say things like, "How about thinking of

it in various different ways?" or "How about thinking a bit harder?" But the people who have come to them for advice have done so because they have already racked their brains about the problem and have not been able to come up with a solution, so this kind of advice is worse than useless to them. It is just like firing an empty gun. Coaching and direction with no ammunition like this is no good at all.

Can You Write Out Ten Kaizens Your Team Has Done?

Our brains respond to outside stimuli, and abstract stimuli only produce abstract, inane responses. On the other hand, concrete stimuli produce concrete responses, so bosses should give their people specific advice. In fact, their ability to guide and direct Kaizen is measured by how specific their advice is. This ability is commensurate with the number of combinations of Kaizen examples and keywords they have in their mental filing cabinet.

Last year, I visited Sango Co. Ltd., a subsidiary of Toyota, that makes tail pipes. I noticed a worker walking and working with around six different machines, without stopping. He just placed parts into one machine and removed a similar part installed from his previous round. In every plant in the past, where I had watched workers in manufacturing cells, the worker was required to stop in front of the machine and press two buttons as a safety precaution. When pressing the buttons the machine knew that the worker's hands were free and could not be damaged by the machine.

How was the worker able to walk, without stopping, and still operate every machine safely? Imagine the manager previously asking the worker to think about finding a way to run each machine without stopping? And following Toyota's advice, how do you do these Kaizens without spending much money?

Answer: the worker installed a little metal lever between each machine. As he walked from one machine to the next machine, the worker would simply move his hand across the lever. This told the previous machine that the worker was safely away and allowed the machine to operate. This little device cost less then $50.00 to install.

The above example shows the power of using words and asking and it shows the power of using one's imagination to solve problems.

Observation
(noticing problems)

- One by one, every time
- Duplicated effort, triplicated effort
- Hanging around,

- Complicated, troublesome
- Tedious, repetitive
- Only X knows how to do it
- Only X can do it
- Rushed, irritating

- Stopped, delayed • Smelly • Noisy
- Shaky, dark • Bumpy
- Heavy • Slow

- Hard to see • Hard to understand
- Easily forgotten • Easily overlooked
- Easily misheard • Easily misread

- Intermittent, irregular, variable
- Large/small quantity
- Manually operated
- Easily damaged • Easily soiled

- Checks omitted
- Failure to communicate/calculate
- Failure to report/record

- Very changeable
- Diverse, of great variety
- Different, individual
- Unmatched, incompatible

- Hard to grasp
- Hard to perform
- Tiring
- Easy to get wrong
- Uncomfortable, illogical
- Unstable, unsatisfactory
- Inconvenient, awkward

Fig. 79 <Key words – Observation.>

Ideation (solving problems: stop/reduce/change)

In advance / beforehand
Different order / chart / at-a-glance
Fix shape / integrate
Decentralize ↔ centralize

Simplify / streamline / combine / make single-touch / prioritize / extract key points only / separate / describe in a manual / standardize / provide samples / gauge instead of measuring / set instead of adjusting

---

Streamline / block off / smooth / isolate / fasten / display / normalize / average / lighten / speed up

---

Make visible / visually control / fix location / highlight / discriminate / partition / enlarge / color-code / mark / illustrate / make apparent / photo / video

---

Average / normalize / make year-round / repeat / audibly confirm / record / decentralize / centralize / mechanize / automate / coat / cover

---

Use serial numbers / checksheets / install windows / link / synchronize / convert (don't transcribe)

Make movable / synchronize / make parallel / use distributed processing / control by exception / analogize / share / commonize / convert / package / bundle

---

Jigs / attachments / divide vertically ↔ divide horizontally / retainers / supports / change work allocation / make hands-free / change person in charge / use functions / change position (left-right, bottom-top) / change shape (round, square, triangular) / change orientation (sideways ↔ vertical ↔ oblique)

Fig. 80 <Key words Ideation

> **Implementation** (prompt, easy, relaxed action)
> - For the time being
> - To be going on with
> - At least
> - Tentatively, for now
> - Start with what we can, and go as far as we can
> - If it doesn't work, try something different
> - If it does work, do another Kaizen
> - Aim for the best but start with the better
> - Start with part of the problem
> - Divide the problem up
> - Try multiple solutions
> - Try local solutions
> - Try partial solutions
> - Try phased solutions
> - Break through at one point

Fig. 81 *<Key words Implementation.>*

☆

As a follow-up to a Kaizen training session, all the supervisors taking part are asked to write reports on around ten Kaizens that have been done in their own workplaces. They then create their own Kaizen training materials based on these. Whether or not they can do so in the short time reveals what they have been giving their attention to in their daily work. Anyone can recollect and report on one or two Kaizens if they think hard enough about it, but not ten. Unless they have been constantly making their people's eyes light up by saying things to them like, "That's a great Kaizen" or "Keep on doing Kaizens like that," they will find it difficult to come up with the goods.

In other words, it is easy to tell whether or not someone has been practicing positive management by seeing whether or not they can write up ten Kaizens that their people have done. Their management style is graphically illustrated by whether or not they are continually thinking of their people's motivation toward Kaizen and their ability to do it. A good manager is always trying to recognize, praise and encourage, in a timely fashion, all of his or her employees.

Kaizen Forms Are a Tool for Kaizen OJT and for Documenting and Sharing

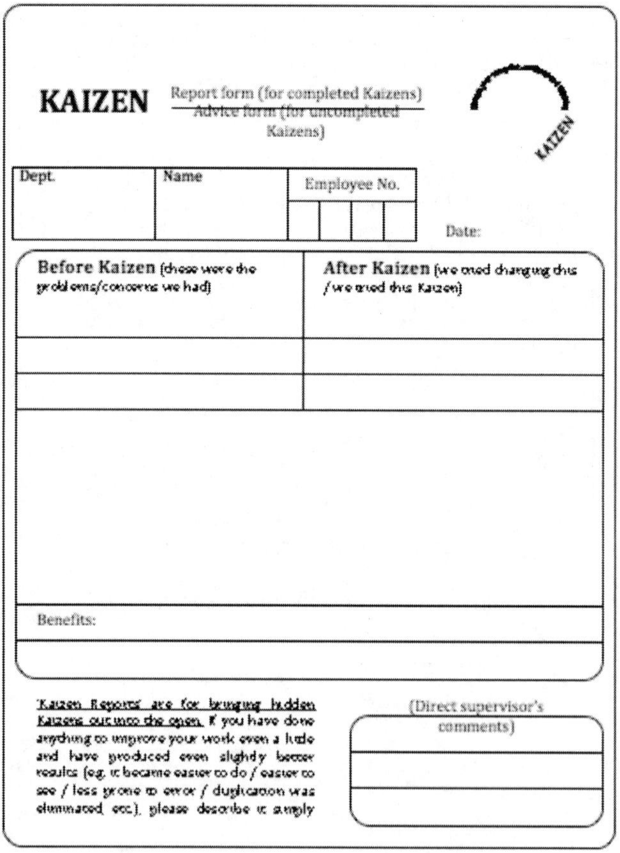

Fig. 82 <A Kaizen form.>

Employee: Adam Alder **Date:** 05/24/09
Department: Medical
Supervisor: Manny Kinshe

Benefits
The forms can now be sent out in windowed envelopes, and there is no need to copy the name and address onto the envelope, saving 34 hours.

Before
Since there is a single standard health insurance certificate for use nationwide, the forms could not be sent out in windowed envelopes.

After
A blank sheet has been added to the form, on which the recipient's name and address is printed.

Fig. 83 <Sending windowed envelopes.>

Chapter XIV

Formulas and Keywords

Words to Help People Notice Problems

'Observation keywords' are words for enabling us to notice, or draw other people's attention to, problems in our everyday work. After a Kaizen program has been going for some time, we begin to hear remarks like, "We've run out of ideas," "We've done all the Kaizens we can," and "There aren't any Kaizens left to do." If this were really true, it would be marvelous. It would mean that all the problems had been solved and the work was being done absolutely perfectly. It would be the ideal workplace, with the nicest surroundings and the highest productivity in the whole world. But such a company doesn't exist. Even the highest-ranked companies do multitudes of Kaizens every year, and there is no way their employees go around saying things like, "Our company has done all the Kaizens it can," "We don't have any more problems," "There is nothing left for us to improve" or "There is no more room to improve anything." Every company, no matter how good, still has problems, and if employees are making those kinds of remarks, all it means is that they haven't noticed them, or that they have become blind to them.

When this happens, some managers try to lecture the employees, telling them that their failure to see any problems has itself become a problem. But, although the people who say this may think themselves very clever, this outdated line has absolutely no effect on the people who hear it.

Here are some clues for Kaizen

Finding Problems in Our Everyday Work

It would be better to make use of the language we use every day – words and phrases such as 'one by one,' 'every time,' 'waiting around,' 'searching about,' 'irritating,' miscommunication,' failed to check,' 'miscalculated,' 'overlooked,' 'hard to see' and 'hard to understand'. These are all words that point to problems in our everyday work – and they do so specifically, not abstractly. They are 'observation keywords,' i.e. words that help us to spot specific problems with our work.

Rather than preaching abstractly to people who are saying things like, "There aren't any problems," or "There's nothing to improve," it is more effective to wait until they say these words or demonstrate these attitudes and point the problem out to them there and then.

Fig. 84 <Here are some clues for Kaizen.>

For example, "You say there aren't any problems, but you have to do that calculation every time you do that job, and sometimes you get it wrong. That's a problem, isn't it? There's room for improvement there, isn't there?" or, "Each time you do that job, you have to check the same kind of thing and report on it, don't you? Couldn't that be improved somehow?"

'Stopping' is the Best Kaizen

Let's say that hearing a keyword has enabled someone to spot a problem. Of course, that in itself has no value. They have to solve the problem they have noticed, because, after all, problems are there to be solved. So the next thing they have to do is come up with some specific ideas and devise some concrete solutions. 'Ideation keywords' are very powerful in this case, because they are words that enable people to change their thinking.

There are many 'ideation keywords,' but the three most powerful are:

Stop

Reduce

Change

All Kaizens are covered by these three concepts. Anyone who knows them can do Kaizen. To begin with, the best kind of Kaizen is one that eliminates unnecessary activity, where we stop doing something we don't really need to do. After all, just discontinuing something takes no time, costs nothing, and can be done right away. Kaizen is all about discontinuing anything we can; that is, stopping doing anything that we don't really need to do. There is no better Kaizen than 'stopping'.

Formulas and Keywords

If You Can't Stop It, Reduce It

Of course, life is not as simple as that. Sometimes we cannot just stop doing something, even when we know it would be better if we could. Sometimes it is difficult to discontinue something because our hands are tied by various restrictions, circumstances or red tape. In such case, the keyword 'reduce' is effective. 'Reducing' can also mean 'partially discontinuing'. If it is impossible to discontinue something completely, all at once, we can discontinue or reduce just those parts we can.

The things we can reduce include:

- Number
- Frequency
- Time
- Variety
- Weight
- Length
- Width
- Thickness

For example, botched jobs that have to be redone once or even twice can be done right first time if everything is set up correctly in the first place. Standardizing parts can reduce the variety of products produced. The greater the variety and frequency, the more complicated and troublesome things become, and the more time and effort are spent dealing with them. The chance of error also goes up. In most cases, 'increasing' makes a situation worse. Conversely, eliminating or reducing makes processes simpler, briefer, concise, and more streamlined. That is what Kaizen is all about.

Change the Elements or Conditions

Of course, everything has its limits, and we sometimes find ourselves up against what seems to be a brick wall, where no more decrease seems possible, or it appears that we cannot simplify the process any further. But, even if this happens, we do not need to stop trying to improve. The third ideation keyword, 'change' is waiting for us.

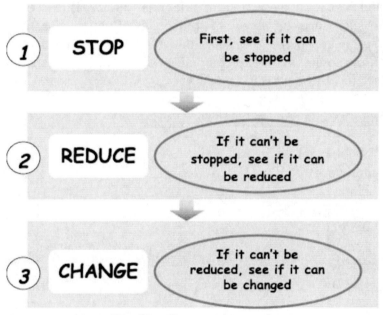

Fig. 85 <Stop – reduce – change.>

For example, we could:

- Change the order
- Change the procedure
- Change the color
- Change the angle
- Change the material
- Change the position
- Change the assembly

Formulas and Keywords 253

In fact, 'stop' and 'reduce' are both covered by 'change'. They have only been cited separately here to emphasize the fact that, while 'change' is qualitative, 'stop' and 'reduce' are exclusively quantitative.

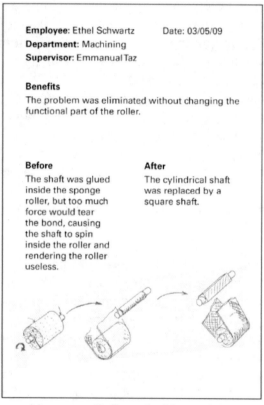

Fig. 86 <The problem was eliminated without changing the functional part of the roller.>

To sum up, Kaizen is all about changing quantities and qualities. It is about changing elements and conditions. What's more, there are various ways in which elements and conditions can be changed, so we can take the keyword 'change' and split it up, using even more everyday words. For example, with 'change the order,' we could use 'in advance,' 'beforehand,' 'already' or 'simultaneously'. In more technical language, these might be called 'setup

externalization' or 'synchronization'. We can usually make ordinary, everyday words more complicated by adding '-ation' to them. Here are some examples:

- Visualization (making something easy to see)
- Actualization (bringing something out into the open)
- Synchronization (making two things coincide)
- Integration (putting two things together to form one thing)
- Conjunction (joining one thing to another)
- Separation (splitting things up)
- Standardization (setting a particular pattern)
- Localization (specifying where to put things)
- Communization (sharing things)

In other words, things can be improved in a great variety of ways. With all these approaches available, we cannot allow anyone to say, "We don't have any ideas" or "We can't think of any ways of improving it."

But simply memorizing these keywords and phrases isn't good enough. Just bandying words about doesn't get us anywhere. If we did no more than that, people would be likely to mock us by saying; "We could read that in a textbook." We should always tie the words to a specific example. By combining them with specific examples, we turn the Kaizen keywords into useful hints and usable know-how. In fact, the number of combinations of keywords and practical examples people know is a precise indicator of their Kaizen leadership ability.

Anyone Can Understand a Kaizen Example from Her Own Workplace

Just describing examples of Kaizen, without using keywords, is also not enough. It is certainly true that people with practical ability can extract the essential points of Kaizens done in other

industries, companies or workplaces and make use of them in their own work, but keywords have to be used to get the essential points across to other people who are not so practically minded. When using combinations of keywords and case studies, it is best to use easy examples that anyone can understand. Complicated case studies that require a lengthy explanation of their background don't work. Even when we have to use complex examples, we should extract just the key.

Throughout the book are examples of easy examples, and these could be used just as they are as materials for teaching Kaizen. But if they were, people who don't understand Kaizen would be bound to say things like, "These are from different industries, so they're no use to us," "They're from companies in a different business to ours, so they can't help us," or "Their circumstances are different, so we can't learn anything from them."

Of course, those who make such remarks are simply declaring to the world at large their lack of abstract thinking capacity and ability to apply concepts to different situations, but it is no good just pointing this out to them, because the last thing that people are willing do is admit their own stupidity. The only way to get people like that to understand is to give them examples from their own company or their own workplace; in other words, we have to describe to them specific examples of Kaizens done on the actual work that they are engaged in.

The only Kaizen training materials that will convince them are those consisting of a combination of the following three elements:

- **Keywords**
- **Simple generic examples**
- **Examples from their own company and workplace**

It is only when these three elements are present that the materials will have any power to persuade; and using the three of them in combination is the most powerful Kaizen training tool.

You start off the process by asking each person to identify two problems and find the solutions from their own work area. Most people can do this but many people will come up with large problems for they think even though you asked for small problems, you really want them to come up with the big problems. But, some of the people will give you wonderful examples, wonderful small examples that you can use as demonstration material. It will take time, but after a short period people will begin to understand what you expect from them.

Keywords for Rapid Implementation

Once someone has come up with a solution to a problem or a proposal for improvement, all they have to do then is implement it. A Kaizen is only worth anything if it is implemented; just thinking or talking about it is worthless. However, some people are very good at putting together a string of fine-sounding words but not very good at putting their ideas into action. Others might be capable of acting but keep on making objections and finding excuses for putting it off.

Drastic changes and major reforms need to be thought about long and hard before being implemented, but Kaizens are merely small, easy changes that only alter the situation a little. The highest priority is to do them quickly. 'Implementation keywords' are words and phrases that encourage people to begin implementing their Kaizens as soon as possible, such as 'for the time being,' 'for

Formulas and Keywords 257

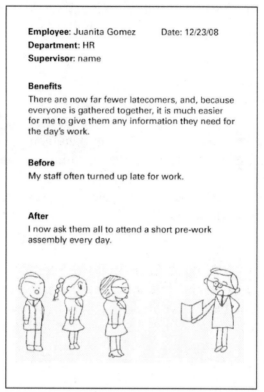

Fig. 87 <There are now fewer latecomers.>

now' and 'provisionally'. They are words that help people to get started without delay.

Then, when the time comes for us to implement a Kaizen, we face all sorts of constraints. Budgetary, regulatory, technical and other issues stand in our way. Those who are no good at Kaizen give up when faced with such problems and go off in a sulk. But masters of Kaizen know that Kaizen is all about overcoming practical constraints. 'Implementation keywords' are words and phrases that teach us tips, tricks and techniques for surmounting the practical constraints and difficulties that face us in order to get started on a Kaizen – words and phrases such as 'Attack part of the problem,'

'Localize the battle,' 'Concentrate on breaking through at a single point,' 'Start with whatever you can,' and 'Take it as far as you can'.

If at First You Don't Succeed...

Even when we manage to do a Kaizen, there is no guarantee that it will work. Sometimes a Kaizen that we think will improve things actually turns out to do the opposite and makes things worse. Sometimes a Kaizen solves one problem only to create a different one. People who are no good at Kaizen give up at this point, but this is when those who are good at Kaizen begin the next one.

In other words, 'implementation keywords' are words and phrases that encourage us to continue attacking the problem with a series of blows, mount a sustained assault, and whip up a chain reaction, e.g. 'If your first Kaizen doesn't work, try another,' 'If that doesn't work either, try yet another,' and 'If your first Kaizen works, do another'. They point to the essence of Kaizen, which is continual improvement.

In Kaizen, we do not try to solve our problems all in one go. We try to improve the situation little by little, by making one small change after another. But this idea cannot be fully communicated by keywords alone; they need to be used in combination with practical case studies and examples. Kaizens come to life and become convincing when illustrated by real-life examples that show people doing Kaizens. Often after solving one problem the situation becomes worse or different problems are created, and then by not giving up but carrying on to do further Kaizens eventually will solve the problems.

Formulas and Keywords 259

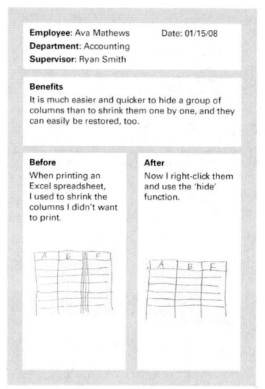

Fig. 88 <It is much easier to hide a group of columns.>

It is therefore recommended that, at the second stage of creating a collection of Kaizen case studies, they include examples of problems being solved in this way by a series of Kaizens (Kaizen 1, Kaizen 2, etc.). When people see many of this type of specific example, they begin to understand that 'If your first Kaizen doesn't work, try another' is not just a slogan but a practical necessity.

Employee: Jan Jenkins   **Date:** 11/23/08
Department: Engineering
Supervisor: Elizabeth Crowley

Benefits
The area looks much tidier, the information is much easier to find, and documents no longer get lost.

Before	After
All sorts of information was stuck haphazardly on the wall, which looked untidy and made it hard to find the information you wanted.	The information sheets have been placed inside transparent file pockets, each with an index tag showing its contents, and the file pockets are stored upright in a filing box which is kept close to where it is needed.

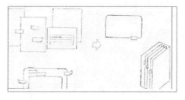

Fig. 89 <The area looks much tidier.>

Chapter XV

The Four Fallacies

A Manual for Annihilating the Four Fallacies

When asked whether Kaizen is good for them or not, most people will reply that it is, because making small improvements to the way they work enables them to do their jobs more easily, comfortably, safely and efficiently.

Nevertheless, some people still stubbornly resist Kaizen. It is funny that whenever I ask a worker, "Do you like your work?" They always say yes. They do like their work, no matter how boring and repetitious the work is, they always say they like their work. I feel it is because they are afraid, because they have been programmed to fear change because they are think they might not succeed and be fired.

To overcome this resistance to change, the manager has to be patient, listen, support, and to challenge people to do new things and to be very careful not to criticize or threaten them.

Let us analyze the illusions and superstitions that such people cling to so obdurately. Here are four fallacies- the typical objections to Kaizen:

① If we do Kaizen and make our jobs easier, they'll give us something else to do and we'll have to Kaizen that. There's no end to Kaizen, so it's not good for us.

② Kaizen tightens the screws on us and takes away any breathing space we might have had. If we eliminate all the waste, we'll create a highly pressurized workplace where everyone is on edge. Waste can be a necessary evil; we need a little bit of inefficiency in our work, just like a car's steering-wheel needs a bit of play.

③ Our work is special, and is subject to various different scenarios, so it's not really suitable for Kaizen.

④ Small, homemade, 'Mickey Mouse' Kaizens aren't cool, they're embarrassing; but large, impressive improvements are difficult to make.

Although it overlaps to some extent with what was explained in the previous chapter, some techniques for quashing these 'four fallacies' have been put together here in the form of a 'Manual of Persuasion'.

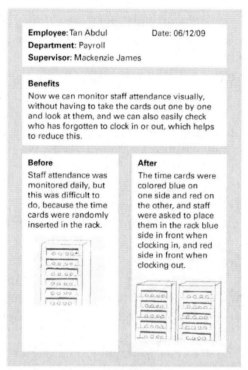

Fig. 90 <Now we can monitor staff attendance visually.>

No. 1 If our jobs get easier, they'll give us something else to do

KAIZEN

People Make Improvements and the Work Increases

People who object to Kaizen come up with the following kinds of arguments:

"If we do Kaizen and our work gets easier, they'll give us some more work to do. As soon as we improve that and relax a bit, they'll give us another job. No matter how many Kaizens we do, our work will never become any easier, so Kaizen is not good for us."

This argument is pretty persuasive. Lots of people who hear it will say, "Yes, yes, that's right. No matter how many Kaizens we do, there's never an end to them." Of course, in the very nature of life there are always problems. Workloads are being continually increased even in workplaces where nobody does any Kaizen. People aren't given more to do just because they've made their existing work more efficient; they are given more to do anyway, whether they are doing Kaizen or not. Every company is in the position now of having to get more and more done with fewer and fewer people, and the workload per employee is increasing even at companies that are expanding and hiring more people.

I received last week the following email from Mark Graban, consultant with LEI and who runs the leanblog.org, sent to him by Mike Wisnefsky.

"Hello Mark,

I'm currently an Industrial Engineering intern at a manufacturing company that pays its workers incentive rates, so the more pieces they make (above the projected 100%) the more money they make.

I was listening to your podcasts (I'm only on #9 right now, working my way through) and I heard a lot of talk about getting employee suggestions and how useful they could be. Currently my company is averaging very few suggestions per employee per year, and I was hoping to increase that. Unfortunately the incentive rate system causes two problems:

    1. Workers are afraid to make suggestions to improve things because significant improvements lead to time studies which lead to changed pay rates.

    2. Taking the time out of their day to make a suggestion either requires sacrificing their lunch break or leaving their work station and taking the pay cut as they end up making fewer pieces.

After talking to my superiors, they've informed me that the workers will not stand for their incentive rate system to be changed (and that's quite a big change for an intern to make/suggest). Is there any way to increase the number of worker suggestions and input into their work systems in a financial system that seems to discourage it?

Thanks,

Mike Wisnefsky"

Yes, Kaizen, at first, might seem to have a negative effect on piecework, but the reality is "If I can make my work easier then I can produce more." If I can reduce defects then I can make more good pieces." Of course, people have to find the time to do their Kaizens and this varies from company to company. At Toyota, the team manager substitutes for the worker on the line, giving the

worker time to do Kaizens. But, at most companies, Kaizens can be done during breaks, before work starts, at the end of the day or even at home. Look, if we ask people to do only one or two Kaizens in a month, they will find time to do them.

Kaizen Does Not Cause Layoffs

Let us say that Kaizen should not cause layoffs. When I brought Iwata and Nakao, two ex-Toyota supplier managers, over from Japan to teach the "Five Days and One Night," workshop now called Kaizen Blitz, we were clearly taught that Kaizen should never result in layoffs. How in the world can you expect people to be involved in improvement activities when the result will be unemployment for them or for some of their fellow employees? It is crazy! But, unfortunately, especially during this economic recession, managers have exploited and denigrated this marvelous tool and laid off people after making improvements. Of course, we have to keep the ship moving; we don't want to ship to sink, and at times when we don't plan carefully and we are not aware of the possibility of recessions, we are forced to make layoffs. We should have envisioned this when we gave so much of our work to China. It was pure short-term thinking.

But, we want to teach people Kaizen and the Kaizen process. When done properly Kaizen will give people more security not less. Kaizen is three key things to me:

1. **Making work easier**
2. **Making work more interesting**
3. **Building skills and capabilities**

When we empower people to make their work easier, more interesting and especially something that allows them to build their skills and capabilities they must end up being more secure. There is an old saying. You can give people food or you can teach them

The Four Fallacies

how to farm. The food very quickly disappears as you eat but as you improve your ability to grow food, you can feed yourself forever.

Toyota has always had a clear focus to operate with "fewer people," but since 1950 they've been able to grow to become the world's largest automobile manufacturer without laying off any fulltime workers. We are now going through an unusual difficult worldwide recession and Toyota has been forced to lay off some of their part-time laborers. Because Toyota continually has planned for the long term over the short-term, they accumulated substantial cash to continue to support their full-time employees. I do hope that it will last into the future and become an example for other companies to learn from.

The per-person workload is continually growing. The amount of work that needs to be done goes on increasing, regardless of the existence of Kaizen. Customers' requirements keep on getting more and more stringent; they never get any easier. And there is competition, too. A company that does not keep on increasing the quantity and improving the quality of its work will soon go out of business. If a company that has been doing a job with ten people goes on doing it with ten people, it is bound to go under eventually, because the world is continually changing. If the company continues to do the job with ten people, it will get left behind. As long as the world keeps on changing, the company will eventually be forced to get the job done with nine people, regardless of whether its employees are doing Kaizen or not. If it does not, it will not survive.

Kaizen doesn't cause restructuring, nor is it the reason for headcount reduction. Kaizen is needed in order to change the existing methods of working in order for the company to be more and more efficient.

In 1979, I started a company called Productivity Inc. I was told that productivity is a wonderful word because it represents that a group of people who are producing more goods and services to share with each other. As a country becomes more productive, it becomes wealthier and has more to share. Productivity means producing more with the same or fewer resources.

We mustn't get it the wrong way round; Kaizen doesn't cause a company to reduce its payroll, but the payroll reductions forced upon the company by outside circumstances do make it necessary for it to practice Kaizen.

At any rate, the amount of work each employee must get done will continue to increase, and we have to cope with the extra work placed upon us. If we don't do Kaizen in these circumstances, our working lives will just get harder and harder.

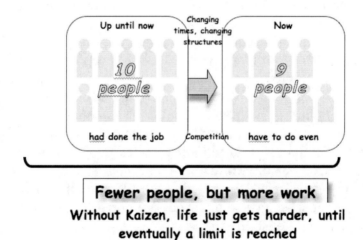

Fig. 91 <Fewer people, but more work.>

No. 2 Kaizen stresses us and takes away our breathing-space

KAIZEN

Use Kaizen to Take the Pressure Off

Some people believe that if we keep on doing Kaizens, we will be left with no room to maneuver, and that we need a little slackness or inefficiency in order to allow us to relax. If we keep on driving out waste through Kaizen, we will end up with a highly pressurized company full of workplaces where everyone is on edge. People who hear this argument find it strangely convincing, and make comments like, "Yes, I see. Doing Kaizen all the time will give us no room to breathe. We need a bit of slack in our work."

But this is a very interesting misunderstanding. In fact, the complete opposite is true. Far from taking the relaxation out of people's lives and work, Kaizen actually puts it in. For proof of this, look at people who are good at Kaizen – they are always working in a quiet, calm, composed way, and they get excellent results. Meanwhile, those who are not good at Kaizen are always rushing around looking stressed out, and the results they achieve fail to match the effort they expend. They keep making the same mistakes over and over and over again.

When you build your skills and capabilities, especially from your own ideas, your work becomes a much more fulfilled experience. Every professional has spent many hours building skills and capabilities. We only want to give the same opportunity to every one of our employees.

Kaizen Releases us from what is Useless

So, why, despite this, do people make the peculiar remark that Kaizen takes away our breathing space? It actually makes work more interesting. Kaizen is about releasing us from doing anything unnecessary. We want to stop doing the unnecessary things so that we can devote all of our time and energy to what is necessary, and give it the careful attention it deserves.

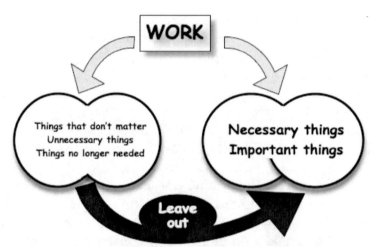

If our time is eaten up by things that don't matter, we cannot pay enough attention to what is essential, we have to do even what is important in a rush, and we have no time to relax.

If we cut out what is unnecessary and focus on what is important, we can do what is important slowly, carefully, thoroughly, and in a relaxed way.

Fig. 92 <Leave out.>

People who don't do Kaizen, and therefore do not release themselves from doing what is unnecessary, work hard at everything indiscriminately. They spend the whole day running around like headless chickens, wearing themselves out doing things that don't matter and that don't make any difference. They are the ones who have no breathing space and no time to relax; and the more time and energy they spend doing unnecessary work, the

less they have for the important stuff. That is why their results don't match the effort they expend.

Kaizen experts, on the other hand, have mastered the art of prioritizing. They put all their energy into what is important and forget about what is not, so they can do their jobs in a relaxed, composed way. In fact, the better someone is at their job, the more calmly they go about it.

It is certainly true that we need a little bit of headroom, a little time to stop and think, in our lives and at work. And that is why we need Kaizen – to relieve us of what is unnecessary and create that breathing space.

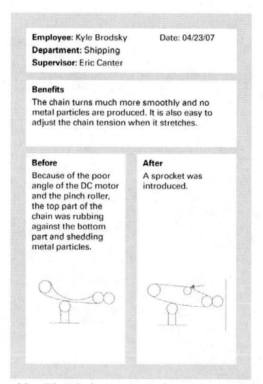

Fig. 93 <The chain turns much more smoothly.>

No. 3 My work is special, so I can't do Kaizen

> KAIZEN

There Are Differences, Yes, but There Are also Similarities

Whenever we talk about other companies' Kaizen programs or examples, somebody almost inevitably says, "Yes, but that's a different type of industry from ours" or, "Yes, but they're much bigger (or smaller) than us." They come up with all sorts of reasons explaining how these examples don't tell them anything and can't help them. Such people seem to believe that they cannot learn anything from anyone else; even when we tell them about examples from companies of the same size and the same industry, they say, "Yes, but their situation is different," "Yes, but their background is different," or "Yes, but that's a different field." All they do is blather on about the differences. It is as if they are confessing their lack of intelligence by saying, "I can only understand examples that fit my own particular circumstances perfectly," and loudly declaring to all and sundry, "I can't apply what you are trying to tell me unless you lead me by the hand and spoon-feed me."

There are an infinite number of differences in the universe, because nothing exists that has every element and every condition exactly the same as something else. But as long as there are differences, there are also similarities. There are many differences between Japanese and Americans, for example – in language, culture and customs. However, we are not one hundred percent different from each other. We are both humans i.e. mammals that walk upright on two legs. We also both use language and both have a culture and customs (albeit different ones). These are things we have in common.

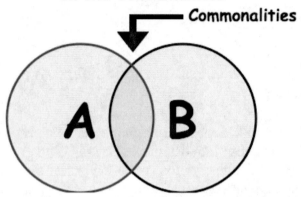

Fig. 94 <We can learn from others if we focus on commonalities.>

The point is that whenever we are able to point out differences, similarities also exist. In fact, it is only because there are similarities that we are able to identify differences.

However, despite the fact that everything is both similar to and different from everything else, some people seem to be incapable of seeing the similarities and do nothing but quibble over the differences. In contrast to this over-reaction, there are also people who focus exclusively on the similarities and forget about the differences. Both are only seeing half of the picture. They are only looking at half of the situation. We have to point out to such people that, "There are differences, yes, but there are also similarities," and "There are similarities, yes, but there also differences."

We can learn from other industries as well as our own if we focus on the similarities; in fact, looking at things from a different perspective can often give us useful hints. It can lead to our changing our ideas and devising original, creative Kaizens.

The Four Fallacies

Probably my most powerful learning experiences have come from my travelling overseas especially from the study missions in Japan. In February 1981, I led my first day mission to Japan.

At the time it was very difficult for me for I did not read or speak Japanese, hardly knew anything about Japanese management, very little about manufacturing. From these visits, year after year, I met some of the most amazing people on the globe and ended up publishing hundreds of books on the Toyota Production System and other advanced Japanese management and manufacturing techniques. These techniques have revolutionized the way goods and services are made in the world.

It is generally said that spotting differences is easy, but that identifying and applying similarities requires the ability to think abstractly.

276 How to Do Kaizen

Employee: Ben Doramian **Date:** 12/11/08
Department: Main Office
Supervisor: Max Bandon

Benefits
I no longer forget to make calls.

Before
I sometimes forgot to return someone's telephone call, or to call someone again later after I had called and they were out.

After
I now stick Post-It notes on the telephone to remind me to make these calls, and take them off when I have made them.

Fig. 95 <I no longer forget to make calls.>

The Four Fallacies

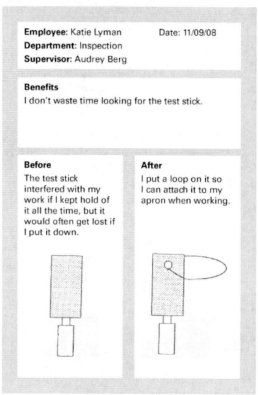

Fig. 96 <I don't waste time looking for the test stick.>

No.4 'Mickey Mouse' Kaizens are embarrassing

KAIZEN

The Best is the Enemy of Kaizen

Everyone knows that 'the best' is what we should be aiming for. If we could achieve it right away, we should go right ahead and do so. But what happens in practice? Isn't it true that various conditions and constraints usually prevent us from doing our best? So, if we took the 'all or nothing' approach and insisted on nothing but the best, we would find it difficult even to begin improving anything.

So, if we insist on nothing but the best, we cannot do any Quick and Easy Kaizens. But 'Quick and Easy' is the lifeblood of Kaizens, and insisting on the best is one of the factors that impede them. This is the reason for saying that the best is the enemy of Kaizen.

When things are explained in this way, someone always objects by saying, "But shouldn't we be aiming for the best in everything? We should 'move forward little by little.' We should set high targets but be very happy that we are always moving in the right direction. It's preposterous to treat 'the best' as our enemy."

This is absolutely right. We should indeed be aiming for the best in everything we do. But 'aiming for' and 'insisting on' (or 'being trapped by') are different. Nevertheless, when we aim for 'the best,' we do tend to get hung up on it and come to think that nothing less will do.

Aim for the Best, but Start with the Better

Because of this, we should make 'Aim for the Best, but start with the Better' a rule of Kaizen. Simply put, we should 'Think Big, but Start Small'. It is true that we should look at the bigger picture, but if that were all we did, we would be no more than a commentator.

Fig. 97 <Aim for the best but start with better.>

What commentators say is certainly correct, as far as it goes. But we rarely hear much about anything they themselves have actually done. They have a wonderfully broad perspective and can certainly see the big picture, but they haven't even made the smallest start on actually doing anything. Of course, their job is to talk about the big picture; that's how they make their money, and there's nothing wrong with that. But businesses don't need commentators; they need people who can get things done. Sitting around commentating won't put a penny on the bottom line.

The Four Fallacies

Whenever I teach a class, I seem to attract someone who wants to play 'devils advocate." Put simple, "nothing is perfect on this earth." You can always find something to criticize. But instead of looking something negative to prevent us from changing we should be always striving to be better. Frankly, I don't want to get involved with the devil no matter what he looks like.

To get rid of the 'commentator employees' from companies, it is recommended that words and phrases like 'for the time being' and 'at least' be introduced. Kaizens always start with doing something 'for now'. Rather than planning all the steps up front, a Kaizen journey starts with a single step, which leads on to the next, and then the next. At any rate, the watchword in companies with strong Kaizen programs is, "Rather than sitting around discussing it, let's give it a go and see what happens. If we try it, we'll find out whether it works; if we don't, we won't learn anything."

Chapter XVI

Simple Kaizen Case Studies

A Collection of Case Studies that 'Tell It Like It Is'

Simple Examples Lead to Sustained Expansion of the Kaizen Program

Any company doing Kaizen is advised to put together a collection of its own simple, practical, easy-to-understand examples to create a set of case-study training materials directly related to its everyday work.

Collect Case Studies Promptly

Strangely enough, it is those companies with the least dynamic Kaizen programs who seem to want to compile polished, impressive-looking case-study collections. This causes them to end up feeling weighed down by responsibility and renders them incapable of assessing situations swiftly, taking rapid decisions and acting promptly. They keep on repeating, "I'll get around to it very soon, I'll get around to it very soon," but nothing ever gets done.

On the other hand, companies with vibrant Kaizen programs take the words 'rapidly,' and 'here and now' as their watchwords. This means that, as soon as they see an interesting Kaizen, out come the scissors and glue, the materials are snipped out and stuck to a sheet of backing paper, the whole thing is copied, and the job's done. A case study really can be put together on the spot, right then and there, with scissors and glue. Since this takes no time at all, any number of them can be prepared, and they can be continually fed back and shared.

This piques the employees' interest and shows them the kind of thing that needs to be done, so they come up with another Kaizen.

This in turn becomes the material for the next case study, and one Kaizen breeds another until the whole program takes off.

People should introduce simple case studies. When they see them, people who don't know what Kaizen is all about may think, "There's nothing new about this sort of thing," "What, is that all there is to it?" and "It's obvious, isn't it?"

People probably balk at simple Kaizen examples because they don't want employees to stay at this level forever, and they hope that they will try doing some more sophisticated ones. But looking at things this way is no less than refusing to face reality. If a company is only producing low-level Kaizens, it indicates that it must have been working in a pretty unsophisticated way before the Kaizens were done. The people in charge are probably reluctant to make this apparent to their superiors, and would prefer to report on excellent Kaizens delivering big results. Unfortunately, however, this divorces the Kaizen program from reality, because only reporting the best Kaizens, done by a select few, obscures what is really going on in the workplace.

Companies that progress their work improvement programs slowly but steadily know that the first step in Kaizen is facing the facts. Using collections of low-level Kaizens at the stage where these are the only ones being done is a way of getting everyone to recognize the low level at which the company had been working until then. Then, asking everyone to do Kaizens and reassuring them that there is no need for them to be any more sophisticated than the simple ones in the case-study collection will motivate them little

Fig. 98 <Reading and understanding case studies.>

by little to start tackling similar deficiencies in their own ways of working. In contrast, companies that eschew Kaizens of this sort find that not even simple Kaizens get done, let alone the sophisticated ones they have been asking for, and so the simple problems remain unsolved and keep on repeating themselves.

Use Simple Examples to Face the Facts

Although some people may describe their colleagues' Kaizens as 'obvious' or ask whether that is all there is to them, the level of the

Kaizens themselves will vary from company to company. Of course, there won't be much difference in the level of thinking that goes on inside people's heads, because the level regarded as 'common sense' by most adult members of society is more or less the same. But there are big differences in the actual level achieved, i.e. the level of implementation, from company to company. This is what sets one company apart from another.

If we look at what actually happens, we see that top-drawer companies are companies where the obvious is done as a matter of course. This is thanks in part to everyone facing the facts by sharing case studies

Highlight the Key Points

One thing you must be sure to do when making simple Kaizen examples is to highlight the key points noticed and the key ideas behind the Kaizens. Of course, people who understand Kaizen can look at simple examples, recognize their value, and the thinking behind them, as well as their standard formula, principles and rules. But most companies are not fortunate enough to have a workforce who all possesses this level of understanding. Organizations contain quite a high proportion of people "just doing their job" mixed up with those who are switched on. Those who don't understand tend to make fun of simple Kaizens, saying things like, "What, is that all?" and "Is that all there is to it?"

Each day the manager should be out talking to her/his employees about their implemented ideas and encouraging them to identify new problems and come up with new solutions. When the manager reviews her/his employee's ideas a whole new dynamic takes place. First, the manager sees a new depth of talent within the worker.

Most workers come to work and do their repetitive job over and over again with very little opportunity to solve problems. Now the manager is asking and empowering workers to participate - to use their brains and what will flow out of the worker will be truly amazing: Claudia was a packer at Technicolor. Her job was to pack the DVD videos to go to Disney, Blockbuster, Netflix, and others. Bending to rip pieces of the bubble wrap was a potential strain on her back.

Fig. 99 <Packing the videos.>

Her improvement idea was take a bar of metal and bend it to hang up the bubble wrap. It was a great idea to prevent her from bending over. She took her idea to maintenance and asked them to help her make the bar. Imagine how Claudia felt when she came up with this idea? The company avoids future workmen's compensation claims and Claudia feels wonderful participating.

Simple Kaizen Case Studies   289

Fig. 100 <Hanging up the bubble rack on a stand.>

Along comes Ken, looks at Claudia's idea and says, "Why can't we eliminate the bubble wrap and just use inexpensive wrapping paper?" Their customers agreed and Claudia's and Ken's ideas saves Technicolor $105,000 per year; wrapping paper is much cheaper then bubble wrap. They also saved on shelf space.

Fig. 101 <Replace the bubble wrap with plain wrapping paper.>

The examples were very small ideas but the results were great for the employees and the company.

Fig. 102 <Bubble wrap shelves are now empty.>

The aim of sharing Kaizens is to get people who don't understand Kaizen to understand it. This is the Kaizen promotion staff's job, so they should not be scaring people off with big and impressive but unrepresentative Kaizens. They should be thinking about how to get people to appreciate the value of simple ones. To do this, they should introduce examples and also append key words and phrases summing up the Kaizens' established formula, principles and rules. Doing this can give everyone some insight into the Kaizen essence underpinning every specific example.

All this applies not just to Kaizen case-study compendia but also to internal Kaizen presentations.

Of course, whenever these simple Kaizens are presented, some brief comments should be made emphasizing their importance and pointing out what the audience should take note of. But, when making comments, don't try to get away with meaningless, cringe-making flattery; all that will do is lose you credibility with the Kaizen promotion staff and senior management. Just as managers' leadership ability is revealed by the comments they make about Kaizen itself; their comments on Kaizen presentations reveal their attitude toward the implementation of the Kaizen program.

Simple Kaizen Case Studies 291

You hear often the word 'innovation.' We have to be more innovative to survive. Of course, you do but you don't know where the next great idea might come from.

Simply teach all employees to look around and look for opportunities to be innovative. Think about the simple pencil.

In essence evolution never stops. Things can always be improved. Just look at the evolution of the writing instrument in my lifetime: At grammar school, I was given a number 2 pencil, which, I would easily break, had to continuously sharpen and, of course, I would always chew on the eraser.

Fig. 103 <A pencil.>

Fig. 104 < Remember the old pencil sharpener?>

Later on I had to buy a pen and ink well. My hands were always inked marked. I thought the ink would penetrate my skin and poison me.

Fig. 105 <Pen and ink.>

Just after World War II the ballpoint pen was created.

Fig. 106 <A ballpoint pen.>

On my last trip to Japan I found a clip-on Zebra pen and pencil set. There are four different colored inks, a retractable pencil, it clips onto my shirt pocket and doesn't leak.

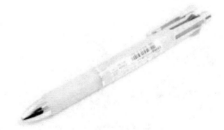

Fig. 107 <Zebra pen with 4 colors and a pencil.>

The old path to innovation looked for the big ideas, the evolution that excites customers, but today there is also a new path to innovation, getting all employees to use their brains and solve problems.

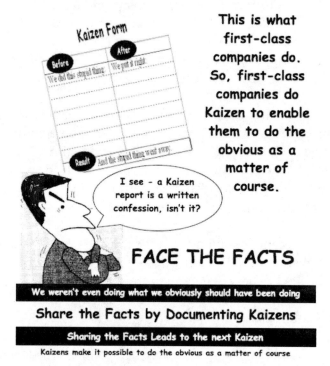

Fig. 108 <Kaizen is about doing the obvious as a matter of course.>

Think We now Know that Top Down Doesn't Always Work.

Toyota and other Japanese companies implemented, in addition, not in substitution to a Top Down, but a Bottom Up system whereby the person closest to the customer and the actual problem could make the decision.

Kaoru Ishikawa invented the concept of Quality Control Circles (QCC), whereby the worker in small teams, were challenged to tackle problems around their work area. The workers were taught quality tools that in the past were in the hands of the Quality Control Manager: pareto diagram, scatter diagram, control charts, check sheets, brainstorming, cause and effect diagram, histogram,

and stratification. These quality teams would normally challenge large problems that affected quality in their work area. A team might work on only two or three problems a year and normally they worked on the problem during their breaks or after hours, rarely were they paid overtime to work on these problems.

One day, I was invited to Tokyo Juki's annual Quality Control Circle program where QCC teams presented their findings to top management. I was sitting next to the president. After a presentation by one team, a worker asked the president to give them feedback. The president rose and said "I am very proud of you; your presentation was excellent."

The worker on the stage looked at the president and said, "What we really want is feedback on what we can do to improve." I was a little shocked to hear that coming from a worker. But, isn't it wonderful that the worker was confident enough to look for criticism not praise?

Toyota and other Japanese companies implemented a Bottom Up system, whereby the person closest to the customer and the actual problem could make decisions.

Yes, we want to empower the worker closest to the customer, closest to the job to be part of the decision making process. Letting them identify problems and implement them on their own is the most powerful way I know of getting continuous improvement.

Top Management in Japan Leads the Suggestion System in 48.2% of the Companies Involved.

To express the importance of having everyone involved in problem solving activities, the senior person of many companies in Japan leads the effort. They will frequently look at the scorecard to see how many ideas were submitted and implemented. They will meet

with the suggestion committees to be kept up to date on the latest ideas. They will go out and talk to as many of their employees as they can and see their Kaizens.

"As with any fire, if you don't feed it the light will go out." Keeping people involved with their creative ideas has been one of the keys to Toyota's success.

Twenty Expressions to Avoid (from the Book 40 Years, 20 Million Ideas - The Toyota Suggestion System)

1. Everyone understands that!
2. We've never done that before, there's no point in trying it.
3. I tried to do that before, and I know it won't work.
4. This isn't up-to-date enough.
5. Is this within the budget?
6. There are just too many plans being made - I'll take a look at your opinion when I have time.
7. Let's talk about this some other time.
8. Let's wait a while and see how things turn out.
9. Why do you want to change? Aren't things going okay now?
10. There is a rule on this, so it's no good doing it that way.
11. I don't think that's technically feasible.
12. This idea is really off the wall, the manager will never agree to it.
13. That's just not done at this company!
14. That might work somewhere else, but certainly not here!
15. The real world is more complicated than that.
16. You don't really understand the situation, do you?
17. Your suggestion is good, but the company can't afford it.
18. This will create problems later on.
19. Even if I give you advice, there's still no way.
20. What is this suggestion? Can't you make it a little better?

Chapter XVII

SUMMARY

I recommend you look around at work and see the current reality and begin to see what is possible in the future for every worker and yourself. Can you make wonderful products and deliver wonderful services to your customers and also create a wonderful place for people to work to be challenged and fulfilled? Ask yourself, "Would I want my children to do the work I see others around me doing?" Or would you want something better for them and for yourself?

I reiterate; if the work is needed then it is good work, but I should have the right to grow and continuously improve what I do. Every day should be filled with learning and opportunities to improve. Your company should become an extension of the school system where learning continues everyday.

Each person has unlimited creative potential to make their work easier, more interesting and to build their skills and capabilities. This is what Kaizen is all about, a very simple process that allows people to feel empowered to fully participate as human beings and to solve the myriad of problems that occur almost every day on the job.

And now it is up to you. Virtually everyone is attempting to be Lean and very few are able to do it properly. Most are missing the people side of Lean, getting all employees involved in improvement activities. Within this book you now have the information, the tools and techniques, to develop a great Kaizen program.

On my second study mission to Japan in November 1981, I found a copy of Dr. Shigeo Shingo's book A *Study of the Toyota Production System from an Industrial Engineering Viewpoint.* I gave a copy to Jack Warne, VP at Omark Industries. Jack bought 500 copies and asked every manager and engineer at Omark to read, in study groups, one chapter at a time. Within a year Omark became the best JIT Company in America. Consider reading this book in study groups, one chapter at a time, and just

SUMMARY

asking each team, "How can we apply Kaizen in our company?" Then sit back and watch the magic happen.

At the last Lean Accounting Summit, I asked the audience, "Did you like my talk about Kaizen?" I received a loud yes. I even asked them all to stand up and make a pledge that they were going to go back and do it. They all gave the pledge.

Will they do it? I hope so. What stands in the way? Whatever stands in the way of change can be overcome with your determination.

Quick and Easy Kaizen is a new path to innovation that empowers everyone to become a problem solver. Yes, we do focus on small ideas when implementing Kaizen but the new great innovative idea might come from one of your engineers or it might come from anyone in the organization. Allow this new process to flow for you.

Now you have wonderful tools to work with to get rid of the fear of making a mistake. Use the mistake board and start immediately your own Quick and Easy Kaizen process. It works! It works very well!

I wish you all well. Please keep me posted on your success.

Just ask people:

1. To look around their work area for opportunities to change for the better and to write up, at least, two improvement ideas to make their work easier, more interesting and to build their skills and capabilities.
2. To make improvement suggestions when problems are found or when new things arise.
3. To write up their improvement ideas on the Kaizen form.

4. To submit this new idea to the supervisor and to their work team.
5. To implement their idea by themselves, with their team members, or with the support of others in the company.
6. To take a picture before the improvement is made.
7. To take a picture after the new idea is implemented.
8. To have the idea displayed for other members to see and to copy for themselves.
9. To have their improvement idea counted and added to the "scorecard" – the statistics of the organization."
10. To talk to other workers about their problems and their ideas to solve those problems.

As Dr. Shigeo Shingo would always say, "Do it!"

Do it!

Do it!

Do it!

Do it!

Do it!

Do it!

Interview with Tom Hartman

Senior Director Lean Consulting, Autoliv Americas

Tom Hartman

BODEK: Autoliv recently won the Shingo Prize for Manufacturing Excellence. I am most interested in learning how Autoliv has applied the Lean concepts throughout the organization especially in the developing your human resources. You have probably the best suggestion system in America; I call this Quick and Easy Kaizen. Thank you for doing this.

How did you get started?

HARTMAN: Note: the point of perspective for the following story is for the Autoliv Brigham City inflator facility. This facility had the most thorough records and was therefore used for purposes of following the progress since 1998.

Since we have been a major Toyota supplier of airbags and seat belts, Toyota assigned Takashi Harada, a seasoned TPS instructor, to work with us from 1998 to 2000. The true beginning of our new suggestion program was established toward the end of Harada's three years as our mentor.

In the beginning, Harada-san taught us the principles of the Toyota Production System (TPS). Then he transitioned to some of the key techniques. In '99, he started to transition to the culture of the Toyota Production System, which embodied Kaizen.

In 1999, we created the suggestion or Kaizen program. Workers used a Kaizen form to write down their observations and recommended solutions. We assigned points to each suggestion based on its perceived value. We tried to prioritize them based on relative importance to the company and/or the customer. In those days, our maintenance and engineering people, who in most cases were actually making the changes as suggested in the Kaizens, were almost totally reactive. We had major operational availability issues (uptime), and therefore our maintenance people were more or less working full time to keep the equipment running to deliver the products needed on a daily basis.

In 1999, we had 3,290 suggestions submitted, but only 493 of them were implemented. Admittedly not all of the suggestions were worthy of being implemented, but due to the strain on our support personnel, we were not in a position to implement even all of the best of them. We had about 1,500 people working at this plant and we were experiencing a period of aggressive growth, which was always challenging to say the least.

We had not yet started training our workers deeply in Kaizen. We were attempting to train our associates and first-line supervision, but our methods were weak. We were primarily focused on training our management, but had little success at the worksite. Management's effort was to learn and introduce TPS simultaneously. It was a very difficult period.

In 2000 and 2001, we focused on "submitted" suggestions, trying to prime the pump, so to speak, with these suggestions. We awarded, a "jet ski," and an all-terrain vehicle. The idea was to create and sustain excitement regarding the Kaizen process.

BODEK: You used themes to stimulate new ideas?

HARTMAN: In 2000, we emphasized lead-time reduction. We wanted to get back to the people in a more timely manner so that they would be directly engaged in the suggestion process on a daily basis. We struggled, because we were still scratching our way up the learning curve regarding equipment reliability, standardizing our machine build, designing for manufacturability, and people development. We wanted to link the Kaizen process to all of these key areas, but the more reactive we were (putting out fires), the less we could focus on the proactive side, which included the ideas of our people.

In 2001, we wanted to raise the excitement level of Kaizen by introducing a "fun month" and special Kaizen nominations (for special recognition). We started to recognize individuals for their contributions and give substantial rewards reflective of the total savings from the Kaizen.
At the same time, we implemented a three-working-day response to their improvement ideas. Again, we struggled to accomplish our goal. In 2001, we submitted about 6,100 suggestions and implemented 3,200. We were trying to generate excitement through both fun-based activities and also monetary rewards. Some of these rewards were a significant amount of money! It was still

frustrating, because we could not implement them fast enough. In effect, we were attempting to retain the excitement despite our troubles with the implementation process. We felt very strongly that we had to maintain the momentum we had worked so hard to achieve. The task of determining the actual savings associated with each Kaizen caused both a backlog with accounting and negative feelings among the team members. The distinction between "tangible cost savings" versus "cost avoidance" was an emotionally charged issue. This was a period of selfishness with competition for individual Kaizens, while sharing ideas and working together, as a team was foreign to this model.

In 2002, we made changes to the system again to focus on reducing stagnation by shifting our emphasis from "submitted Kaizens" to "implemented Kaizens," since that was the goal all along. The results for 2002 showed that we had 11,000 submitted and 6,900 implemented. This represented about five ideas implemented per person.

We had shown quite an improvement when compared with two per person implemented in the previous year. We were making real progress! We also simplified rewarding employees with a fixed payout of nominal value regardless of the cost savings for an implemented Kaizen. This reduced the implementation time of each Kaizen substantially.

In 2003, our target was to implement six Kaizens per person. We redesigned the system so that it was more consistent and we refocused our management to be able to implement the employees' ideas more quickly. We developed a Kaizen Database, where employees could enter their ideas via a computer. Management could approve or deny Kaizens from their office. We thought it was great because it made it easy to evaluate and approve Kaizens, which decreased our time of implementation. The downside was it took away the day-to-day interaction and communication of management interfacing with the associates. It was very impersonal. Our management team would spend a good deal of

their day in the office responding to suggestions. This violated the concept of building a "trusty team" (as taught by Harada-san) where management and the workforce are constantly interacting, teaching and improving through Kaizen.

BODEK: This is radically different from my past understanding. I had been taught that the worker who comes up with the idea implements their own idea, but you are saying that it is also management's responsibility to see that the ideas are implemented - that management not only supports the workers but could assign others to help the worker implement their idea.

When we think more clearly about this a very powerful dichotomy takes place. The worker produces the product. The worker producing the product brings the sales dollars to the company, not management. It is obvious that management's role is to support the worker not the reverse. And since the worker does their job over and over again, they should have a great depth of knowledge on how to produce the product faster, at lower costs and at higher quality; that knowledge was rarely tapped into in the past. But, for some strange reason, your management has been willing to support and serve workers fully.

HARTMAN: At this time, in 2003, our maintenance processes were substantially more robust, equipment runs properly when needed, than in prior years. Therefore, our maintenance and process support technical people now had more time available to help the workers implement their ideas. Our equipment was becoming more standardized, despite the ongoing challenge of more successfully designing the products for manufacturability.

Regarding our Kaizen results for that year: we had almost 17,000 submitted and about 11,000 implemented. We were succeeding in closing the gap between the two.

Another tremendous advantage that we now enjoyed was that our associates were being trained every month on a new topic. (See APS Strength Areas chart) This practice began back in 2001, but strengthened significantly each successive year. By 2003, our people were truly catching the "spirit of Kaizen." They now understood how the suggestion process was vital to the success of our business (and their own job security). The impact of their suggestions on our business performance reflected that growing understanding.

In late 2002 and early 2003, we first began using the "hoshin kanri" or policy deployment process. By making our goals and our performance more dramatically visual to all workers, we helped to focus their suggestions. Because our people now understood the needs of the business it enabled them to add more value and validated the importance of their individual responsibility for meeting our common goals.

In 2004, all of our mature facilities adopted a common Kaizen process. We also reduced our payout for suggestions to a smaller amount. We feared that this change might dampen the enthusiasm, but we were pleasantly surprised that it did not! The annual numbers showed 24,000 submitted and almost 16,000 implemented.

BODEK: Is that one plant, or company-wide?

HARTMAN: These numbers are again reflective of a single facility, our Brigham City inflator facility. We saw similar results in other facilities however. Our maintenance process was becoming increasingly more robust and therefore our equipment was more reliable. Our management was adopting more of a "facilitator/training" role, whereas in the past, management had acted in more of a "directive" role.

Management was now spending progressively more of its time helping the workers to implement their ideas. The effect was

illustrated by our ability to sustain the implementation rate of Kaizens.

In 2005, we changed the focus from individuals to teams. The concept was to go away from a process based on individual Kaizens to one that rewarded each team as they met their team goal. This was accomplished by rolling employee Kaizen expectations into our policy deployment process. Our goal was to help our people grow and learn from interacting with one another. This required our teams, consisting of five to ten people, to be more capable of self-management, thereby putting more responsibility on them to achieve their goals. The associates began to understand the power of everyone working together to benefit the company so that we could continually exist as a company, thereby providing ongoing job security for the entire team. While this sounds like a lofty concept from a textbook on Organizational Management, this is exactly how we evolved.

In that year, we saw submitted Kaizens drop a little to 19,000 and the implemented Kaizens were more or less flat at about 15,000. The transition to a "team-based" approach hurt the numbers, but not the impact.

Regarding 2005, I overlooked an important point; we made a concerted effort to get each and every person involved. Prior to that, we had created Kaizen "supermen or superwomen" who were "Kaizen machines," but we also found that certain people were holding back. By shifting to a team-based focus, our goal was to get everyone "off the bench and into the game." This team focus has continued since that time.

In 2006, we submitted 23,000 Kaizens while implementing 18,000. At this point, we were implementing about eight per person. We eliminated the Kaizen database and adopted a simple Kaizen card at this time. The benefits were many: the visual status of each Kaizen at the cell, the ability to easily escalate a slow Kaizen implementation, an increased emphasis on management and

technical support interaction at the cell and finally, the elimination of countless hours spent updating the database.

In 2007, we adopted a common Kaizen standard company-wide. We standardized our Kaizen methods across the entire corporation. The process was simplified and made more visual, with a very strong focus on team performance. (See Suggestion Form Flow slide)

In 2007, we submitted 43,000 suggestions and implemented 41,000, almost one to one. We saw a huge jump in suggestions implemented per employee as we achieved about 25 per person.

In 2008, we continued the focus on shortening the lead-time and emphasizing team recognition. While our implementation rate rose from 25 to 34, the total number actually went down in 2008 because we had fewer people due to a drastic drop in volume due to a drastic downturn in the economy.

I would like to shift the emphasis to additional drivers of this improvement, which were developing in parallel with the growth of the Kaizen suggestion system.

BODEK: With the team efforts, the teams supported each other.

HARTMAN: Whereas in the beginning the focus was more on the individual, we realized that only by emphasizing teams could we engage everyone. Only when we shifted to a team-focused process, were we able to sustain the excitement.

As we transitioned to team management some of our people found themselves in the position of being outsiders because they didn't want to be involved and they didn't feel comfortable. This situation was resolved by them either adapting to become more comfortable or leaving voluntarily. We didn't let any employees go because they refused to work with the team. It just happened naturally.

BODEK: Tell me a little bit more about the teams.

HARTMAN: Well, the teams were organized by manufacturing line. Please note that all of the figures and examples are operations-based.

The team I'm talking about at this point is the manufacturing line itself. So it would be a team of five to ten people, with one of the team members being the team leader.

BODEK: Right.

HARTMAN: This leader was a working leader. All the teams had common goals categorically in the areas of Quality, Cost (Productivity), Delivery, Safety and Morale. We posted the team's performance prominently at the worksite and measured the performance as a team. With all measurables in common, the team then would be in a position where it would succeed or fail as a team - not as individuals.

Management was diligent in performing its daily follow-up. Management at the "group leader" level, which is the next level up from the "team leader," would have anywhere from eight to twenty lines. When the "group leader" would perform his or her daily management audits reviewing performance at the worksite itself, he/she would use the abnormal conditions that were found as "teaching opportunities." By teaching the team, the manager would achieve a key goal: to raise the skill and ability of each team.

This is one of the distinguishing characteristics that are critically important for understanding our culture and I therefore want to cover that topic in detail.

Because success was achieved through a combined effort, individual members soon developed a strong team identity. This resulted in the recognition of a common responsibility to perform

that was felt by each member of the team. No one was ever intentionally singled out.
Every day, there was a team meeting at the beginning of the shift.

BODEK: For how long?

HARTMAN: Not very long. Ten minutes. If there were a major project, we would organize an APS workshop (Autoliv Production System Workshop). That's our equivalent to a "Kaizen Event." These workshops by definition are management-directed. Only in this case do the workers receive any significant amount of time to be able to be involved in any concentrated manner, where they might be in a meeting for an hour focusing on that Kaizen.

Except for the workshops, their Kaizen input is daily interaction during the work time, on their breaks and lunches, and also in a one-hour monthly team meeting called an Action Plan Review.

During this hour, they are taught APS topics on a revolving basis. The instructor (the production manager) uses standard training modules from our APS University.

The people develop their Kaizens communicating with one another while they're working, during daily meetings at the beginning and the end of the shift and while they are cleaning up at the end of the shift. As you can see there just isn't a lot of time allocated for these Kaizens. No matter whether the implementation of the Kaizen is performed by the maintenance or process engineering organization, the workers are directing the management and the support groups as to how to improve the operations.

What has transpired here is that the workers are now directing the implementation of their ideas as management consistently honors their knowledge at the work site by actually implementing those ideas? **The workers are directing the improvement and management is transitioned into a support role.** These improvements occur between the shifts or during the third shift, if

there isn't a three-shift operation. If there is a three shift operation, the Kaizens are implemented over the weekend, again most often by maintenance and engineering.

BODEK: What percentage of the ideas was implemented by the workers who identified the problem and came up with the solution?

HARTMAN: It's hard to give you an exact number, but, as we matured, the implementation of the ideas would be directed by the workers and implemented by management. In the beginning, most of the implemented Kaizens were initiated by management and then implemented by the support group.

The involvement of people in the implementation does increase progressively. In the beginning, we burned through a lot of what I will call the "creature comfort" kind of Kaizens. "This would be easier for me if we did that." Those were easy and immediate.

We transitioned very rapidly to, "I could be more efficient if we did this." "I could build higher quality if we did that." "We could have more reliability on the equipment if we did the other."

Regarding equipment improvement, in the 2004, 2005, 2006 time frame, we started learning TPM. Once learned, TPM radically improved the ability of the worker to add value.

In the latter part of that time frame, when we had TPM events, they were like APS workshops; we would shut the line down for as much as three or four hours at a time to do nothing but TPM. All of the workers were involved throughout the period. A lot of the robust improvements came during the TPM workshops.

We also had quality workshops; we would shut the line down for an hour or two at a time and the whole team would implement these Kaizens.

So again, there is a dichotomy going on here. Workshops were conducted where the line was stopped. If there was a shut down, the team was more likely to be involved as a group. When we speak of the Kaizens, which were more or less bubbling up autonomously, they were more likely to be directed by the workers, implemented almost solely by the management and the support groups. You would have a member of the team directing management regarding the execution of the Kaizen. You might have five people implementing it, four of them being maintenance, management and engineering, one of them being the leader, commonly being the working team lead.

So you had this reversal of roles where in the Kaizen you had the workers directing management on how to implement the Kaizen, at the Kaizen site. On the other hand regarding APS workshops or "Kaizen events," it is more the opposite, where management leads the team.

But as we enabled the team to add more value through our management style, the teams were able to add more value.

Now, the other major development during the period of 2005 - 2007 was that the worksite became radically more visual. It is not that we weren't emphasizing transparency and visual management at the worksite prior to that time, but it was strongly emphasized in an unprecedented manner during this period. Also, at this time the performance of the entire North American organization became much more transparent. As this occurred the value of the Kaizens radically improved. Logically we would expect this to happen.
his is when the Kaizen "implementation" and "submission" numbers became more and more similar. They began to approach 100%, because the people now truly understood the critical needs of the organization for the very first time. As they became more knowledgeable, their Kaizens became more directly aligned with the goals of the organization. This was also the time frame when policy deployment, or hoshin kanri, really kicked in. (Hoshin Kanri, or policy deployment, was mentioned above)

At this time, management began to do a much better job of conveying the needs of the organization in a more transparent manner. They understood in an unprecedented way, how to add value to effectively meet the needs of the organization.

Now one other thing, throughout the entire period, we had an active "gain sharing program" where the people could earn a bonus as a portion of their salary. It was very frustrating to them prior to this time, since they were incentivized to be able to help the organization meet its goals, but they didn't really know how to accomplish this.

As you recall, '05 was also when we shifted to the team focus. So you had all this happening concurrently. From this point onward, we had people who were incentivized and enabled through visual management to add more value. Not so surprisingly, from this time forward, the value of their Kaizens were more directly aligned to the organization and the results of the organization reflected that fact.

In addition to that, since 2000 we have been training our people in the culture of APS on a daily, weekly and monthly basis. Standardized management is taught on a daily and weekly basis as management audits occur identifying abnormal conditions. On a daily and weekly basis we also have our team meetings where key issues are taught and reinforced. On a monthly basis we present our monthly APS topic such as 5S, heijunja or any one of the structural building blocks of our APS house. In addition, we teach all of the topics represented by the pillars (of the APS House) such as "just in time," "quality first" and "employee involvement" based on key needs of the organization at that specific time.

As the workers become more knowledgeable, they become better prepared to participate in the Kaizen process. At the same time, our support groups are focused on a proactive rather than reactive management orientation.

BODEK: Instead of putting out fires, you were now focusing on how to better support the workers to prevent those fires from occurring, being proactive.

HARTMAN: Beginning in 2007, over half of our maintenance time was proactive. All of these resources were then engaged in improving our current position in the marketplace on a continuous basis rather than just maintaining our position. This is a critical difference between companies that will continue to thrive regardless of market conditions and those that will become casualties.

BODEK: You turned the management pyramid upside down.

HARTMAN: Sure, we then had more of our support assets available to be deployed to the worksite to support the workers at the worksite itself.

As we engaged a progressively higher proportion of the organization in continuous improvement, our performance began to increase exponentially.

In 2006, we implemented a plant-based Autonomous Manufacturing Organization (AMO). The chair of the AMO was the plant manager. On his staff there was a technical support/maintenance manager, a finance manager, multiple AMC managers, an APS manager, a quality manager and a human resources manager.
The Autonomous Manufacturing Center manager (AMC) had responsibility for 30 to 50 manufacturing lines. The AMCs were managing with key support personnel either directly or indirectly reporting to them including the following: quality supervisor, technical support supervisor and production control supervisor.

Reporting to the AMCs were the "AMGs" or Autonomous Manufacturing Groups. We talked about these groups previously. On the AMG leader's staff were the following: quality engineer,

process engineer, maintenance technician and APS technician. AMG leaders had 15 to 20 lines within their areas of responsibility.

Reporting to the AMG leaders were multiple Autonomous Manufacturing Teams. The AMT's were the working team leaders for the individual manufacturing lines and coordinated the activities of the line associates.

By virtue of this organizational structure we redirected the management's attention toward the worksite.

This is also the period when we implemented manager-standardized work. This helped us accomplish multiple objectives, the **first** being to force management to address issues one on one, personally, with the team.

A **second reason** for implementing manager standardized work was to get managers/supervisors out of their offices and onto the floor. Many of the AMG and AMC offices were relocated to the floor.

The **third reason** was to facilitate management being personally involved in solving problems at their systemic roots, with systemically effective solutions. This had been emphasized previously but never to this degree. This also increased our ability to support Kaizen at deeper levels of problem solving, working together as a plant to meet our short, medium and long-term goals and objectives.

The **fourth and final reason** for manager standardized work was that of building team member trust. This was accomplished through direct manager interaction with the workers and their teams.

In the case of maintenance downtime, we began implementing standard management protocols in about 2000. In 2006, we

coupled this with our standard work for managers within the AMO organizational scheme. For example, if we were down for 15 minutes the AMG maintenance support leader was notified. At 30 minutes, it escalated to the AMG leader, at 60 minutes to the AMC leader, and at 120 minutes to the plant manager. We actually developed software with its own notification protocol, where all appropriate leadership would receive pages around the clock in order to be able to provide the proper guidance and support as required.

Also in 2006 we began using standard management protocols in non-maintenance applications. One example was the heijunka process, if the number of cards stacked up beyond the "green zone," there was an automatic requirement for the AMT to call the AMG notifying him of the "yellow zone" status. If the situation progressed to the "red zone," the AMC leader was notified.

We did all this to strengthen our standards at the worksite and to ensure that management interacted with the process at the worksite on a timely basis. As all of this happened, the workers became more trusting of management because they saw management's actions as proof of their high level of commitment to the daily achievement of performance goals.

Now as you can appreciate, all of these improvements have been feeding the worksite to make it stronger. As you look deeper into the organization you find that those organizations that are logically separated from the worksite such as product design engineering become more intimately involved and answerable to the worksite. This is also true of the other support groups such as finance and procurement.

BODEK: It's wonderful.

HARTMAN: I've tried to organize this to demonstrate the rippling effect of support, almost like throwing a rock into a pond, and how

everybody focused progressively more on the worksite over time, enabling the workers to add more value.

One of the very first things to happen on our journey, actually preceding Mr. Harada, was that we reoriented the organization. Instead of operations being "one" of the missions of the organization, it became the center of the universe around which everything else revolved.

As the ability of the organization to support the worksite increased, the workers benefitted greatly.

Starting in 2005, we began transforming middle managers, which were no longer needed to manage processes now being managed by the workers, into launch managers/engineers overseeing the design and fabrication of our own equipment. We also redeployed them into our product development organization to develop products that were more manufacturing friendly. We also trained them as APS facilitators who then were members of the AMG team working full-time teaching and implementing new ideas at the worksite. A great example of our success in this area is related to "new program launch." In 2000, poor launches cost us as much as $1 million a month in premium freight (during the peak launch period). Today we spend a fraction of that amount on an annual basis.

We redeployed those middle managers so, (A) they wouldn't be an obstruction to the workers and, (B) so they could strengthen the worksite by adding value using their many years of experience with our people and our products.

BODEK: It's an amazing story. Managers have taken on an entirely new role. They no longer are the controllers, telling people what to do, but now are there to train and support the workers who have added much responsibility to monitoring the workplace.

HARTMAN: Every day in the managers' standardized work, they were at the worksite, auditing associate standardized work, 5S condition, quality performance or any of the other missions of the worksite. As the worksite progressively became more visual, the manager's role on a daily basis became to identify abnormal conditions. Each of these findings became an opportunity to raise the skill and ability of the team regarding its ability to systemically resolve the root cause of those abnormal conditions.

Managers became more adept at every level of asking "the five whys," of teaching the workers. All of our leaders are teachers. Within Autoliv, if you cannot teach, you cannot lead. Therefore, when an abnormal condition is found, a leader takes the responsibility to teach the team.

For example: a leader might say: "Okay, we have this issue today. Now, I want to make sure everyone understands." He or she will shut down the line right there so everyone on the team understands the issue and has a chance to give input on the resolution. That's very much in the spirit of our Jidoka ("stop and fix") process in our Kaizen culture.

Every time a worker shuts down the line for a quality issue, we call that a Jidoka event. We highlight the best of these examples, by taking the picture of the person or team and we display the picture on the wall near the lunchroom for all to see. We explain what they did and we thank them publicly for their actions. In Mexico, it was not as culturally natural for workers to feel confident in stopping the line. To add extra emphasis, we had a "Jidoka breakfast," where the workers would explain to management why they stopped the line and where they then could be applauded for doing so.

We reinforce using abnormal conditions as teaching opportunities. We train at each and every opportunity, continuously reinforcing the systemic resolution of issues. Workers learn to think more systemically. This systemic thinking is reinforced by daily-

Interview with Tom Hartman

standardized management, resolution of problems in a systemic fashion, and then meetings on a daily basis where problems are discussed, at the beginning and ending of the shift. During weekly meetings where the performance for the week is reviewed and the most important things are highlighted, these problems and resolution methods are again discussed.

We are continually teaching and raising the associate's skill and ability and at the same time we're enabling the greater organization to implement the worker's ideas much more quickly and in a more effective fashion.

BODEK: How often do the workers rotate?

HARTMAN: They rotate every 24 to 26 minutes (depending on the plant and the process).

BODEK: Wow.

HARTMAN: There is truly no significance to frequency of the rotation, although more often is generally better. It was originally an hour, and we were challenged "why not do it on pitch?" Now, every time the heijunka runner delivers more heijunka cards, and every time they record their performance against expectation, they rotate.

And in fact, in the Ogden Module Assembly plant, they are cued to rotate with music. When workers at this facility hear "Louie, Louie," they rotate.

BODEK: That only takes a few seconds, to rotate?

HARTMAN: Yes. It's about 10 seconds.

BODEK: While you still have some energy, back to standardized work.

HARTMAN: At the worker level, it is defining the critical parts of the process. Toyota helped us dramatically on this, because formerly we had lumped everything contained within the control plan into the standardized work. There were multiple pages and no one read them. There were no pictures, all verbiage. So basically it was there to satisfy an auditor and that was about all.

Toyota taught us that this is a tool to enable your workers to do work in a flawless manner, by doing it exactly the same every cycle, every day. Picking a part up with the left hand, putting it in the machine in front of you, then removing another part with your right hand in the following machine, then turning around and picking up a third part with your right hand which is inserted into the machine behind you before returning to your original position and starting "the dance" again.

So the definition of standardized work went from being focused solely on quality-related tasks, to detailed descriptions of the operation that emphasized repeatability, which, of course, drove quality but also drove safety and productivity and predictability in all of its forms.

BODEK: I went to Toyota Gosei and stood in front of a worker. She had a wooden board in front of her as she assembled small rubber hoses with the exact steps, the quality standards, even examples of bad products.

HARTMAN: In our process, that's a job breakdown sheet. We also learned that from Toyota.

We attached one of the tools we used for management at the cell, because we have multiple "maps," we call them. These "maps" are GPS-like guidance for the operator as noted above. These maps tell the operator exactly what to do and in what order. These "maps" are different depending on the customer demand. The line leader (AMT) adjusts the number of people based on the actual customer demand. But that's just part of the standardized work.

Interview with Tom Hartman

Toyota taught us to identify the critical elements of the operation and do two things.

1) Incorporate those critical elements into your equipment logic and your poka-yokes. Make it easier to follow the standard work perfectly, cycle after cycle. 2) Take the critical elements from your standardized work and raise them to a new level of visualization with pictures and highlights. These illustrated highlights are then hung at each workstation. Each shift, every worker, confirms the standardized work as they rotate through each workstation.

If there is a modification of the standardized work, the whole team is trained by their leader. The leader is trained by the engineer so that the leader understands not only the "who, what and where," but also the "why." This way the leader can explain all of this to all team members. The leadership team changes the standardized work documents with the appropriate highlights as noted above, prior to training the team.

Admittedly, over time, even these highlighted documents may become somewhat dull, prompting us to retrain the workers every month or so on the standardized work. This may actually be an audit of their standardized work, but it serves the same purpose. When training, we use the "I do, You do, We do, Follow-up" method which is where the trainer does the work while the operator watches (I do), then trainer tells the operator what to do and observes to make sure it is done perfectly (You do). The trainer then watches and makes necessary corrections as the operator does the work (We do), and finally a daily audit is made to ensure that work is done correctly (Follow-up).

Periodically, every worker is requalified based on an audit of his or her standardized work. If the worker has a quality issue, that person is retrained until he or she can achieve the expected requirement. The same conditions apply to a productivity issue. Every day, the team leader audits standardized work, and teaches accordingly.

As the workers interact with their standardized work they can identify items that seem cumbersome and may require a change that is an opportunity for Kaizen. They submit their ideas for change. Management reviews the Kaizen, approves it and implements it. Then management comes out and trains the whole work team to the new standardized process -- dynamic. Please note that there is no unauthorized experimentation on the line, only the standard process is used to make product that is shipped our customers.

BODEK: Do you calculate the savings that comes from your Kaizen system?

HARTMAN: The answer is no (laughter). It's all the positive financial performance we can't otherwise explain. It actually is a nice problem for the managers and even our president, because with a culture of continuous improvement that is very effective at driving lower cost. There are cost reductions that "surprise you." They are the direct result of continuous improvement occurring at all levels of the organization in every discipline, every day.

BODEK: What you've given me is absolutely brilliant. I mean there is so much work for me to fully understand. And all I did is really ask you one question when you got started.

HARTMAN: It is all driven by the fact that we're under the gun for cost reductions. The Kaizen culture is how we've been able to keep our profitability in this incredibly destructive environment. If it weren't for our culture of APS and Kaizen, we would find it extremely difficult to meet the financial challenges of today's market.

BODEK: As GM goes bankrupt, what does that mean to you?

HARTMAN: We expect GM to emerge from this financial crisis in good shape. GM is one of our largest customers and we intend to

Interview with Tom Hartman

support them in every way possible. We are a four-time running recipient of GM's "Supplier of the year" award and have an excellent relationship with them.

Autoliv is a major supplier of safety products to all major carmakers worldwide. We have worked very hard for many years to be able to provide the products and service necessary to earn our current market position as the world's largest supplier of Automotive Safety Products. In 2008, we won Toyota Global Quality award. To the best of our knowledge we're the only non-Japanese company to win this award.

BODEK: I have a goldmine of information with what you gave me today. You're a real gift. I do thank you very much for sharing your knowledge with us and I wish you continued success.

Autoliv Kaizen examples:

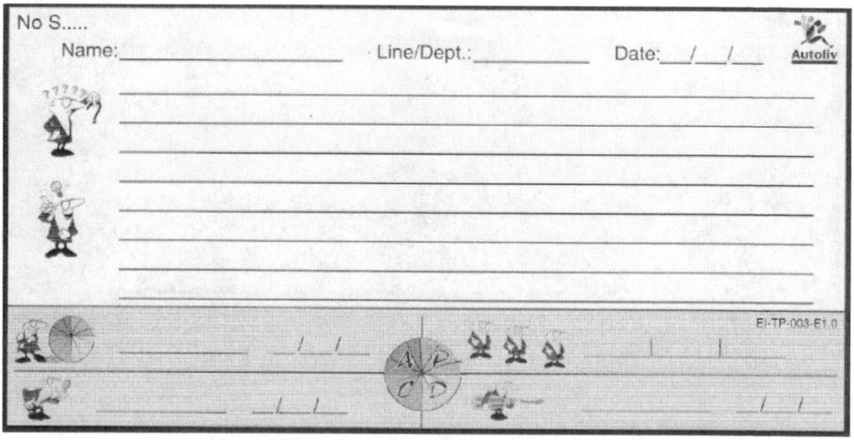

Fig. 109 <Autoliv Suggestion Form.>

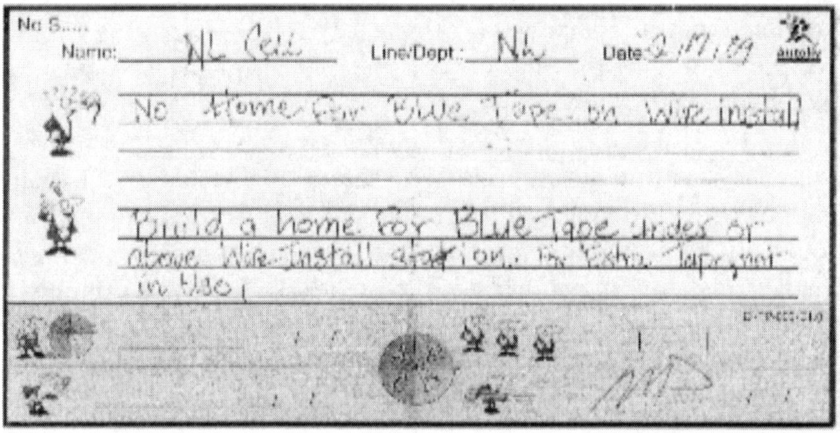

Fig. 110 <No Home for Blue Tape on Wire install>

Build a home for Blue Tape under or above Wire Install Station for extra tape not in use.

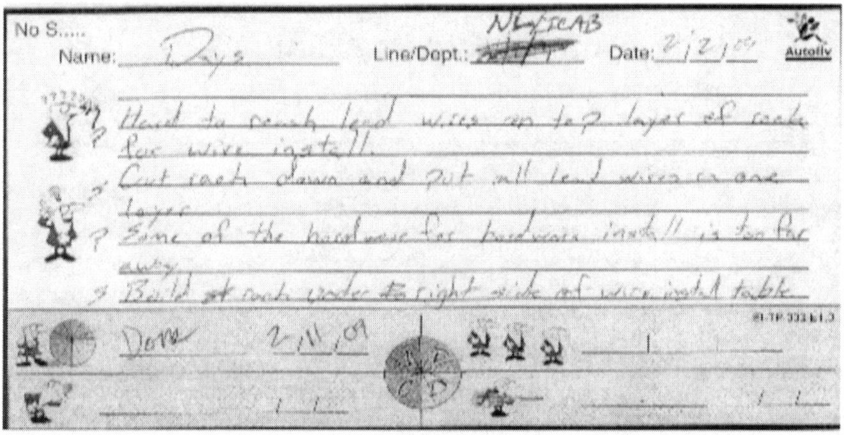

Fig. 111 <Problem: Hard to reach lead wires on top layer of rack for wire install>

Solution: Cut rack down and put all lead wires on one layer.

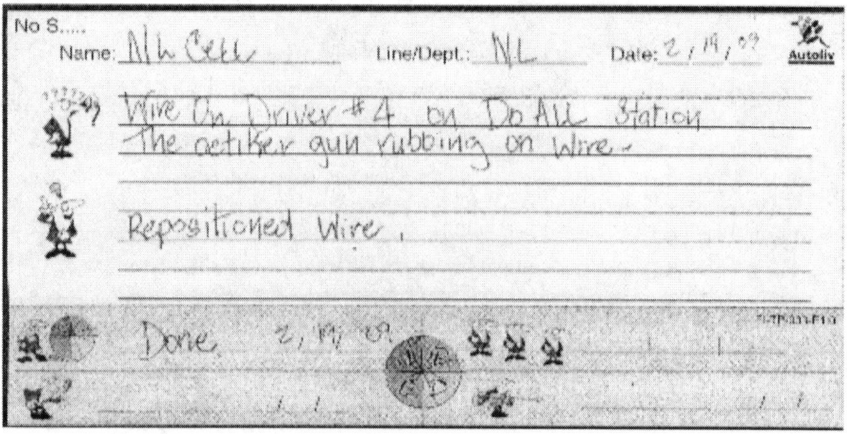

Interview with Tom Hartman

Fig. 112 <Problem: Wire on Driver #4 on Do All station. The octiker gun rubbing on wire.>

Solution: Repositioned wire.

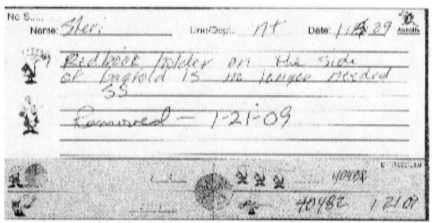

Fig. 113 <Problem: Redbook holder on the side of the bag fold is not longer needed.>

Solution" Removed 1-21-09

Fig. 114 <Problem: On Wire Rack boxes w/wires won't come forward, needs rollers.>

Solution: Replace gray sliders with rollers.

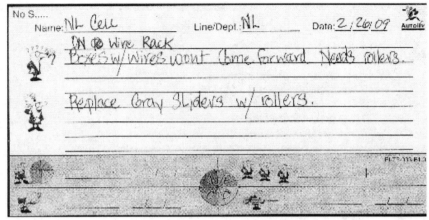

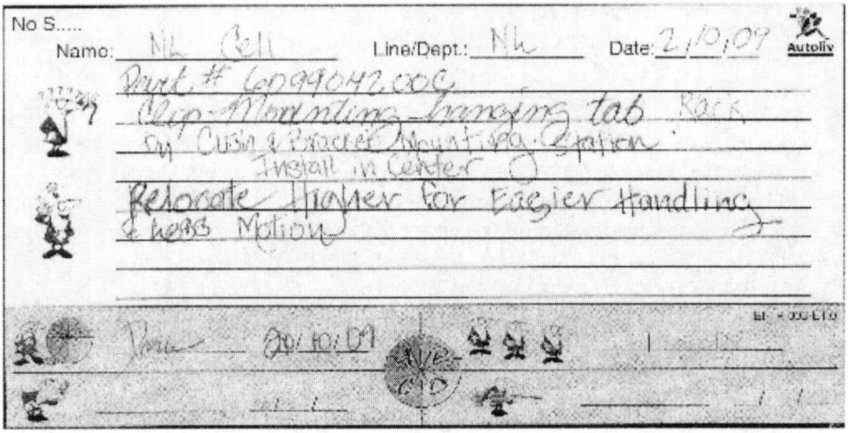

Fig. 115 <Problem: Clip mounting hanging tab.>

Solution: Relocate higher for easier handling and less motion

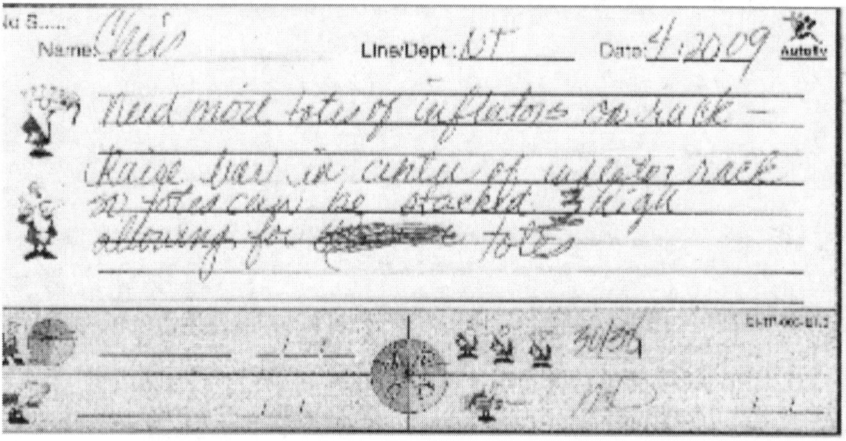

Interview with Tom Hartman

Fig. 116 <Problem: Need more totes of inflators on rack.>

Solution: Raise bar in center of inflator rack so totes can be stacked 3" high allowing for totes

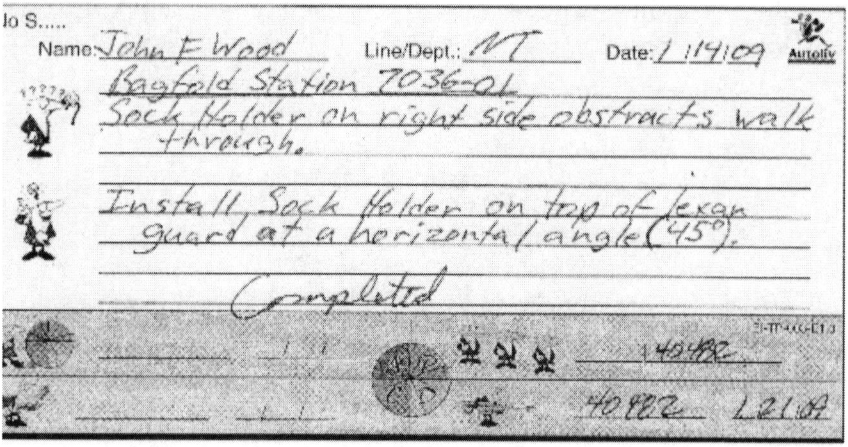

Fig. 117 <Problem: Sock holder on right side obstructs walk through.>

Solution: Install sock holder on top of lexan guard at a horizonal angle (45 °)

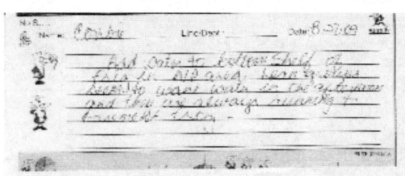

Fig. 118 <Problem & Solution: Add water to bottom shelf of refrigerator in A/P area. Lean groups seem to want water in the afternoon and they are always running to basement refrigerator.>

The ideas are small but just imagine having a culture where everyone is looking for improvement opportunities every day. The ideas are small but when they are added up they save both the employee's time and the company saves millions of dollars. Autoliv's goal in this plant in Utah this coming year is 96 ideas per employee. Wow!

Interview with Tim Ambrey

Director, Autoliv Production Systems, Autoliv Americas

Bodek: I thank for your graciousness in allowing me to interview you for my new book. I had the privilege of interviewing Tom Hartman and this interview is sort of a follow-up. I would like you to talk more about the management system that supports your suggestion process, which has been so highly successful for Autoliv.

I would hope you might also talk about how the suggestion system adds to the quality of work life for your employees.

How does your Kaizen process relate to the quality of work life for the average employee in your company as opposed to employees in other companies?

Ambrey: I can't really speak about other companies per se, but I can speak about Autoliv. We have about 60 plants worldwide. So obviously there are some plants that do well with all attributes of the Kaizen suggestion system, and there are plants that aren't quite as far along their journey.

In the plants where it's done very well, the suggestion system forms a really good give and take relationship between management and the people working on the manufacturing lines. It's a common language and a means of communication.

Bodek: Toyota calls this "Respect for People." Toyota talks about two pillars. One pillar is Just In Time, representing all of the tools and techniques; and I believe we are very familiar with the tools in America: kaizen blitz, 5 S, etc., but the second pillar formerly called Jidoka changed recently to Respect for People. Please do talk about this.

Ambrey: Well, I understand the second pillar still to be Jidoka, quite honestly. Respect for People is the purpose of the entire combination of Just In Time and Jidoka into the system called Toyota Production System (TPS.)

Respect for People is basically best summed up by a question one of the Toyota individuals asked me on the floor one time when I was a plant manager. He was analyzing the work that was being done by somebody in the conveyance department and he asked me, "Is that a dog job or is that a cat job?" that the person is doing.

Interview with Tim Ambrey

I didn't figure it out. It was a flip of a coin. I didn't know what he was getting at. But I said, "All right. I'll take a stab at this. That's a cat job." And he said, "You're correct."

I said, "All right. Let me ask how this is a cat job or how I guessed correctly." He said, "Well, what I can tell you is that it is not a job for a human being."

So the point of the matter was, how are you going to create a job which takes advantage of what humans do well, which is see, think, and then act, and give them the opportunity to make this a more fulfilling job by setting the expectation to eliminate waste in their system, utilizing their expertise.

Bodek: Wonderfully explained. How do you create jobs not based on the old Taylorism where work is boring and repetitive? How can you do it in your climate?

Ambrey: How can we get the people to make suggestions to better the work that they do? Is that your question?

Bodek: Well, most of the work that I see is cat and dog work. It is not made for the capabilities of people. I just wonder how do you rethink the way you manufacture to get the high productivity and quality and low cost and also start to give people really value at work in using their talents? I know you have a great suggestion system, probably the best in America, but please go beyond this and look at the way people work and what they do.

Ambrey: Toyota always kind of indicates, in any conversation about Kaizen, to give priority to work Kaizen over equipment Kaizen. The number one sentence in any introduction of Kaizen in Toyota is that " work Kaizen should stem from improving upon existing standardized work". Standardized work, or better-stated, standardized motion, defines working methods that are recognized as " the best way we know today." Kaizen activities reorganize

and redistribute work, arrange items, and changes the equipment tool layouts. This is all with the intent on improving the workers' movements throughout the plants.

The biggest thing we're trying to do, as I think Tom might have indicated, is to use the Kaizen suggestion system to accomplish three things, or three components, to make it successful. That is to generate a continuous flow, of acceptable ideas, being rapidly implemented.

So if you are to look at those three concepts, (continuous flow, acceptable idea and rapid implementation), continuous flow means to generate a pull system. Material is pulled from shop stock and then refilled. If you're looking at ideas, it's pulling ideas from the peoples' work experience in some repetitive manner, almost like with a takt time.

Acceptable ideas means that in order for something to be acceptable, it has to be held up to a standard of normal versus abnormal. And so in order to do that, you need to define well for the people what it is that you're expecting of them as far as what defines a good idea, an acceptable idea.

The expectation can be made to analyze the current standardized work, and to say that we're looking to eliminate waste in motion that might exist in the current working method. So all your ideas should be normalized against a reduction in motion waste, for instance.

Rapid implementation is nothing more than process lead-time. In factories we talk about the process lead time from turning raw materials into finished goods. In the Kaizen system, the process should be designed to take an idea that has been suggested, pull it into the process and have it come out with the necessary change on the manufacturing line through the assistance of management.

Interview with Tim Ambrey

In order to reduce the types of non-value added work that exists in all of our standardized works, the experience of the team members must be accessed. They have knowledge and the desire to meet the expectations of the company.

Bodek: Tom Hartman, your associate, flipped me around 180 degrees. I teach the Japanese suggestion system all over the world now, but Tom explained something that you do so unique. I've been teaching that the worker comes up with an idea, and then it's the workers obligation to implement that idea. So he's not a burden to management.

With the interview with Tom, it's completely different, because the focal point is different. It means in your system the managers' prime job is to support workers, not to control workers.

You totally recognize that the worker is the one that produces the value, produces the wealth of the company, and it's management's role to support that in every possible way.

Ambrey: Exactly. Well, if you look at a manufacturing facility in Autoliv, they're fully self-sufficient in the fact that they have everything that a small business or any business might have. The staff consists of a plant manager and then all the traditional support functions. So the plant is wholly self-sufficient, not relying on any kind of central management outside of the factory for its day-to-day operations.

When you have that kind of autonomy within the factory, as a plant manager you have certain responsibilities, the first of which in all instances is to assure that 100% good parts in the required quantities are going to the customer on time. So until you get to that point, you really can't work on a whole lot of anything else.

You get to that point through whatever methods you need. And the next obligation is to make sure that your manufacturing system is then formalized. You take all these individual problems that you've solved, define the processes, which drove towards solutions, and inject them into some kind of formalized way of doing business. Obviously, we consider ours to be the Autoliv Production System.

And once the Autoliv Production System is put in place, then you have a vehicle to go assess the work on a daily basis, through daily-standardized management. There can be up to, let's just say for conversation, 20 or 30 things that the plant manager is looking at in a daily fashion, to see what is happening on the plant floor.

One of those items is always checking on the health of the Kaizen system in various areas of the plant. And what are you looking for? You're looking to see that there is a continuous flow of ideas coming from the people. You're looking to see that they understand the types of ideas you are requesting from them, based on whatever your focus might be for the day/week/month, however you've set out your policy deployment in this regard. And then you're also checking to see that the implementation lead-time is low and that the support is there.

Lots of plants, if they're in a struggling situation, they've got mitigating circumstances causing them to spend all their time firefighting. The Kaizen system has a tendency to kind of get pushed off to the side. So it only goes without saying that the most successful Kaizen suggestion systems in Autoliv are those where the plant has already formally established their methodology on daily management and they have processes to engage, to understand the work floor and what is going on.

Bodek: Maybe give me some more examples of that, these 20 or 30 things that the plant manager is looking at.

Ambrey: The manager is looking to see first and foremost; can he go to the shipping dock and without speaking to anybody determine whether all of the shipments that are due to go out today are along whatever pathway to get them to the departure hour. Is work proceeding ahead or behind schedule, yes or no?

If yes, then he goes on to another part of the plant. If no, he's got to stop and begin to go ahead and ask questions of the people and of the process.

Say it's 9:00 in the morning; has there been a successful start up based on whatever attributes define success? Can he do that visually? Are the manufacturing cells ahead, behind or on pace for the requirements for the day? What is the condition of conveyance within the factory? Has there been any material downtime on the floor? If so, where and why? Are there any quality issues at the customer that have come up over the last 24 hours?

Bodek: How do you know this?

Ambrey: This is all to be gathered from the visual control tools that have been put in place to replicate the processes that drive towards the end result.

So there are many, many attributes that are checked on. What is the condition of the returnable packaging? Are we on time with our receipts? Are we behind on our receipts? Are we equal to where we should be at this point in time? Just In Time means very simply timing control. That's all it means.

So everything that we are looking at in a factory is based on timing control. What time is it and where should we be at this time based on our processes?

Bodek: What percentage of the time does this manager spend on the floor doing this?

Ambrey: If all the checks and balances are correct, this walk through of the floor takes typically no longer than 45 minutes. This timing is based on the condition of the plant being" normal".

If things are abnormal, of course you have to stop and understand the nature of the abnormality and understand the reaction protocol that is being put in place.

Bodek: Now this is the leader, this is the plant manager. What does the plant manager have underneath him? How many supervisors or sub-managers are in the plant? And are they doing the same kind of thing?

Ambrey: Yes. Most definitely. We're in the process of trying to get this down through ultimately what is one, two, three layers of manufacturing shop floor management below the plant manager.

Bodek: How many people in your average plant?

Ambrey: Well, we don't have an average plant. We go from 2,000 people on the high side to 100 people on the low side. Where Tom Hartman works in northern Utah there are about 1,000 people.

Bodek: I want to go back to this daily-standardized management. Maybe you can talk a little bit about that?

Ambrey: Standardized work for managers is what we call it.

It's all come about by virtue of having systems in place, that are visually understood by the workers and the managers. A type of tool might be Kanban. So the whole nature of Kanban is a visual control tool that should be used for three purposes.

Kanban provides a means to instruct production and conveyance on the specifics of their work quantities and work timing. Secondly, it should be used as a visual control tool to be able to tell whether processes are occurring equal to, behind or ahead of takt time. Once again, timing control. And then lastly, Kanban should be used as a tool for Kaizen.

What this means is that you should be able to see abnormalities in the system if they are well visually represented. So you can see opportunities for improvement.

So standardized work for management is something that comes about through or by virtue of an interaction with visual control tools.

Bodek: Very good. I want to go back to just two things; one is this whole skill development idea.

What I saw at Canon, this respect for people, really excites me to see the way they look at a human being and their unlimited capability to grow. So very often, the worker has a very limited amount of work that they do and it's very repetitive, over and over again.

Now I understand you do rotate, what, like, every 24 minutes or something like that?

Ambrey: Correct.

Bodek: And to what extent do those workers' skills grow? I mean, how many different skills -- is there a skill development program so that you can end up something like what Canon does, where one worker can make the whole copier?

Ambrey: I don't think we have any plans to go where one worker makes a whole air bag, because it doesn't mesh with our capital equipment. It doesn't mesh with one-piece flow. It doesn't

mesh with moving product through the factory with some kind of velocity.

The question would be stated something like this. Today is Tuesday the 30th of June at 9:57 a.m. Where should you be in relation to your production right now?

Bodek: How do you know that?

Ambrey: The Kanban system breaks the orders into small lots, and defines the timing for completion of each lot. These Kanbans are visual on the lines, and are placed on a sort of timeline. They are then used to determine whether the line is proceeding ahead, behind, or equal to the timing control. Are you ahead or are you behind? We're behind by 20 pieces.

Bodek: How will you make up that quantity by the end of the day?

Ambrey: We don't have enough hours at normal time to do that. That's why we split some shifts and allow them to stay over today to catch those ten pieces up, rather than try to wait until a Saturday to bring them in to catch them up, or wait until the last two days of the month prior to the order to let them catch up.

Bodek: How many shifts do you have? Do you have two shifts?

Ambrey: The ideal situation for us is two shifts. We do have some instances where we are running three shifts because we have short-term spikes in demand and we don't want to capitalize additional equipment. Toyota runs two shifts with a split between the two shifts, typically.
And that split is designed for one major -- or I should say two major purposes. It's designed so that when the manufacturing line has a problem and goes down due to equipment breakage, during the course of the day, the line is stopped and stop gap

measures are put in place to get the line back up and running, by the maintenance department.

But the maintenance department doesn't just put these Band-Aids on and walk away. They have to go keep the line running until the end of the shift, at which point in time that split allows them to conduct a more detailed root cause analysis, and a detailed corrective action that attacks the root cause. That's one of the primary reasons for splitting the shifts.

The second is, if in fact the line is struggling due to some other reason, perhaps, the manufacturing line will stay over and work additional hours, man hours, to get caught up, or get close to caught up during that split. Let's say the shift starts at 8:00, and by 10:00 in the morning they're behind. At this time it's known that there will be 47 minutes of overtime at the end of their shift because that's the only way they can catch up. They're not going to run the equipment more quickly because they have a very well defined takt time. But they're going to put more hours into the equation.

Bodek: I do thank you for your kindness.

POKKA CORPORATION NAGOYA FACTORY

Fig. 119 <Pokka Corporation Nagoya Factory.>

Kaizen Examples

Kaizens (Before and After)

A 'Collection of Case Studies' is the best possible, most powerful textbook. A workplace's case-study collection makes the state of its Kaizen activities clear at a glance. Introducing large numbers of examples clearly shows the situation before and after Kaizen, and the contrast makes people want to do more and more Kaizens. Documenting Kaizens and sharing them by compiling and distributing case studies keeps the 'virtuous circle' of Kaizen turning.

1 'Gone Home' Sign Introduced
Toyo Seiki Kogyo
Before: When their PC was off, there was no way of telling if the person had gone home or was somewhere in the factory.
After: Now, when someone goes home, they place a 'Gone Home' sign in the shape of a cat on their computer's keypad.
Benefit: No more time is wasted asking around or making announcements on the public address system, only to find the person has gone home.

2 Unnecessary Notices Removed and Necessary Ones Laminated
Nihon Kazai
Before: The notice board was cluttered with untidy, torn and out-of-date notices.
After: The unnecessary information was removed, leaving only the required notices, which are protected by laminating.
Benefit: The notice board is tidy, people can easily find the information they need, and they know it is important.

3 Moving Die Safely with Block and Tackle
Miyazaki Rubber
Before: When lifting the die, it was often tilted, so it was in danger of being dropped and had to be adjusted until it was level.
After: The centre of the rope was marked with white tape, so now the die is always level when lifted.
Benefit: Lifting is safer, and time is no longer wasted adjusting the die's position.

4 Positioner for Use when Picking Up Pallets with a Forklift Truck
Hikari Miso

Kaizens (Before and After)   343

Before: The truck drivers used to rely on their own judgment to decide how far to insert the forks when picking up pallets. Sometimes they damaged the goods by inserting the forks too far.
After: White bands were painted on the forks to show them how far to insert them.
Benefit: Now all the drivers know how far to insert the forks and there is less damage.

5 Display of Defectives
Mikuro Hatsujo
Before: The weekly number of defectives was published, but it meant little to the workers.
After: Each week's defectives are displayed in boxes in the cafeteria, together with a note of their value.
Benefit: People can now physically see how many defectives are being produced, and they know how much money is being wasted. They take more care, and produce fewer defectives.

6 Mirror for Improving Dress Standards
Mikuro Hatsujo
Before: Although dress standards had been set, they were not always scrupulously observed.
After: A mirror was mounted on the wall where people would see their own reflection when they exited from the changing room.
Benefit: People have become more conscious about the way they look, and now stop for a moment to adjust their appearance. Dress standards are adhered to better.

7 Method of Checking the Amount of Miso in the Hopper
Hikari Miso
Before: The miso-blending hopper was too tall to see inside, so it was difficult to fill it with the right amount of miso
After: Two mirrors have been mounted above the hopper, making it easy to see how full it is.
Benefit: It is much easier to fill the hopper with the right amount of miso, and no time is wasted climbing up a ladder to peer inside.

8 Method of Checking Tool Position on NC Machine Tool
Sangoban
Before: The operator had to stick his head inside the machine to check the tool position. This was dangerous and ergonomically undesirable.
After: The operator now uses a mirror to check the tool position without peering inside.
Benefit: The job has become safer, easier and more convenient.

9 Warning of Icicle Hazard
ChinonTech
Before: There was no sign to warn people of icicles, which pose a risk when driving out of the factory (although icicles are regularly cleared away, new ones can form overnight).
After: A sign has been installed warning drivers to watch out for icicles.
Benefit: The sign has reduced the risk of drivers colliding with an icicle.

10 Fire Extinguisher Sign Made Visible from Far Away
Hikari Miso
Before: Since the fire extinguisher is in a low position behind some other equipment, it is hard to see. This could be dangerous in the event of a fire.
After: A red 'Fire Extinguisher' sign with a downward-pointing arrow was installed on the wall above the extinguisher
Benefit: It is easy to see where the fire extinguisher is located, so it is safer.

11 Display for Controlling Inventory
Takashima Sangyo
Before: People would forget to order the materials, and they would run out.
After: A sign was made saying 'Please order new clips,' which automatically comes into view when it is time to order more.

Benefit: Nobody forgets to order fresh clips now, and they never run out.

12 Marking Out of Consumables Shelves and Control Chart for Consumables
Kyoei Kogyo
Before: Consumables were simply placed at random on the shelves in their boxes, so it was impossible to see how much there was of what item. This meant that items ran out and rush orders had to be placed.
After: Places have been marked out for each consumable on the shelves, and a chart showing item, model number, manufacturer, supplier, order point, etc. has been made.
Benefit: The consumables are now under control, ordering them is easy, and they do not run out.

13 Labeling Containers for Products That Use Alumina Powder
Misuzu Kogyo
Before: Products are placed in these plastic boxes for shipping to business partners, but there was no distinction between the boxes used for products coated with alumina powder and those used for uncoated products
After: Some boxes were labeled to be used exclusively for coated products.
Benefit: Everyone can now see at a glance, which boxes are to be used for coated products, so there is less risk of uncoated products being put in them and becoming contaminated with alumina powder.

14 Making It Easier to See the Size Label of Parts by Putting It On Top
Sangoban
Before: The size labels were on the sides of the parts containers and could not be seen, so the containers had to be lifted out of the box each time to check the size of the parts.

After: The labels were transferred to the lids of the containers.
Benefit: The sizes of the parts can now be checked without picking the containers up. This has made the job easier and more efficient.

15 Seeing At a Glance Which Pamphlets Are in Which Envelope
Takashima Sangyo
Before: Pamphlets are stored in used envelopes with the titles of the pamphlets written on the outside of the envelopes, but we still often had to look inside to see which pamphlets were in there.
After: Instead of writing on the envelopes, we now stick one copy of the pamphlet onto the outside of the envelope.
Benefit: We can now see at a glance which pamphlets are in which envelope, which saves us a lot of time.

16 Using a Buzzer and Flashing Light to Indicate When the Job Is Finished
Yamato Denki Kogu
Before: A timer was used to indicate how long a process should go on for, but the operator had to keep looking at the timer to see when the job had finished.
After: A timer is still used, but it is now connected to a buzzer and flashing light.
Benefit: The operator can now go off and do another job because he/she no longer has to keep an eye on the timer. This has improved efficiency.

17 Preventing the Door from Being Left Open (1)
Nomura Unison
Before: The factory door was of the ordinary aluminum-framed sliding type. Although there was a rule to say that it should be kept closed, people were always leaving it open.
After: We installed a homemade pulley-and-weight mechanism to close the door automatically.
Benefit: The door is now always kept closed.

18 Preventing the Door from Being Left Open (2)
Nomura Unison

Kaizens (Before and After) 347

Before: The large, heavy door to the clean-room store was always being left open, in contravention of the rule.
After: A sensor and siren were installed, to sound an alarm if the door was not shut.
Benefit: The siren is very loud, so everyone always shuts the door now.

19 Combining a Swab and Tweezers
Chinontech
Before: The worker used to first pick up the Texwipe swab, then put it down and pick up the tweezers. This took time.
After: We joined the handles of the Texwipe and the tweezers together, so the workers now just have to turn the combination tool around in their hand and use the other end, without having to put anything down or pick anything up.
Benefit: Time has been saved.

20 Special Nippers for Removing Caps from Defectives
Miyama
Before: Ordinary nippers were used to remove the sealed caps from defective products, but these applied too much force, and the products often got damaged.
After: A hole was drilled through one of the nippers' handles and a screw was inserted to act as a stopper, preventing the nippers' jaws from closing too hard on the product and damaging it.
Benefit: The products don't get damaged any more, and the screw can be adjusted so that the nippers can also be used to hold the product while testing the strength of the cap weld on the completed product.

21 Simplifying the Counting of O-Rings and Making It More Reliable
Sangoban
Before: O-rings are counted into plastic bags, but sometimes people lost their place and had to recount, or put the wrong number of O-rings in the bags.

After: A special case with the right number of receptacles was designed to hold the O-rings.

Benefit: The number of O-rings can now be seen at a glance, and both recounting and miscounting have been eliminated.

22 Special Chute for Activated Charcoal
Kits Microfilter

Before: The activated charcoal was used directly from the bag it had been delivered in. It was hard for the person responsible for replenishing it to see how much was left, so it sometimes ran out and caused production stoppages.

After: A special container holding columns of 10 was made, and the charcoal is placed in this before being used.

Benefit: It takes less time to take the charcoal out, and it is easy to see how much is left. Fresh charcoal is now always ordered on time, and production flows smoothly. (The chute was made from scrap plastic.)

23 Stabilizing Valve Unit During Installation
Mikuni Kogyo

Before: There was nothing to support the inlet valve unit when it was being installed on the main assembly, so it moved around, making the job difficult.

After: A specially designed polyurethane block was made, and this is placed under the valve unit to support it when installing it.

Benefit: The valve unit doesn't move around, and the job is much easier.

24 Preventing Cable Damage When Closing Control Panel Door
Toyo Seiki

Before: During testing, cables dangle out of control panel and can easily be damaged if the door is inadvertently closed on them.

After: A clip-on protector bracket was designed and installed to protect the cables.

Benefit: The cables cannot now be damaged even if someone tries to close the door. This saves the time it would take to find out which cable had been damaged and replace it.

Kaizens (Before and After) 349

25 Preventing Parts from Coming Off
Ingusushinano
Before: Parts sometimes came off when the assembly was being fitted.
After: The order of installation of the trigger fitting and trigger packing was changed.
Benefit: Installation errors have been eliminated, and the assembly work goes more smoothly.

26 Optimizing the Height and Angle of the Discharge Conveyor
Mikuro Hatsujo
Before: The conveyor inside the oven was slightly lower than the discharge conveyor, so parts would sometimes get stuck and the operator would have to drag them out.
After: The discharge conveyor was adjusted to the best height and angle.
Benefit: The parts always discharge smoothly and the operator doesn't have to waste time getting them out.

27 Making it Easier to Reset the Machine Counter
Taiyo Kogyo
Before: There was an aperture in the panel door that enabled the figures on the counter to be seen, but the door had to be opened to reset the counter.
After: The aperture was enlarged so that the counter could be reset without opening the panel door.
Benefit: The parts always discharge smoothly and the operator doesn't have to waste time getting them out.

28 (1:13:26)
Taiyo Kogyo
Standardizing the Heights of Pallets and Wheeled Dollies
Before: The heights of the pallets and dollies in the goods loading area were different, so the stack would tilt when transferred from dolly to pallet.

After: Off-the-shelf standard-height pallets and dollies were purchased.
Benefit: Goods can now be transferred easily and safely.

29 (1:14:50)
Kits Microfilter
Setting Switch at a Better Height
Before: The start switch for the next process was higher than the switch for the previous process. The operators had to move their hand a long way when starting the next process, and they sometimes knocked their hand against the switch box or fumbled the switch, delaying the start of the next process.
After: The switches were set at the same height.
Benefit: It is much easier and quicker to start the next process, so operators now rarely fumble or hit their hand on the box and there are no more delays.

30 (1:17:07)
Raito Koki Seisakujo
Preparation of Documented Procedure for Restoring Heater
Before: Every time a heater stopped working, the supplier was called out to fix it.
After: Documented procedures for fixing the heaters have been prepared and placed by each heater, and the people in each area have been authorized to do whatever they can to fix the heaters themselves.
Benefit: The procedure for fixing the heaters is now clear to everyone, and the supplier does not have to be called out so often.

31 (1:19:12)
Takashima Sangyo
Improved Company Guidance for University Graduates
Before: The only materials taken to presentations about our company at employment fairs for university graduates were a video presentation and pamphlets introducing the company.
After: A portable display case containing product samples as well as introductory pamphlets was prepared for use at presentations.

Kaizens (Before and After)

Benefit: Because we can now demonstrate our actual products to them, graduates can understand our technology much better.

32 (1:21:44)
Yamato Denki Kogyo
Improving Tidiness and Operability by Fixing Marker Pen Cap

Before: A marker pen is used for marking the products, and the worker had to keep taking the cap off and putting it back on again. When the cap was taken off, there was nowhere to put it, so it was just left untidily on the worktable.

After: The cap was fixed to the edge of the table, so it is always in the same place. Now the worker just takes the pen out and puts it back each time.

Benefit: The work is more efficient, because the pen can be taken out and replaced with one hand; the work area is tidier, because the cap is always in the same place; and better use is made of the space available on the table.

33 (1:24:01)
Miyama
Easier-to-Grasp Door Handle

Before: The recessed door handle was a nuisance, because it was hard to get hold of and pull out.

After: I had the idea of tying a piece of rope to the handle. Now the handle can be pulled out easily.

Benefit: Although it only saves a small amount of time each time the door is opened, a source of irritation has been eliminated.

34 (1:25:55)
Ingusu Shinano
Preventing Wires from Being Damaged

Before: When cutting off the cable sheathing and unnecessary wires, necessary wires were sometimes cut off by mistake.

After: The necessary wires are now clipped together before cutting, leaving just the wires that must be cut sticking out.

Benefit: The wires and sheathing can be cut more cleanly, and the wrong wires are no longer cut off by mistake.

35 (1:27:38)
Yamato
Installation of Cover to Prevent Scattering of Chips
Before: The chips and oil flew out and were scattered all over the floor, so a lot of time was wasted continually cleaning up.
After: A cover was installed to contain the chips.
Benefit: The floor doesn't get dirty any more, so life is much easier and a lot of time is saved.

36 (1:29:29)
Shintoku
Containment of Cutting Debris
Before: The cutting debris used to squirt out of the machine and spread all around, even into the aisles. It got stuck to the soles of people's shoes when they walked on it, and was carried all over the factory. It took a lot of effort to keep the floor clean.
After: Screens were erected to contain the debris.
Benefit: The debris is confined to a small area. We no longer have to spend so much time cleaning the floor.

37 (1:30:52)
Marugo Kogyo
Improved Method of Filtering Waste Water from Wire-Cutting Tank
Before: Stocking material was used to filter metal debris and metal dust from the waste water, but the smallest particles could not be removed even with 30 or 40 layers of material, the filter had to be replaced frequently, and it took about a day to maintain and clean the machine..
After: The tank was partitioned into three compartments. Large debris settled in the first compartment and small debris in the second, leaving only fine metal powder to be separated by the filter.
Benefit: The life of the filter was extended from 200 hours to 400 hours, the filter only has to be replaced once every 3 months

instead of monthly, maintenance only takes 4 hours instead of 8.5 hours, the stocking material doesn't have to be adjusted, and the wastewater can be cleaned during operation.

38 (1:32:46)
Kyoei Kogyo
'Serving Boxes' for Parts

Before: Small parts were counted into plastic containers before assembling, but large parts would not fit in the boxes so were taken straight from the racks. This was a waste of time and led to operators occasionally omitting to install all the necessary parts.

After: We made 'serving boxes' with compartments for all the parts needed to make the product, with a photograph on each compartment showing what parts should be placed in it.

Benefit: The operators save time by not having to go to the racks to pick up parts so often, and they no longer occasionally leave out parts.

39 Reservation Chart for Pool Cars
Hiraide Seimitsu

Before: People used to reserve the pool cars by scribbling notes on the whiteboard anywhere they could find space.

After: A permanent reservation chart was marked on the whiteboard.

Benefit: Everyone knows where to mark their reservation, and all the reservations can be can seen at a glance.

40 Compact Vacuum Generator to Reduce Setup Time for Vacuum Testing
Marugo Kogyo

Before: A high-capacity vacuum pump or the factory's central vacuum system was used when conducting the vacuum test, and it used to take a long time to set everything up.

After: We made a compact vacuum generator (measuring 100 cm x 70 cm x 50 cm) in-house, using spares parts we had in stock.

Benefit: Setting up for the vacuum test is now far quicker and easier.

41 Making Ladder Non-Slip
Hikari Miso

Before: A ladder is used to climb to the top of a 2-meter-high tank, but the rungs were slippery when wet, so there was a risk of someone's foot slipping off and the person falling and injuring themselves.

After: Non-slip tape was affixed to the rungs.

Benefit: There is now no danger of slipping.

42 Providing Signed Storage Location for Lifting Chains
Taiyo Kogyo

Before: We use hooked chains for attaching dies to the hoist when lifting them, but there was no special place to put them, so people used to hang them on the wagon handles, where they would dangle into the aisle and create a trip hazard.

After: We fixed hooks to the pillar where the chains could be hung up clear of the aisle, and marked out the aisle with tape.

Benefit: A trip hazard has been eliminated.

Kaizens (Before and After)

Completed

Idea # 2009 - 366

Date Submitted*	08/03/2009	Submitted By*	Allshouse, Cindy A.
Department*	Patio Doors	Shift*	First

Problem/Need*	With the new screen handle, There are all kinds of new parts, plus the existing parts in boxes laying on the floor around the screen rack
My Idea/ Solution*	Make a table with enough slots for all the parts, 3 types of hangers, 6 different screws, 3 different color handles, and 3 colors of thumb screws
Result*	More organization
Can I implement this myself*	No	If no, who might help me:	Woodshop
Impact of the Idea*	Cost/Time Savings
Idea Support:	

* Indicates required field.

Idea Result:	Implemented	CompletionDate	08/12/2009
Final Idea Comments:			

Before Picture	After Picture

How to Do Kaizen

Completed

Idea # 2009 - 360

Date Submitted*	08/02/2009	Submitted By*	Cramer, Karen L.
Department*	Paint	Shift*	First

Problem/Need*	Constantly turning sash (some big and heavy) to tape and mask.
My Idea/Solution*	A moveable, elevated table to tape, clean and mask all in one movement.
Result*	Faster and less muscle work to flip windows.

Can I implement this myself*	No	If no, who might help me:	woodshop
Impact of the Idea*		Cost/Time Savings; Quality; Safety	
Idea Support:			

* Indicates required field.

Idea Result:	Implemented	CompletionDate	08/03/2009
Final Idea Comments:			

Before Picture	After Picture
	(image)

Support Documents:	

Kaizens (Before and After)   357

Completed

Idea # 2009 - 412

Date Submitted*	08/03/2009	Submitted By*	Shaffer, Thomas G.
Department*	Storms	Shift*	First

Problem/Need*	Tripping over air lines at work table
My Idea/Solution*	Plastic coiled air lines that retract out of your way.
Result*	Work is safer and easier. Air line is tucked out of work area and even look neater.
Can I implement this myself*	No	If no, who might help me:	maintenance
Impact of the Idea*	Cost/Time Savings; Quality; Safety		
Idea Support:			

* Indicates required field.

Idea Result:	Implemented	CompletionDate	08/11/2009
Final Idea Comments:			

Before Picture	After Picture
Support Documents:	

Stored Gas ASH F-Cell

Before: E-check machine is not required for all part numbers. Operators have to take 5 steps around this machine every time they produce a part that does not require E-check.

After: Installed wheels on E-check which allows it to be pushed out of the way and installed sliding rollers to bring the work to the operator when E-check is not required.

Results:
 Eliminated 5 steps per part or 2,250,000 steps a year.

Bunji Tozawa - Biography

Education: Schooled in Kita, Kyushu, Japan. Graduate of Kagoshima University, Kagoshima, Japan, majored in Geology and Economics.

College joined Kawasho Trading Company, a division of Kawasaki Steel. Twenty-five years later, in 1981, he joined The Japan HR Association as a writer. Today Mr. Tozawa is the CEO of The Japan HR Association, with offices in Tokyo and Osaka, Japan.

How to Do Kaizen

Instructor: Started to teach Kaizen in 1990 and has taught over 1000 seminars, now running approximately 120 three-hour seminars per year on Quick and Easy Kaizen throughout Southeast Asia. In Bangkok, Thailand, February 2001 he expected around 30 to 50 people for a seminar; 400 people arrived.

Publications:

Editor: Kaizen monthly magazine, Japan HR Association

Author of the following books:

PHP
Business Kaizen Techniques
Handbook of Kaizen OJT (On the Job Training)
Manual for Promoting Kaizen Activities

Sanno Daigaku Press
Through 5S with Kaizen
Simple Kaizen of Office Work
Marketing/Sales Kaizen

Asuka Press
Keys for Quick and Easy Kaizen of Work
Work Kaizen for Building a Strong Company

Kodansha Bunko
Kaizen in Cartoon Fashion

Kotsu-Shimbunsha
Successful Work Kaizen

Nikkankogyo-Shimbun
    Defiant Work Kaizen
    Kaizen Tale
    Kaizen Q & A
    Kaizen Promotion Starts with Examples and Ends with Examples
    Know-How of Quick & Easy Kaizen (3 Parts)
    How to Make Kaizen (3 Parts)
    Kaizen Teian (3 Parts)
    Kaizen Reporting System
    Kaizen Seminar Video Text

Gyosei
    Work Kaizen Manual for Public Workers

Dojidaisha
    Kaizen for Healthcare Workplace

Japan HR Association
    Kaizen Teian Handbook
    Service Kaizen Teian Handbook
    Collection of Kaizen Examples

Consulting clients:
    More than 230 companies including Shin-Etsu Chemical, Sony, Motorola, Sumitomo 3M, Matsushita Electric Industrial, Kyocera, Toyota, Roland, Chiba-Geigy, Yamaha Motor, Pioneer Electronic, Seiko Instruments, Epson

Norman Bodek - Biography

Education: New York City Public School system, Yonkers, New York School system, University of Wisconsin, New York University, New York University Graduate School of Business, and New York University College of Education

Military service: Two years active duty with the U. S. Army Audit Agency and four years in reserve.

Lecturer: American Management Associations, Control Data Institute, President Regan's Productivity Conference Washington, DC, PPORF Conference - Japan, Institute of Industrial Engineers,

American Society for Quality, APICS, AME, Productivity, Inc. Conferences and Seminars, IEE, WCBF, International Lean and Six Sigma conference, Lean Accounting Summit, FAA, DCAA, Dresser Mfg., Union Carbide, AVCO Corporation, BAE, Gulfstream, Clark Metal Products, Gorell Windows, Jeppersen, Larsen & Turbo - India, Productivity - Madras (Chennai), India, London - England, Jutland – Denmark, Sweden, Malaysia, Shingo Prize conferences, etc.

Adjunct Professor, Portland State University, Portland, Oregon teaching "The Best of Japanese Management Practices."

Recipient of The Shingo Prize[*] for Manufacturing Excellence and also created the Shingo Prize with Dr. Vern Buehler sponsored by Utah State University. Received a Six Sigma Grand Master medal from ICBUPR.

Professional Career: Public Accountant and Insurance Broker, Vice President Data Utilities, New York City, and Barbados, West Indies, President Key Universal Ltd. with offices in Greenwich, Connecticut and Grenada, West Indies

    1979-1999 Started Productivity Inc. & Productivity Press with offices in Norwalk, Connecticut, and Portland, Oregon.

    Newsletters: PRODUCTIVITY, Total Employee Involvement (TEI), The Service Insider, Quick Change Over (QCO), and Total Productive Maintenance (TPM)

    Study missions to Japan, led around 35 missions visiting over 250 manufacturing plants

---

[*]For information on the prize: http://www.shingoprize.org/shingo/index.html

Conferences: Over 100 conferences on productivity and quality improvement including Productivity The American Way, Best of America, Quality, Quality Service, TPM, and TEI

Seminars: Hundreds of seminars on TPM, TQM, TEI, QCO, Visual Management, 5S, JIT and others.

In plant training events: From Japan brought over Dr. Ryuji Fukuda, Dr. Shigeo Shingo, Shigehiro Nakamura, and many others including Ohno's assistants from Japan (Iwata and Nakao) and ran Five Days and One Night (now called Kaizen Blitz), Maintenance Miracle, Quick Changeovers, Visual Factory, and benchmark plant visits and seminars with American Manufacturing companies.

Books Published: Dr. Shigeo Shingo's - Toyota Production System, SMED, Poka-Yoke, Non-Stock Production, etc., Taiichi Ohno - Toyota Production System (JIT), Henry Ford – Today and Tomorrow, A New American TQM, Yoji Akao – Quality Function Deployment (QFD) and Hoshin Kanri, Dr. Ryuji Fukuda – Managerial Engineering, CEDAC and Building Organizational Fitness, Shigeichi Moriguchi – Software Excellence, Shigeru Mizuno - Management for Quality Improvement (The 7 New QC Tools), Seiichi Nakajima – Total Productivity Maintenance (TPM), Michel Greif – The Visual Factory, Ken'ichi Sekine – One Piece Flow, Shigehiro Nakamura – The New Standardization, and many other books on world class manufacturing and total quality management. See the full list in the bibliography.

1990 - Industry Week called him "Mr. Productivity."

2001 – Called "Mr. Lean" in Quality Progress Magazine

1999 - Started PCS Press with a monthly newsletter, keynoting conferences and running training workshops on Quick and Easy Kaizen, Zero Defects, and Improving Customer Service.

Books written:
The Idea Generator – Quick and Easy Kaizen,
PCS Press 2001

The Idea Generator – Workbook,
PCS Press 2002

Kaikaku: The Power and Magic of Lean
Shingo Prize winner
PCS Press 2004

All You Gotta Do Is Ask
Co-authored with Charles Yorke
PCS Press 2005

Rebirth of American Industry
Co-authored with William Waddell
PCS Press 2006

How to do Kaizen
Co-authored with Bunji Tozawa
PCS Press 2010

Articles published in:
Quality Digest Magazine
Solutions – IIE Magazine
Target – Association for Manufacturing Excellence (AME)
Quality World
The Journal for Quality and Participation
T + D Magazine - ASTD

Manufacturing Engineering – SME's magazine
Timely Tips for Teams – monthly
NWLean
HR.COM
And others, over 40 articles published in the last two years.

Radio – ran an interview program in New England.

E-learning – course developed with Society of Manfacturing Engineers to teach Quick and Easy Kaizen. Ran a number of webinars for various groups.

Bibliography

The following are books that Norman published at Productivity, Inc. - Press

Akao, Yoji (ed). - *Quality Function Deployment: Integrating Customer Requirements into Product Design* – Productivity Press, 1990
———. *Hoshin Kanri: Policy Deployment for Successful TPM* – Productivity Press, 1991
Akiyama, Kaneo. - *Function Analysis: Systematic Improvement of Quality and Performance* – Productivity Press, 1991
Asaka, Tetsuichi and Kazuo Ozeki (eds.) - *Handbook of Quality Tools: The Japanese Approach* - Productivity Press, 1990
Barrett, Derm – *Fast Focus on TQM: A Concise Guide to Companywide Learning* - Productivity Press, 1994
Belohlav, James A. - *Championship Management: An Action Model for High Performance* - Productivity Press, 1990
Bodek, Norman – *The Idea Generator: Quick and Easy Kaizen* – PCS Press, 2002
Boyle, Daniel C. – *Secrets of a Successful Employee Recognition System* - Productivity Press, 1995
Camp, Robert C. - *Benchmarking: The Search for Industry Best Practices that Lead to Superior Performance* - Productivity Press, 1989
Campbell, John Dixon – *Uptime: Strategies for Excellence in Maintenance Management* - Productivity Press, 1995

Christopher, William F. and Carl G. Thor - *Total Employee Involvement – Handbook for Productivity Measurement and Improvement* - Productivity Press, 1993

Cooper, Robin and Regine Stagmulder – *Target Costing and Value Engineering* – Productivity Press co-published with The Institute of Management Accountant, 1997

D'Egidio, Franco. - *The Service Era: Leadership in a Global Environment* - Productivity Press, 1990

Ford, Henry. - *Today and Tomorrow* – Productivity Press, 1988 (Double Day 1926)

Fukuda, Ryuji – *Building Organizational Fitness: Management Methodology for Transformation and Strategic Advantage* – Productivity Press, 1994

————. *Managerial Engineering: Techniques for Improving Quality and Productivity in the Workplace* – Productivity Press, 1983

————. *CEDAC: A Tool for Continuous Systematic Improvement* – Productivity Press, 1990

Grief, Michelle. - *The Visual Factory: Building Participation through Shared Information* - Productivity Press, 1991

Gotoh, Fumio. - *Equipment Planning for TPM: Maintenance Prevention Design* – Productivity Press, 1991

Gross, Clifford M. – *The Right Fit: The Power of Ergonomics as a Competitive Strategy* - Productivity Press, 1991

Hartley, John R. – *Concurrent Engineering: Shortening Lead Times, Raising Quality, and Lowering Costs* - Productivity Press, 1992

Hatakeyama, Yoshio. - *Manager Revolution! A Guide to Survival in Today's Changing Workplace* - Productivity Press, 1986

Head, Christopher W. – *Beyond Corporate Transformation: A Whole System Approach to Creating and Sustaining High Performance* - Productivity Press, 1997

Hirano, Hiroyuki. - 5 *Pillars of the Visual Workplace: The Sourcebook for* 5S *Implementation* - Productivity Press, 1995

————. *JIT Factory Revolution: A Pictorial Guide to Factory Design of the Future* – Productivity Press. 1989

————*JIT Implementation Manual: The Complete Guide to Just-In-*

Time Manufacturing - Productivity Press, 1990

———. *5S for Operators: 5 Pillars of the Visual Workplace* Productivity Press, 1996

Horovitz, Jacques. - *Winning Ways: Achieving Zero-Defect Service* – Productivity Press, 1990

Ichida, Takashi (Compiler) – *Product Design Review: A Method for error-free Product Development* - Productivity Press, 1996

Ishiwata, Junichi. - *IE for the Shop Floor 1: Productivity Through Process Analysis* - Productivity Press, 1991

Jackson, Thomas L. and Constance E. Dyer – *Corporate Diagnosis: Setting the Global Standard for Excellence* (Based on the work of Shigehiro Nakamura and Dr. Ryuji Fukuda) - Productivity Press, 1996

———. And Karen R. Jones – *Implementing a Lean Management System* - Productivity Press, 1996

Japan Institute of Plant Maintenance, eds.- *Autonomous Maintenance for Operators* - Productivity Press, 1997

———.TPM *Encyclopedia.* Atlanta: Japan Institute of Plant Maintenance – Productivity Press, 1996.

———. *Focused Equipment Improvement for TPM Teams* - Productivity Press, 1997

———.TPM *for Every Operator* - Productivity Press, 1996

———.TPM for Survivors - Productivity Press 1996

Japan Management Association - *Kanban and Just-In-Time at Toyota: Management Begins at the Workplace.* - Productivity Press, 1986

———. *Total Productivity: The New Science of TP Management* (Based on the work of Shigehiro Nakamura) – Productivity Europe, 1996

———. The *Canon Production System: Creative Involvement of the Total Workforce* – Productivity Press, *1987*

Japan Union of Scientist and Engineers (JUSE). - *TQC Solutions: The 14-Step Process* – Productivity Press, 1991

Kanatsu, Takashi. - *TQC for Accounting: A New Role in Companywide Improvement* – Productivity Press, 1991

Karatsu, Hajime. - *Tough Words For American Industry* - Productivity Press, 1988

———. *TQC Wisdom of Japan: Managing for Total Quality Control* - Productivity Press, 1988

Kato, Kenichiro. - *I.E. for the Shop Floor 2: Productivity Through Motion Study* - Productivity Press, 1991

Kaydos, Will. - *Measuring, Managing, and Maximizing Performance* - Productivity Press, 1991

Kirby, J. Philip and David Hughes – *Thoughtware: Change the Thinking and the Organization Will Change Itself* – Productivity Press, 1991

Kobayashi, Iwao - *20 Keys to Workplace Improvement* - Productivity Press, 1990

Lewis, C. Patrick – *Building a Shared Vision: A Leader's Guide to Aligning the Organization* - Productivity Press, 1996

Liebling, Henry E. – *Handbook for Personal Productivity* - Productivity Press, 1989

Liker, Jeffrey, ed. - *Becoming Lean: Inside Stories of U.S. Manufacturers* - Productivity Press, 1997

Louis, Raymond J. - *Integrating Kanban with MRPII: Automating a Pull System for Enhanced JIT Inventory Management* – Productivity Press, 1997

Lu, David J. - *Inside Corporate Japan: The Art of Fumble-Free Management* - Productivity Press, 1987

Maskel, Brian H. - *Performance Measurement for World Class Manufacturing: A Model for American Companies* – Productivity Press, 1991

———. *Making the Numbers Count: The Management Accountant as Change Agent on the World Class Team* - Productivity Press, 1996

———. With Learner First - *Putting Performance Measurement to Work: Building Focus and Sustaining Improvement* - Productivity Press, 1997

———. *Software and the Agile Manufacturer: Computer Systems and the World Class Manufacturing* - Productivity Press, 1994

Mauer, Rick – *Feedback Toolkit: 16 Tools for Better Communications in the Workplace* - Productivity Press,

Bibliography

1994
———. *Caught in the Middle: A Leadership Guide for Partnership in the Workplace* - Productivity Press, 1994

Merli, Giorgio - *Total Manufacturing Management: Production Organization for the 1990s* – Productivity Press, 1990

———. *Co-Makership: The New Strategy for Manufacturers* – Productivity Press, 1991

Merrill, Peter – *Do It Right the Second Time: Benchmarking Best Practices in the Quality Change Process* – Productivity Press, 1997

Michalski, Walter J. - *40 Tools for Cross-Functional Teams: Building Synergy for Breakthrough Creativity* - Productivity Press, 1998

———. *Tool Navigator: The Master Guide for Teams* – Productivity Press, 1997

———. *40 Top Tools for Manufacturers: A Guide for Implementing Powerful Improvement Activities* – Productivity Press, 1998

Miltenburg, John – *Manufacturing Strategy: How to Formulate and Implement a Winning Team* - Productivity Press, 1995

Mizuno, Shigeru (ed.). - *Management for Quality Improvement: The 7 New QC Tools* – Productivity Press, 1988

Monden, Yasuhiro and Michiharu Sakurai (eds.). *Japanese Management Accounting: A World Class Approach to Profit Management* - Productivity Press, 1990

———. *The Toyota Management System: Linking the Seven Key Functional Areas* – Productivity Press, 1999

———. *Cost Reduction Systems: Target Costing and Kaizen Costing* - Productivity Press, 1995

———. *Cost Management in the New Manufacturing Age: Innovations in the Japanese Automobile Industry* – Productivity Press, 1992

Moriguti, Shigeiti (ed.) – *Software Excellence: A Total quality Management Guide* - Productivity Press, 1997

Nachi-Fujikoshi (ed.). - *Training for TPM: A Manufacturing Success Story* - Productivity Press, 1990

Nakajima, Seiichi. - *Introduction to TPM: Total Productive*

Maintenance - Productivity Press, 1988
————.*TPM Development Program: Implementing Total Productive Maintenance* - Productivity Press, 1989
Nachi Fujikoshi Corporation. - *Training for TPM: a Manufacturing Success Story* - Productivity Press, 1990
Nakamura, Shigehiro – *The New Standardization: Keystone of Continuous Improvement in Manufacturing* – Productivity Press, 1993
————. and Hideyuki Takahasi – *Go-Go Tools: Five Essential Activities for Leading Small Groups*- Productivity Europe
Nikkan Kogyo Shimbun, (eds.) - *Poka-Yoke: Improving Product Quality by Preventing Defects* - Productivity Press, 1989
————. *Factory Management Notebook Series: Mixed Model Production* - Productivity Press, 1991
————. *Factory Management Notebook Series: Visual Control Systems: Visual Control Systems* - Productivity Press, 1991
————. *Factory Management Notebook Series: Mixed Model Production* - Productivity Press, 1991
————. *Visual Control Systems - Factory Management Notebook Series:* Productivity Press, 1995
————. *TPM Case Studies* - Productivity Press, 1995
Northey, Patrick and Nigel Southway – *Cycle Time Management: The Fast Track to Time-Based Productivity Improvement* – Productivity Press, 1993
Ohno, Taiichi. - T*oyota Production System: Beyond Large-Scale Production* - Productivity Press, 1988
————.*Workplace Management* - Productivity Press, 1988
————. and Setsuo Mito - *Just-In-Time for Today and Tomorrow* – Productivity Press, 1988
Ono, Ken'ichi – *Visual Feedback: Making Your 5S Implementation Click* - Productivity Press, 1996
Perigord, Michel. - *Achieving Total Quality Management: A Program for Action* – Productivity Press, 1991
Psarouthakis, John. - *Better Makes Us Best* - Productivity Press, 1989
Puri, Subhash C. – *Stepping up to ISO 14000: Integrating Environmental Quality with ISO 9000 and TQM* –

Bibliography

Productivity Press, 1996

———. *ISO 9000 Certification: Total Quality Management* – Productivity Press, 1995

Productivity Press Development Team – *Just-In-Time for Operators Learning Package* - Productivity Press, 1998

Robinson, Alan. - *Continuous Improvement in Operations: A Systematic Approach to Waste Reduction* - Productivity Press, 1991

Robinson, Charles J. and Andrew P. Cinder. - *Introduction to Implementing TPM: The North American Experience* - Productivity Press, 1995.

Robson, Ross E. - *The Quality And Productivity Equation: American Corporate Strategies For The 1990s* – Productivity Press, 1990

Sakurai, Michiharu – *Integrated Cost Management: A Companywide Prescription for Higher Profits and Lower Costs* - Productivity Press, 1995

Sarita Chawla and John Renesch – *Learning Organizations* - Productivity Press, 1995

Scanlan, Phillip M. – *The Dolphins Are Back: A Successful Quality Model for Healing the Environment* - Productivity Press, 1995

Sekine, Keniche, Keisuke Arai, and Bruce Talbot. - *Kaizen for Quick Changeover: Going Beyond SMED* - Productivity Press, 1992

———.*One-Piece Flow: Cell Design for Transforming the Production Process* - Productivity Press, 1992

———.and Keisuke Arai.- *TPM for the Lean Factory: Innovative Methods and Worksheets for Equipment Management* – Productivity Press, 1998

Shetty, Y.K and Vernon M. Buehler (eds.). - *Competing Through Productivity and Quality* – Productivity Press, 1989

Shiba, Shoji, Alan Graham and David Walden – *A New American TQM: Four Practical Revolutions in Management* - Productivity Press, 1993

Shingo, Shigeo - *A Revolution in Manufacturing: The SMED*

System – Productivity Press, 1983

———. *Zero Quality Control: Source Inspection and the Poka-yoke System* – Productivity Press, 1986

———.. *The Sayings of Shigeo Shingo: Key Strategies for Plant Improvement,* - Productivity Press, 1987

———. *Zero Quality Control: Source Inspection and the Poka-Yoke System* - Productivity Press, 1986

———.*A Study of the Toyota Production System from an Industrial Engineering* Viewpoint - Productivity Press, 1989

———. *Quick Changeover for Operators* – Created by Productivity Press from Shingo's SMED System, 1996

———. *Mistake-Proofing for Operators: The ZQC System* - Created by Productivity Press from Shingo's SMED System, 1996

Shinohara, Isao (ed.) - *New Production System: JIT Crossing Industry Boundaries* – Productivity Press, 1988

Shirose, Kunio. - *TPM for Workshop Leaders* - Productivity Press, 1992

———.*TPM Team Guide* - Productivity Press, 1996

———. And Yoshifumi Kimura and Mitsugu Kaneda – *P-M Analysis: An Advanced Step in TPM Implementation* - Productivity Press, 1995

———. and Keisuke Arai *Design Team Revolution: How to Cut Lead Times in Half and Double Your Productivity* - Productivity Press, 1999

Steinbacher, Herbert R. and Norman L. Steinbacher – *TPM for America: What it is and Why You Need It* - Productivity Press, 1993

Suehiro, Kikuo – *Eliminating Minor Stoppages on Automated Lines* – Productivity Press, 1992

Sugiyama, Tomo. - *The Improvement Book: Creating the Problem-Free Workplace* – Productivity Press, 1989

Suri, Rajan – *Quick Response Manufacturing: A Companywide Approach to Reducing Lean Times* - Productivity Press, 1998

Suzue, Toshio and Akira Kohdate. - *Variety Reduction Program (VRP): A Production Strategy for Product Diversification* – Productivity Press, 1990

Suzuki, Tokutaro (ed.) – *TPM in Process Industries* - **Productivity**

Bibliography

Press, 1994

Swartz, James B. – *The Hunters and the Hunted: A Non-Linear Solution for Reengineering the Workplace* - Productivity Press, 1994

Tajiri, Masaji and Fumioh Gotoh - Autonomous Maintenance in *Seven Steps: Implementing TPM on the Shop Floor* - Productivity Press, 1997

Tateisi, Kazuma. - *The Eternal Venture Spirit: An Executive's Practical Philosophy* – Productivity Press, 1989

Tel-A-Train and the Productivity Press Development Team – *The 5S System: Workplace Organization and Standardization* – 1998

Todorov, Branimir – ISO 9000 Required: Your Worldwide Passport to Customer Confidence - Productivity Press, 1996

Tozawa, Bunji – *Kaizen Teian 1: Developing Systems for Continuous Improvement Through Employee Suggestions* – Productivity Press, 1992

———. *Kaizen Teian 2: Developing Systems for Continuous Improvement Through Employee Suggestions* – Productivity Press, 1992

———. *The Idea Book: Improvement through TEI (Total Employee Involvement)* – Productivity Press, 1988

———. *The Improvement Engine: Creativity & Innovation Through Employee Involvement* - Productivity Press – 1995

———. *The Service Industry Idea Book: Employee Involvement in Retail and Office Improvement* – Productivity Press, 1990

Tsuchiya, Seiji – *Quality Maintenance: Zero Defects Through Equipment Management* - Productivity Press,

Uchimaru, Kiyoshi, Susumu Okamoto and Bunteru Kurahara – *TQP for Technical Groups: Total Quality Principles for Product Development* - Productivity Press, 1993

Watson, Gregory H. - *Benchmarking Workbook: Adopting the Best Practices for Performance Improvement* - Productivity Press, 1992

Yasuda, Yuzo. - *40 Years, 20 Million Ideas: The Toyota Suggestion System* - Productivity Press, 1991

* The above list includes all of the books I published at Productivity Press, most have my introduction. In addition we published 60 books in our Management Master Series each around 60 to 75 pages.

"Only by much searching and mining are gold and diamonds obtained, and man can find every truth connected with his being if he will dig deep into the mine of his soul." - **James Allen**

Index

2
20 Million Ideas 296

5
5 Why's 21

A
Aisin Seki 17

B
BAE 6, 364
Bic Camera x
Boeing 29, 191
Buddhist parable 153

C
Canon 17, 36, 37, 169, 208, 209, 337, 371
Circuit City .... ix, x
Claudia 288

D
Dana 12, 382
DCI 93, 235
Detroit Ordinance Depot 107
Dionicio 92

F
Frederick Taylor 88

G
Gary Convis 207
General Motors .... vi, 28, 81, 126, 131, 203, 204
Gulfstream. 1, xv, 5, 12, 15, 18, 42, 46, 71, 73, 83, 92, 100, 175, 203, 364

H
Henry Ford 88, 365
Hino 46, 67, 68, 134

K
Kai*aku* 181
Kaikaku .... v, 29, 215, 366
Kaizen Blitz 4, 8, 80, 112, 121, 365
Kaoru Ishikawa 293
Key words 242, 243, 244
Kodak 16, 39

M
Mistake Board 68, 71, 73

N
Northwest Airlines 82
NUMMI 81

O
Ohno 7, 10, 16, 30, 80, 81, 102, 125, 126, 172, 173, 180, 365, 374
Oki Denki 122
Oldsmobile 202
On Error Training 19

P
Poka-yoke .... xv, 30, 71, 94, 175, 176, 177, 178

Q
Quality Control Circle 294

R
Ritsuo Shingo 30
Rory Bowman 89

Rudi 27
Ryuji Fukuda 19, 49, 365

S

Shigehiro Nakamura ... xv, 36, 365, 371
Shigeo Shingo 8, 30, 126, 298, 365, 376
Six Sigma 99
Stew Leonard viii
Subaru 5

T

Taiho Kogyo 8, 80

Taiichi Ohno 3
Technicolor 11, 288, 289
Tiger Woods 205

U

US Navy 41

V

Value Stream Mapping 122

W

W. Edwards Deming 134
Work smarter, not harder ... 204